Walking

the

Blue

Ridge

WALKING

THE

Blue Ridge

A GUIDE TO

THE TRAILS

OF THE

BLUE RIDGE

PARKWAY

REVISED EDITION

Leonard M. Adkins

The University of

North Carolina Press

Chapel Hill & London

© 1991, 1992, 1994
Leonard M. Adkins
All rights reserved

The paper in this book
meets the guidelines for
permanence and durability
of the Committee on
Production Guidelines
for Book Longevity of
the Council on Library
Resources.

Printed in the United
States of America

96   95   94
5   4   3   2

Library of Congress
Cataloging-in-Publication
Data

Adkins, Leonard M.
   Walking the Blue Ridge :
a guide to the trails of the
Blue Ridge Parkway /
Leonard M. Adkins.
—[Rev. ed.]
     p.   cm.
   Includes bibliographical
references (p.   ) and index.
   ISBN 0-8078-4401-2
(pbk. : alk. paper)
     1. Hiking—Blue Ridge
Parkway (N.C. and Va.)—
Guidebooks. 2. Walking—
Blue Ridge Parkway (N.C.
and Va.)—Guidebooks.
3. Trails—Blue Ridge
Parkway (N.C. and Va.)—
Guidebooks. 4. Blue Ridge
Parkway (N.C. and Va.)—
Guidebooks. I. Title.
GV199.42.B65A34   1992
917.55—dc20   92-17117
                              CIP

To my parents

for making everything possible

and to Laurie

for making me happy

In the woods is

perpetual youth.

–Emerson, *Nature*

Contents

Acknowledgments

I could have never completed this book by myself. Because of their invaluable assistance, I wish to gratefully acknowledge:

Cindy Carpenter, information assistant, Pisgah National Forest – thanks for your help.

Art Frederick, Blue Ridge Parkway ranger – I would have been unable to follow the route of the Roanoke Valley Horse Trail without his assistance.

Ann Messick – fewer wildflowers would have been identified without her help.

Phil Noblitt, Blue Ridge Parkway staff interpretive specialist – a most patient person who cheerfully answered any question I asked.

Mary Ann Peckham, former Blue Ridge Parkway staff interpretive specialist – her encouragement helped me decide to write the book.

West Virginia Scenic Trails Association – for use of the association's measuring wheel.

Bob Ellenwood, Laurie and Bill Foot, Cheryl Maynard, Marti McCallister – thanks, folks, for your friendship and for opening your homes to me.

Suzanne Bell, Sandra Eisdorfer, and David Perry, University of North Carolina Press – thank you.

The Blue Ridge Parkway, with its hundreds of miles of meandering pathways, has provided me with innumerable days of walking pleasure. I would like to thank all of the people, past and present, who have worked long and hard to make my amblings possible.

Abbreviations

AT	Appalachian Trail
BRP	Blue Ridge Parkway
FS	Forest Service
FSR	Forest Service road (usually unpaved)
NC RT	Roadway in North Carolina
VA RT	Roadway in Virginia
US RT	Branch of federal highway system

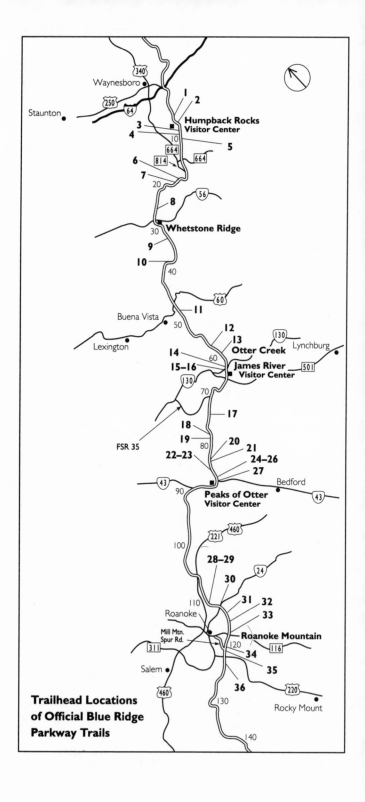

**Trailhead Locations
of Official Blue Ridge
Parkway Trails**

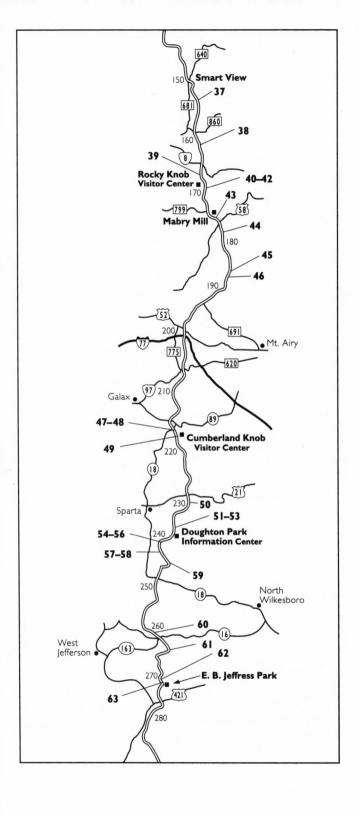

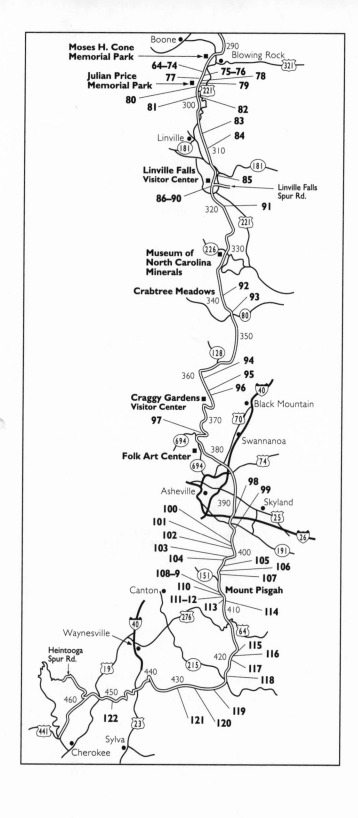

Walking

the

Blue

Ridge

Introduction

What is it about these Blue Ridge Mountains that continues to draw me to them time after time and year after year? I have now hiked their full length, from northern Georgia to central Pennsylvania, three times. I have driven each mile of the Skyline Drive and the Blue Ridge Parkway. Yet, after each excursion to the Blue Ridges, I find the yearning to return even stronger than before.

Maybe it is the sense of discovery I feel each time I venture into the mountains. The place names alone are a constant source of enticement and entertainment. How can I resist not trying to find out what happens in Bear Wallow Gap or what Rough Butt Bald really looks like? Will Graveyard Fields be as spooky as it sounds? Will tears come to my eyes when I walk over Onion Mountain? What the heck is The Lump? Does a rock castle actually exist in the gorge, and does anyone maintain the Craggy Gardens?

The idea of walking all of the trails of the Parkway occurred to me while I was on one of these small, personal quests. Wanting to understand the geology of the mountains, I was on the Greenstone Self-Guiding Trail (BRP mile 8.8) trying to concentrate on the information presented on the trail signs. Yes, I was gaining knowledge on the origins of the mountains, but I was also being thrilled by the beauty of the surroundings. The bright sunshine, filtering through the leaf canopy of the oak and hickory trees, danced about to create varying shadows on the underbrush of mountain laurel and rhododendron. Warm air rising from the hazy green of the Shenandoah Valley wrapped around my skin like a welcomed shawl against the coolness of an early spring day. A couple of wildflowers were just beginning to break through the coarse, rocky soil next to the trail, adding a dash of color to the brown and gray forest floor.

If I could derive such pleasure from walking just one little .3 mile trail, how much more would I enjoy and get to know these mountains if I walked all of the trails on the Parkway?

The Blue Ridge Parkway, administered by the National Park Service, is 469 miles long. There are over 100 Park Service trails along the Parkway and dozens of Forest Service pathways coming in close contact – in other words, ample opportunities to explore, enjoy, and experience the mountains.

The Park Service has done an excellent job in making the Blue Ridges accessible to everyone, even the most casual of walkers. A large number of the trails are easy or moderately easy to walk. Many are self-guiding trails on which much information can be learned about the natural history of the Blue Ridge Mountains.

For those inclined to put forth a little more effort, the rewards are greater. Parkway trails will bring you along spiny ridge lines to views of verdant isolated valleys or out to soaring mountain peaks covered in the dark-green growth of spruce, firs, and mountain laurel. Other trails can lead you through tunnels of rhododendron to end at rushing waterfalls tumbling over steep, precipitous mountainsides. Still others will deliver you onto gentle, rolling plateaus of open fields and meadows, where you may revel in warm sunshine and cool mountain breezes.

The Parkway can be a lesson in human history, too. The ridges and valleys of the Blue Ridge Mountains were inhabited when the Park Service began to obtain land for the Parkway. Isolated from the rest of the country by the rugged terrain, these mountain people had developed into a self-reliant and independent population. Their way of life, their daily chores, and their hopes and aspirations may be discovered and studied by following some Parkway trails to farms and communities reconstructed by the Park Service. Even on trails secluded and far removed from where you would expect someone to have lived, you may stumble upon the rock foundation of a cabin no longer in existence or a crumbling stone wall once used to contain livestock. Pay attention when hiking; you might be walking through an old fruit orchard or by someone's long-abandoned flower garden.

Also, be willing to visit a trail more than once, and don't limit your excursions to just the warmer months. A trail walked in the spring will certainly look different in the fall. The cooler temperatures of winter will keep you from sweating as you huff and puff up a steep hill, and the absence of insects will be most welcomed. I had walked trails in the Peaks of Otter area so many times that I assumed I had seen everything they had to offer. But one winter afternoon, after a light snow had fallen, I came upon the tracks of a gray fox. Excited, I followed the small paw prints and caught a glimpse of the fox dashing across an open meadow above the Johnson Farm.

Another excellent way to enjoy your visit to the Parkway is to take advantage of the interpretive programs offered by the Park Service. During the heaviest tourist months, Park Rangers (and knowledgeable volunteers) conduct guided walks on the Parkway trails, focusing on a myriad of subjects ranging from endangered plants to old-time methods of farming. Campfire programs are also presented on a regular basis at the campgrounds. I have been awe-struck by stunning slide shows about the Parkway, enjoyed concerts of mountain music on lap dulcimers and autoharps, and been amused by the antics of a ranger dressed up as an old mountain woman imparting her knowledge of local medicinal plants.

Since that day a number of years ago when I stood on the Greenstone Self-Guiding Trail, I have walked all of the trails of the Blue Ridge Parkway (and was married on the Abbot Lake Trail at the Peaks of Otter!). It is my sincere hope that this guidebook will entice you enough to lace up those comfortable old walking shoes of yours, put one foot in front of the other, and begin your own love affair with the mountains by walking the Blue Ridge. Happy Trails!

A Short History of the Blue Ridge Mountains and the Parkway

At various times through the ages, the area now known as the Blue Ridge Mountains, stretching from northern Georgia to central Pennsylvania, has risen to great heights from the sea or has sunk to become the floor of a vast ancient ocean. For millions of years, along with the rest of the North American continent, the land has been alternately subjected to the effects of the movements of the earth's crustal plates, rising and falling seas, erosion from wind and water, and advancing and receding glaciers.

Each time the crustal plates collided North America would take on a new face. Giant land masses grinding into each other would cause the earth's surface to break, crack, and fold upward, creating mountains. At the same time, large slabs of the lower portion of the crust were sliding underneath one another, raising the surface even higher.

About 200 million years ago the plates began to split and drift apart, forming the Atlantic Ocean. Several theories maintain that, at that time, the Blue Ridges may have been as rugged and tall as the Rocky Mountains. What happened to create the Blue Ridge Mountains we see today? Erosion by wind and water has been wearing away these mountains bit by bit. Rock that was once part of a high, lofty peak has been washed down the mountainside and swept away in a spring thaw, violent summer thunderstorm, or gentle fall rain. The tiny particles of the mountains may become deposited in the valleys, move on to create the rich soil of the Piedmont, or even be carried out to sea. Some of the sand particles a child uses to build a sand castle on Virginia Beach may have once been part of a rock outcropping on the crest of the Blue Ridges.

Glaciers have also played an important role in the creation of the present-day landscape. Scientific theories suggest that as the great sheets of ice advanced from the north, they forced many plants to migrate southward. The Ice Age's cooler temperatures allowed northern trees, such as birch, beech, fir, and spruce, to begin to compete with, and even gain a foothold against, the traditional southern hardwoods like oak, poplar, and hickory. Once the glaciers began to recede and warmer air returned, most of the northern plants died out, unable to tolerate a southern climate. However, the cool temperatures on the higher peaks and ridge lines of the southern Blue Ridges have allowed many of these trees to remain and prosper, cut off from their relatives several hundred miles to the north.

No studies have established exactly when the first occupants arrived in the Blue Ridge Mountains. Archaeological evidence does show that the mountains were inhabited at least 10,000 years ago. These first Appalachians were hunters and nomads, gathering fruits and nuts during

A trail in winter. (Courtesy of the National Park Service, Blue Ridge Parkway)

the warmer months only to retreat to the valleys and low-lands with the return of fall and winter. Not much else is known about these archaic Indians.

The Catawba, Algonquin, Iroquois, Shawnee, Delaware, and Cherokee Indians were all living in, or making use of, the Blue Ridge Mountains when explorers first arrived in the New World. The Cherokees had large villages established in northern Georgia and eastern Tennessee, but most of the tribes used the mountains as a rich and diverse hunting ground, taking advantage of the tremendous numbers of elk, deer, and buffalo.

Traveling southward from Pennsylvania or westward from the coast of North Carolina, the first settlers began arriving in the 1700s. Their numbers increased after the Revolutionary War, and soon small communities were established throughout the mountains. Isolated from urban centers, these settlers and communities became proficient in the skills of self-sufficiency.

Owing to the rugged terrain, modern transportation methods developed slowly in the Southern Appalachians. Even as late as the 1920s and 1930s, most roadways were little more than narrow, rutted, hand-built dirt paths. Melting winter snows and spring rains would turn them into quagmires that could be traversed only on horseback or by oxcart.

In 1933 President Franklin Roosevelt made an inspection tour of the first Civilian Conservation Corps camp to be established in Virginia. The corps was building the Skyline Drive in Shenandoah National Park. Roosevelt not only enjoyed the beauty of the park but was pleased with the progress and potential of the Skyline Drive. A U.S. senator from Virginia, Harry F. Byrd, suggested to the president that a scenic highway be built linking Shenandoah National Park with the Great Smoky Mountain National Park in North Carolina and Tennessee.

(History does not record if Senator Byrd was the originator of the idea for the Parkway. Others have also claimed that distinction. Possibly it should go to Colonel Joseph Hyde Pratt, whose construction of a "Crest of the Blue Ridge Highway" was halted by the outbreak of World War I.)

Roosevelt approved the idea of the Parkway. After much arguing and maneuvering by the politicians of Virginia, North Carolina, and Tennessee (who realized its economic benefits), construction of the Blue Ridge Parkway began on September 11, 1935. Congress placed the Parkway under the jurisdiction of the National Park Service in 1936.

The Parkway was, of course, built in bits and pieces. The first portion was built near the North Carolina–Virginia border. Other stretches were added as the Park Service was able to obtain the necessary rights-of-way. In addition, scores of rivers and creeks had to be bridged and more than twenty tunnels blasted through the mountainsides.

With the construction of the Linn Cove Viaduct on the side of Grandfather Mountain and another small portion of roadway, the task was accomplished. On September 11, 1987, a gala ceremony on the viaduct officially declared the completion of the 469-mile Blue Ridge Parkway, fifty-two years after the project was started.

The National Park Service estimates that the Parkway now receives more than 25 million visitors annually.

How to Use This Book

The trails are presented in the order they appear geographically on the Parkway – by milepost, beginning with mile 0, where US RT 250 intersects the BRP a few miles east of Waynesboro. Over the course of each BRP trail and some of the side trails, I give descriptions and directions by decimal mile point.

Although the Parkway does meander in all directions, it can be considered to be generally aligned in a north-south configuration. Directions given are assuming you are traveling south on the Parkway. Therefore, trails or roadways identified to the west will be on the right side of the Parkway, and those listed to the east will be on the left side. Additionally, overlooks will have a northern and southern end corresponding to northbound and southbound on the Parkway.

Ranging from pleasant, easy nature strolls of two minutes to challenging climbs of 5,000- and 6,000-foot peaks to multiday backpacking trips, the trails along the Blue Ridge Parkway make it possible for anyone to enjoy the beauty and pleasures of the Blue Ridge Mountains. To help you choose the trails appropriate for your interests and ability, I have given each walk one of the following grades of difficulty:

An *easy leg stretcher* is a very short walk that simply gets you out of the car to enjoy a view, learn a little bit of history, or observe some significant feature.

A walk rated *easy* will last no more than a few minutes and have little or no change in elevation.

A *moderately easy* walk is an extended easy one with slight changes in elevation. (With a little effort all of the easy and moderately easy trails should be within range of anyone – even those who are not in the best of shape.)

A trail rated *moderate* has either a number of gradual changes in elevation or a few steep ascents and descents. Also, the trail will probably be longer in length than those of the previous ratings.

A *moderately strenuous* trail will involve quite a number of ups and downs on a rough and/or rocky pathway.

A *strenuous* hike should be undertaken only by those in good physical condition with experience in negotiating steep ascents and descents on rocky, and possibly dangerous, terrain.

Please remember these ratings are just general guidelines. Individual perceptions of trail difficulties vary widely from person to person. What may be moderate to you may be strenuous to someone else. Also, you may be feeling especially vigorous one day and walk a strenuous trail rather easily. Another day an easy trail could become an arduous journey requiring more effort than you had imagined. Do not let all of this deter you from enjoying the enchantment of wandering through the mountains. The more you walk and hike, the better you will be able to determine your own abilities and limitations.

Side trails – those that intersect the main trails discussed – are marked with a bullet (•).

This guidebook does not cover just the "official" trails of the Blue Ridge Parkway. In order to present as many walking opportunities as possible, I have also provided information on Forest Service, state park, and private trails that come into close contact with the Parkway or any of its trails. The Park Service does not list any of the Parkway trails by letter or number. In order to simplify identifying these trails, I have assigned them numbers in brackets, i.e., [BRP 1]. These numbers are relevant to this guidebook only and will not correspond to any outside resources or information. The Forest Service, however, does assign numbers to their trails, i.e., [FS 161]. These numbers will match up with those on Forest Service maps and in most other national forest trail guides. Please note that as a general rule, Forest Service and other trails are not as well maintained as the Parkway trails.

To give detailed information on every one of the non-Parkway trails is, of course, impossible. Enough information is provided to allow you to decide whether or not you wish to walk them. Information on additional resources is included.

You will note, however, that I do present mile-point information on a number of the Forest Service trails. These detailed descriptions are included because those pathways possess a high degree of scenic value, are exceptionally isolated or secluded, present possible campsite opportunities, or are just personal favorites.

In order to record as accurately as possible the full lengths and mile points of the Parkway Trails and those Forest Service trails that have descriptions, I pushed a measuring wheel while I walked them.

You may note that my mileages differ slightly from some Parkway mileages or distances mentioned in other sources. It is always hard to get different sources to agree on the exact same distance. The National Park Service may have measured a trail from a visitor center, a trail sign, or some other point. Other sources may have begun measuring a trail at a parking area or a contact station. My distances are accurate in that they begin at the point I say to start walking at mile point .0.

Advice and Precautions

EMERGENCIES

An emergency should be reported to the nearest ranger station (see Appendix B) or to the PARKWATCH number (800-727-5928). It is important to know your location (BRP mile) so Rangers may respond as quickly as possible.

WATER

If you are going to be hiking much more than an hour, it would probably be a good idea to bring along some water. It is not wise to assume that the crystal clear mountain streams, or even the springs, will be safe without being treated. Gone are the days when a hiker could drink from such sources with impunity. The increase in the numbers of people visiting the natural areas of North Carolina and Virginia has brought a corresponding increase in the appearance of Giardia. This water-borne parasite has varying effects on the human body – some people never feel any effects, others experience slight discomfort and maybe a mild case of diarrhea, while others are incapacitated to the point of requiring hospitalization.

Water sources can also become tainted by viruses, bacteria, and other pollutants, such as runoff from roadways.

If you are only out for day hikes, you have nothing to worry about – just bring enough water with you. If you're going to be out overnight, though, it will be tough to carry all of the water you need. Most water sources you encounter can be made potable by boiling. However, only a water filter can effectively remove man-made chemical pollutants. A great variety of light-weight backpacking filters are available, but some work better than others. Talk to backpacking friends or consult a trusted retail outdoors outfitter before deciding which filter will be best for you.

You can help not add to the water problems by camping at least fifty feet away from any source. Bury human waste at least 400 to 500 feet away.

SNAKES

With a wide variety and large number of snakes living in the Blue Ridge Mountains, encountering one is a possibility. Only two, the copperhead and rattlesnake, are poisonous. It would be wise to learn how to identify them.

There are a number of things you can do to reduce the possibility of an encounter. Stay on the authorized pathways. Avoid rocky areas. Do not put your hands into places you can't see into. Step on a log first instead of just walking over the top of it. Walking with a group will also reduce the possibility of encountering any snakes. If you are hiking alone and want to avoid an encounter, tap the ground in front of you with a stick in order to alert any snakes of your presence. They're just as reluctant as you are to have an altercation and, given enough warning, time, and room, will usually be gone long before you arrive.

Remember, the mountains are a snake's natural habitat. Please refrain from killing one; just walk around it, giving it a wide berth, and continue on your way.

Important: All snake bites contain bacteria; seek medical attention for any type of bite.

BLACK BEARS

The Blue Ridge Mountains are also the home of a large number of black bears. The chance of seeing one or more, especially on the longer and more remote trails, is a very real possibility. The best times of day to catch a glimpse of a bear is early morning or early evening, but they are also known to be roaming about throughout the day.

Seeing a bear in its natural surroundings is definitely an exciting experience. This experience, however, brings some responsibility to you. Although black bear attacks on humans are extremely rare, there are several things you can and should do to keep it this way. Remember that bears are wild animals and do not like to be approached at close range (if you must take a photo, do so from quite a distance away). Do not try to feed a bear. Not only does this endanger you, it also endangers the bear. Once a bear becomes used to close human contact it may begin wandering into campsites or housing developments looking for free handouts. This often results in the bear having to be destroyed by the authorities.

Probably the most important safety rule concerning bears: do not get between a mother bear and her cubs! If this happens to you, turn and walk away – don't run – as quickly as possible. In fact, this is the best advice for any encounters with bears; give them plenty of room and leave them alone.

INSECTS

Warm weather brings no-see-ums, gnats, fleas, mosquitoes, deerflies, ticks, and more. You should bring repellent.

There is still some controversy as to whether conventional insect repellents will work against ticks. To protect yourself you should try to stay away from overhanging underbrush where the ticks are most likely to be encountered. Tuck your pants into your socks or boots, and, possibly, consider wearing a long sleeve shirt and a cap. After each outing it would be wise to check yourself closely, or better yet have someone else check you. Remember, the things you are looking for are rather small.

PLANTS

Poison ivy is prolific throughout the Blue Ridge Mountains. You should definitely learn how to identify it. Unfortunately, it appears in a number of different forms.

The most common is a woody shrub of up to two feet high that will grow in large patches, often lining or overtaking pathways. Just as likely, it will grow as a hairy root-covered vine that clings to the trunk of a tree, climbing far up into the branches. Sometimes, the main trunk of this vine will become so strong and thick that it will support itself. The poison ivy is then hard to distinguish from a small tree.

All parts of the poison ivy plant contain the poison. This is true even in winter when it appears that the plant has died a long time ago. Appearing in the fall, the poison ivy's white berry is especially toxic to certain people.

Poison oak also grows in the mountains, but less frequently than poison ivy.

Stinging nettle will grow in large patches and encroach upon pathways that are not well maintained. Brushing up against the plants will give the tiny thorns an opportunity to scratch your legs and deposit a poison that will probably itch you for the rest of the day. One bout with this plant will teach you to be on the lookout for it from then on.

SUN

By now we have all heard of the dangerous effects of the sun, especially with the continued deterioration of the earth's atmosphere. More and more doctors are suggesting that you apply a high-strength sun-block lotion whenever you will be outdoors for an extended period of time.

MAPS

Most of the Parkway trails are so short or so well marked that it is really unnecessary to obtain any maps for them.

The Park Service has free maps available for the major recreation areas on the Parkway – Otter Creek, Peaks of Otter, Roanoke Mountain, Rocky Knob, Cumberland Knob, Doughton Park, Moses H. Cone Memorial Park, Julian Price Memorial Park, Crabtree Meadows, Craggy Gardens, and Mount Pisgah. In order to get a good overview and not become possibly confused by the maze of trails in these areas, it is suggested you obtain copies of the maps. Maps for each area may be picked up at that area's ranger's office, campground contact station, or visitor center.

If you are going to be hiking any trails in the national forests, you should probably acquire a map. Information on obtaining the proper national forest map is provided in Appendix F.

In my opinion, the national forests maps provide all of the information you need to hike any of the national forest trails described in this guidebook. However, if you are a map enthusiast, you may wish to obtain detailed topographic maps of the areas you will be exploring. Write to the U.S. Geological Survey (Distribution Branch, Box 25286 Federal Center, Building 4, Denver, CO 80225) and ask for the free index maps of Virginia and North Carolina in order to determine which maps you will require. Unfortunately, you may need to order several of these maps in order to cover just one trail, and they currently cost about three dollars each!

PROPER CLOTHING AND EQUIPMENT

Like any large mountain range, the Blue Ridges are susceptible to wild fluctuations in weather. Warm sunny days can become cold and rainy in just a matter of minutes. Additionally, don't be surprised if a pleasant spring or fall day changes quickly to one with sleet or snow. Hypothermia, probably one of the major causes of death for campers and hikers, is a condition in which the body loses heat faster that it can produce it. Amazingly, hypothermia often strikes at temperatures in the fifties and sixties simply because many people do not anticipate changes in the weather. Be prepared for these conditions by carrying raingear and an insulating layer of clothing, such as a wool sweater, in your daypack. Winter hiking, of course, means you need to carry several layers of insulating clothing. (Layering is a more effective means of keeping warm than wearing just one thick or bulky layer.)

In addition to raingear and extra layers of clothes, your daypack should probably contain a small first-aid kit, flashlight, knife, compass, space blanket, toilet paper, and some waterproof matches.

Also, if you're camping, be prepared for cool nights, even in the summer.

There is really no reason to invest in a pair of heavy-duty mountaineering-type boots in order to enjoy the benefits of walking in the Blue Ridge. Excluding those people who have ankle or foot problems, sturdy and comfortable running, walking, or tennis shoes should be adequate for most day hikes. Unless you are carrying an extremely heavy pack (which you should not be) lightweight hiking boots will suffice for overnight backpacking trips.

Wearing a wool or part-wool sock over a thinner inner sock of polypropylene, silk, or similar material will reduce friction and rubbing on your feet. To assure a proper fit, wear this sock combination when shopping for new boots. Before embarking upon any extended hike, be sure to break in new boots or shoes so as to avoid any discomfort or blisters. Applying moleskin (available at most pharmacies and outdoors outfitters) to any "hotspots" on your feet will go a long way in preventing blisters from developing.

Obviously it is not within the scope of this guidebook to be a backpacking or hiking "primer." A number of good books are available if you feel the need for further information. One of the most complete and concise introductions to backpacking, related equipment, and wilderness ethics that I've ever come across is the first third of *The Complete Backpacking Guide to Canada*, by Elliot Katz (Toronto: Doubleday, 1980). *The Complete Walker III*, by Colin Fletcher, is not only informative but also makes for some very entertaining reading.

Blue Ridge Parkway Regulations

All of these regulations apply while you are within Parkway boundaries. The regulations in the national forests are not quite as rigid, but the Parkway's rules are wise guidelines to follow anywhere.

SPEED LIMIT

The Blue Ridge Parkway is not an interstate. The speed limit is 45 miles per hour.

NATURAL FEATURES

All of the plants and animals within the boundary of the Parkway are protected by law. Picking flowers or digging plants is prohibited. Berries, nuts, and fruits can be picked, but only for personal consumption.

Please do not deface any natural features such as rock facings or road cuts. You should contact a Park ranger before engaging in any rock climbing activities; rock climbing is prohibited on road cuts.

PETS

All pets must be kept under physical control (caged, carried, or on a leash no more than six feet long) at all times. Pets are not permitted in the Parkway's public buildings.

WEAPONS

It is illegal to use or carry a weapon (rifles, shotguns, handguns, bows, airguns, slingshots, etc.) on the Parkway. They may be transported in automobiles provided they are packed, cased, stored, or broken down to prevent their ready use.

It is also against the law to trap or net on the Parkway.

CAMPING

Parkway campgrounds are usually open from May to October. Some sites do stay open year round, but these can change from year to year. Call 704-259-0701 for the most up-to-date information. See Appendix D for a listing of the campgrounds on the Parkway.

Camping is permitted only in the designated campgrounds. Drinking water and rest rooms are provided; shower and laundry facilities are not. There are no hookups, but each campground does have a sanitary dumping station.

Please remember that camping is prohibited along all of the "official" Parkway trails. You are permitted to camp along the Forest Service trails, and I alert you of this fact in the descriptions of these pathways.

There are two backcountry campsites within Parkway boundaries – BRP miles 169 and 241.1. Permits are required and can be obtained free of charge at ranger stations nearby.

FIRES

Fires are permitted only in designated areas such as picnic areas and campgrounds, must not be left unattended, and are to be completely extinguished after use. The Parkway superintendent may issue a no-fire rule during periods of high fire danger.

Wood for campfires may be gathered only if it is dead, lying on the ground, and within .25 mile of the campground. Cutting trees that are dead but still standing is prohibited.

UNATTENDED VEHICLES

If you must park on the shoulder of the Parkway, make sure that you are completely off the road but no further than ten feet from the pavement. Use an overlook or parking area whenever possible.

The Parkway has experienced an increase in vandalism and theft in the last several years, so it is wise to leave your valuables at home. Place whatever valuables you do have out of sight and lock the car.

If you're going to leave your vehicle at an overlook or parking area overnight, be sure to give a Park ranger your vehicle's make and license number, the length of time and place you will be leaving it, and the name of each person in your party.

SWIMMING

Swimming is prohibited in Parkway waters.

FISHING

You must possess a valid state fishing license in order to fish along the Parkway. Local fishing regulations do apply, and some Parkway waters may be closed from time to time. Contact the nearest Parkway facility or the main Parkway office (704-259-0701) to be sure which regulations are in effect at any given time.

2

Rockfish Gap to the Roanoke River

BLUE RIDGE PARKWAY MILES 0–114.8

Beginning just a few miles east of Waynesboro, Virginia, the Parkway winds back and forth between the eastern and western sides of a single, narrow ridge line that makes up the Blue Ridge Mountains from BRP mile 0 to mile 114.8. Spur ridges, stretching like knobby-knuckled fingers, descend into the valleys. Many places provide points where you may view all of this from just one spot – the Blue Ridge extends north to south as you peer over the flat lands of eastern Virginia or turn your gaze to the west and focus on the distant Allegheny Mountains in West Virginia.

Dictated by the narrow topography, the trails of this section have only two choices as to where they may go. They either closely parallel the Parkway, rising and descending according to the whims of the undulating ridge line, or they plummet quickly from the crest of the mountains onto the edge of the Piedmont or into the Shenandoah Valley.

Ninety percent of this section is bounded by either the George Washington or Jefferson National Forest. Extensive trail systems join up with many of the Parkway's trails, allowing you to work out quite a number of extended, overnight excursions. Backcountry camping is allowed almost anywhere in the national forests, but please be aware that these trails may not be as regularly maintained as the Parkway trails.

The national forests and the steep mountainsides have kept modern civilization's encroachment to a minimum. It is possible to walk many of the trails without encountering any signs of present-day inhabitation. Even the views into the Piedmont and various valleys show that the bulk of human activity is currently concentrated in areas quite some distance from the Parkway. Often trails (such as the White Rock Falls Trail, BRP mile 18.5) stay within a half mile of the Parkway, yet all sounds of the roadway are blotted out by dense forest growth, an obstructing knob, or a briskly moving stream.

These mountains were inhabited at one time, however – not in the distant past, but just a short time ago. Certain trails (like the Humpback Rocks and Mountain Trail, BRP mile 6) go past crumbling stone walls, while others (BRP mile 85.9) pass through orchards that still bear fruit. A number of the trails will even deliver you to Park Service reconstructed cabins and farms where you can participate in living history demonstrations.

Not forgetting the natural world, the Park Service has provided self-guiding trails (BRP miles 8.8, 63.6, and 85.9), which give detailed but easily understood information on the natural history of the central Blue Ridge Mountains.

Mile 0. Shenandoah National Park is located to the north of the Blue Ridge Parkway. The Skyline Drive, the main roadway through the park, joins the BRP here in Rockfish Gap. A number of guidebooks (available in Shenandoah National Park visitor centers) detail the vast network of hiking trails in the park.

Mile 0. Appalachian Trail. Approximately 100 miles of the more than 2,000-mile-long Appalachian National Scenic Trail parallel the Blue Ridge Parkway. See Chapter 3 for details.

Mile 5.9. Mountain Farm Trail [BRP 1]

Length: .25 mile, one way

Difficulty: easy

Highly recommended

The Mountain Farm Trail is an easy, self-guiding pathway that begins at the Humpback Rocks Visitor Center. Signposts along the way explain the various structures (including log cabins, weasel-proof chicken houses, and gear loft) and farm tools (such as maul and frow, beatlin block, and ash hopper). A garden is planted for the growing season, and live demonstrations are presented during

Log cabin along the Mountain Farm Trail at Humpback
Rocks. (Courtesy of the National Park Service, Blue Ridge
Parkway)

the spring, summer, and fall. Check at the visitor center
for times and dates, as well as a detailed pamphlet about
this trail (available for a small fee).

This walk presents a good overview and introduction
to the former inhabitants of the Blue Ridge Mountains.

Mile 6. Appalachian Trail. See Chapter 3.

Mile 6. Humpback Rocks and Mountain Trail [BRP 2]

Length: 3.75 miles, one way

Difficulty: strenuous

This steep and rocky section of the Appalachian
Trail climbs steadily for a view from Humpback Rocks
and an even better view on the summit of Humpback
Mountain. In addition to other views, the trail also passes
a couple of mountain laurel thickets which, along with the
azaleas, makes for a colorful walk in late spring. In early
spring trillium may be abundant.

A relocation is planned for this section. Contact the
Appalachian Trail Conference or the Old Dominion Ap-
palachian Trail Club for the most recent information. (See
Chapter 3.)

A blue-blazed side trail [BRP 3] gives access to the
Humpback Rocks picnic area, enabling you to have someone pick you up instead of walking back on the same path.

Some people prefer to walk just to the Humpback
Rocks, a hike of 1 mile, one way.

.0   Begin an immediate ascent at the southern end of the parking lot, which is on the eastern side of the BRP.

.06   Here are good views overlooking the BRP and Shenandoah Valley.

.15   Come to a bench and a final view over a meadow.

.2   Reach the ridge line; continue to ascend at a more gradual rate. The fall flowers are particularly abundant here.

.5   The signpost is at a confusing intersection. Do not go left! (To the left is the old trail – very steep, dangerous, and badly eroded. Please let this land try to heal itself by continuing to the right on fairly level ground.)

.55   Ascend on wooden steps.

.6   Begin a series of short switchbacks on a trail that is now steeper, rougher, and rockier.

.8   At a wonderful, old, double-trunked oak tree, the trail switches back and becomes even rockier and steeper.

.9   Intersection. To the left are Humpback Rocks and a commanding view of Shenandoah Valley (800 feet). Even though the rocks are marred by graffiti, this spot is still magnificent. After enjoying the rocks, return to the intersection and continue on the trail.

1.1   Level out and pass through a mountain laurel thicket. Soon come to an old stone wall, where there are good views from the rocks on the right side of the trail.

1.3   A large greenstone talus slope appears on the left; continue to ascend.

1.4   On top of the ridge line, cross through an old stone wall and continue; good wintertime views into Rockfish River Valley.

1.7   Drop into, and ascend out of, a gap.

2   Arrive at the summit of Humpback Mountain, where there are good views of Rockfish Gap and Shenandoah National Park to the north, Shenandoah Valley to the west, and Rockfish River Valley to the east. Begin a gradual descent.

2.6   Note the old stone wall on the right.

3   The southward view from a rock ledge is of Wintergreen Ski Resort and Bald Mountain. Drop through mountain laurel.

3.2   Leave mountain laurel and drop more steeply.

3.75 Arrive at a trail junction and the end of this walk. The Appalachian Trail continues to the left for about 4 miles to arrive at the Three Ridges Overlook. To reach the Humpback Rocks picnic area parking lot, turn right onto the blue-blazed trail [BRP 3] for .3 mile.

Mile 8.4. Blue-Blazed Side Trail to the Appalachian Trail from Humpback Rocks Picnic Area [BRP 3]

(See Cotoctin Trail [BRP 4] for directions to the beginning of this trail.)

Length: .3 mile, one way

Difficulty: moderate

This pathway goes through a mixed hardwood forest and passes by a fine example of the old "hogwall" stone fences used by farmers to keep their razorback pigs from wandering too far.

.0   Begin to the left of the Cotoctin Trail on the pathway identified by blue blazes and an Appalachian Trail symbol.

.1   Note how the builder of this stone wall incorporated the rock outcropping into the wall.

.26 Level out.

.3   Trail intersection joining the Appalachian Trail. To the left is the Humpback Gap parking lot (3.75 miles); to the right is the Three Ridges Overlook at BRP mile 13.1 (about 4 miles).

Mile 8.4. Appalachian Trail. See Chapter 3.

Mile 8.4. Cotoctin Trail [BRP 4]

Length: .2 mile, one way

Difficulty: moderate

The Cotoctin Trail is located at the furthest point in the Humpback Rocks picnic area parking lot. It is identified by a sign pointing to "Overlook into the Valley." This short trail is well worth the walk, for the pay-off is a magnificent view into the Shenandoah Valley. A nice spot for a quiet, secluded picnic.

.0   Ascend slightly and cross small concrete bridge.

.13 Level out.

.2   Arrive at the rock outcropping overlook.

Mile 8.8. Greenstone Self-Guiding Trail [BRP 5]

Length: .2 mile, round-trip

Difficulty: moderate

Winding through an upland hardwood forest, the Greenstone Trail is a self-guiding trail with signposts explaining the volcanic origins of the Northern Blue Ridge Mountains. An easy pathway, this trail is one of the first you should walk. The information learned here will add greatly to your future walks and drives along the Parkway.

.0 Start at the northern end of the parking lot and bear to the right.

.05 Passing by Virginia pine, mountain laurel, and rhododendron, drop down on stone steps and continue to descend.

.1 Drop down again and begin to loop back.

.15 There are good views into the valley here. Begin to ascend on stone steps.

.2 Return to the parking lot.

Mile 9.6. Appalachian Trail. See Chapter 3.

Mile 13.1. Appalachian Trail. See Chapter 3.

Mile 16. VA RT 814 descends to the west of the Parkway to enter George Washington National Forest. The national forest around Sherando Lake and the St. Mary's Wilderness Area presents many opportunities for circuit hikes and, since camping is allowed throughout the area, the option for excursions of several days in length.

The trails are characterized by long, narrow ridge lines for ease of walking and good views, steep ascents and descents for challenging hiking, old mining areas to explore, and plenty of water to quench a hard working walker's thirst. This is a highly recommended area in which to spend some time.

More information may be obtained by contacting:

District Ranger
Pedlar Ranger District, USFS
2424 Magnolia Avenue
Buena Vista, VA 24416

The trails in this area are described in *Hiking the Old Dominion: The Trails of Virginia*, by Allen de Hart.

Mile 17.6. The Priest Overlook Trail [BRP 6]

Length: 300 feet, one way

Difficulty: easy leg stretcher

A very short path begins on the south end of the parking lot, crosses a small field, and in 300 feet arrives at a bench overlooking Torry Ridge. This leg stretcher is so short that no one should miss it. At the very least you can always boast to your friends that you actually got out of your automobile to walk on one of the trails of the BRP.

Mile 18.5. White Rock Falls Trail [BRP 7]

Length: 2.7 miles, one way

Difficulty: moderate

The first portion of the hike is an easy, gently sloping pathway to a cool, shaded spot beside a small stream. The pathway, which was built by the Youth Conservation Corps in 1979 and is now maintained by volunteers of the Tidewater Appalachian Trail Club, then becomes rockier and steeper. However, once it reaches the falls, it ascends at a gradual rate.

A pleasant day hike of five miles could be accomplished by combining the White Rock Falls Trail with the Slacks Overlook Trail [FS 480A]. Also, the falls could be approached from the other end – Slacks Overlook, mile 20 – in a hike of about 1 mile, one way.

.0   The pathway begins on the east side of the Parkway in White Rock Gap. There is only a grassy parking area here, and the trail sign is hidden below the roadway, so be on the lookout for the parking area and a tree blazed with an orange diamond. Begin by gradually descending on the pathway.

.15   Cross three small footbridges and notice the jumble of large boulders in the valley below.

.3   Pass old, crumbling stone walls.

.5   Pathway joins old roadbed.

.65   Be alert! The trail makes an abrupt turn to the right, off of the old road, and ascends gradually through mountain laurel and pine. Sassafras is particularly abundant.

.8   Pass a number of old trees that have been attacked
       by woodpeckers; continue with slight ups and downs.

1.2   Cross a small stream (nice spot for a rest break) and
       parallel it by ascending very steeply. Be sure to watch
       for the beginning of some switchbacks.

1.4   End the switchbacks and ascend more steeply along
       a ravine lined with hemlock.

1.5   Pass under large boulders and walk below stone
       outcropping.

1.6   A trail intersection. Three hundred feet to the right
       along the rock wall leads to White Rock Falls – a
       most magical place. The sun, beaming through hem-
       lock and mountain laurel, dances on the steep walls
       as the water cascades downward thirty to forty feet.
       After stopping at this enjoyable spot, return to the
       intersection and continue to ascend.

1.8   Switch back to the right.

1.9   Reach ridge line and descend.

2   The rocks to the right afford good valley views.
       Cross a small footbridge and ascend gradually.

2.2   Be alert! No matter how inviting it looks, the trail
       does not enter the hemlock grove; rather, it makes an
       abrupt right, crosses the creek, and ascends.

2.3   Under some stately hemlocks, cross creek on
       footbridge.

2.7   Arrive at the BRP. The Slacks Overlook is 150 feet to
       the left (BRP mile 20).

Mile 18.5. The White Rock Gap Trail [FS 480]

Length: 2.5 miles, one way

Difficulty: moderate

Markings: orange blazes

This trail descends from the western side of the BRP
for .5 mile to an intersection with the Slacks Overlook
Trail [FS 480A] (BRP mile 20). It continues another 2 miles
to the upper Sherando Lake campgrounds.

Mile 20. Slacks Overlook Trail [FS 480A]

Length: 2.2 miles, one way

Difficulty: moderate

Although there is nothing particularly spectacular
about this trail, it is an extremely pleasant walk through a

mountainside environment of hardwoods, berry bushes, and mountain laurel. If done in the direction described, it is, except for the final half mile, a gradual descent the whole way.

.0   Begin by taking the unmarked trail past the picnic table at the north end of the parking lot. In 250 feet, at the intersection of two unmarked trails, turn left downhill and intersect with a pathway blazed with blue diamonds. Turn right and slab the hillside.

.25   Walk around a spur ridge; continue to slab hillside.

.4   Amid abundant berry bushes, walk onto and begin following another spur ridge.

.6   Switch back to the right, cross a ridge line, and begin to descend.

1   Cross a (usually) dry water run.

1.4   Descend more rapidly.

1.6   Turn left onto an old roadbed.

1.8   Come to the White Rock Gap Trail [FS 480] with orange diamond blazes (to the left it is about 2 miles to Sherando Lake). Turn right and ascend through hemlock.

1.9   Arrive at an old homestead site where raspberries should be plentiful in season!

2.0   A sign here identifies the spring as the headwaters of North Fork Back Creek.

2.2   Arrive at BRP mile 18.5 in White Rock Gap.

Mile 22. Torry Ridge Trail [FS 507] and Slacks Overlook Trail [FS 480A]

Length: 1.9 miles, one way

Difficulty: moderate

The trailhead involves a little searching to find, but this hike is a standout because of its ease of walking, the numerous viewpoints, intimacy with a ridgetop environment, and a good feeling of isolation. The trailhead is about 1 mile up FSR 162 (near Bald Mountain Overlook, mile 22.1). The road may be gated, and it may be necessary to walk, gradually ascending, the 1 mile. At the first road intersection turn right, and in less than .1 of a mile, the yellow diamond-blazed trail begins on the left side of the road.

.0   Descend through a hardwood forest.

.16   A break in the vegetation reveals a good view of

Torry Ridge dropping to the valley floor. Begin walking through rhododendron.

.25   At the top of a small knoll is a view back to the BRP.

.4   As you descend from the knoll, note the telegraph pole. Before radio, telegraph was the only means of communications for the fire tower on top of Bald Mountain.

.7   A rock slide provides a couple of nice views.

.8   With a telegraph pole on the right, descend through a large rock jumble. The trail is then less rocky and mountain laurel and rhododendron thicker.

1.2   Trail intersection. (The Torry Ridge Trail continues descending along the ridge line to arrive, in about 3 miles, at Sherando Lake.) Turn right onto the Slacks Overlook Trail, with blue diamond blazing. After passing through so many thickets of rhododendron, it is conspicuously absent on this gently sloping pathway.

1.4   Cross a small rock field.

1.5   Cross second rock field.

1.7   Pass a small gully. The hillside becomes much steeper, but the pathway remains wide and level.

1.9   Be alert! Look for double blue blazes, and just beyond them turn to the right (unmarked trail) to ascend to the Slacks Overlook parking area. (The Slacks Overlook Trail [FS 480A] continues straight for 2.2 miles to reach White Rock Gap at mile 18.5; see BRP mile 20.)

Mile 22. Bald Mountain Trail [FS 500E]

Length: 2.2 miles, one way

Difficulty: moderate

This wonderfully isolated hike passes through the St. Mary's Wilderness Area. It receives very little traffic, so there is a good possibility of not seeing anyone for the full distance. Also, being in the wilderness area, you can camp here.

The trailhead is located on FSR 162 (near Bald Mountain Overlook, mile 22). This road may be gated and therefore have to be walked. About .75 mile up the road are two horizontal yellow blazes. A sign on the left side of the road identifies the trail.

.0   Begin by entering the wilderness area and gradually descend.

.4   An open place in the vegetation offers the first view.

.5   Switch back to the right and enter the head of a valley. This isolated spot seems far away from the BRP and virtually undiscovered. Hemlock thickly lines the creek, which you will cross and then parallel on a rocky, descending pathway.

.6   Cross the creek again as the valley begins to open up.

.7   Cross the creek once more and continue to descend through a thick growth of rhododendron.

1   At a pleasant campsite, leave the creek and begin the ascent on an old roadbed.

1.3   Pass through a hemlock tunnel and over a water run. Enter a different world as the rhododendron gives way to a very open forest floor.

1.5   Reach a ridge line; continue to ascend, but at a gentler pace.

1.9   Be alert! At the double blazes the trail leaves the old road and makes an abrupt right turn onto a pathway lined with azaleas and sassafras.

2.2   Intersect the Mine Bank Trail and turn left; walk 300 feet to reach the BRP across from the Fork Mountain Overlook, BRP mile 23. (The Mine Bank Trail [FS 500C] drops for 2 miles to reach St. Mary's Trail [FS 500] in the wilderness area.)

Mile 26.3. Big Spy Mountain Overlook Trail [BRP 8]

Length: .1 mile, round-trip

Difficulty: easy leg stretcher

Highly recommended

This short trail ascends through clover to a grassy knob for good views of the Shenandoah and West River valleys. It is especially good at sunrise, sunset, or star-gazing times.

Mile 29. Whetstone Ridge Trail [FS 523]

Length: 12 miles, one way

Difficulty: moderately strenuous

The approximately 12-mile-long pathway gradually descends along the crestline of Whetstone Ridge (named for the fine-grained sharpening stones it provided to early mountain settlers) from the wayside parking lot to a parking area on VA RT 603. The far end of the trail is reached by automobile by exiting the BRP to the west near the wayside and following VA RT 603 for about 9 miles to the marked trailhead parking area. The trail, which much of the way is along the original route of the Appalachian Trail of the 1930s, has few vistas during the summer. Yet, once the leaves drop off the trees in the fall, the views are almost continuous. Water sources are practically nonexistent, so be sure to carry plenty of fluids.

Mile 34.4. Yankee Horse Overlook Trail [BRP 9]

Length: .1 mile, round-trip

Difficulty: easy leg stretcher

A good place to visit on a hot summer afternoon. The pathway leads to a cool, shaded grotto in which Wigwam Falls plunges thirty feet over the rock facing. The trail makes use of a small portion of the bed of a narrow gauge railroad. At one time the Blue Ridge Mountains were laced by these narrow gauge tracks, allowing the harvesting of timber and other resources in otherwise inaccessible areas.

.0   Ascend to the railroad tracks on steps, turn right, and cross the stream. Turn left uphill.

.06   Cross another stream on a footbridge and arrive at the waterfall. The water, hemlocks, and cool shades of green ferns and mosses make this an enchanting spot.

.1   Turn left onto the railroad tracks and return to the parking lot.

Mile 38.8. Boston Knob Trail [BRP 10]

Length: .1 mile, round-trip

Difficulty: easy leg stretcher

Abundant dogwood trees make walking this circular path a pleasure and a thing of beauty just about any time of year. Spring brings forth their pink and white leaf bracts and flowers, while in summer the trees provide some welcome shade. In autumn the hillside is ablaze with the dogwood's bright red berries and rust colored leaves.

Mile 47.5. Indian Gap Trail [BRP 11]

Length: .2 mile, round-trip

Difficulty: easy leg stretcher

Indian Rocks, along the Indian Gap Trail. (Courtesy of
the National Park Service, Blue Ridge Parkway)

Late spring and early summer is the time to best enjoy this quick trail. It twists and winds its way through a
maze of rhododendron tunnels, and nothing quite equals
the enjoyment of negotiating the maze when the plants are
in full bloom. The interesting rock formation on top of the
knoll is an added bonus.

.0   Begin the ascent on a stone walkway through mountain laurel.

.06 Cross over the ridge line.

.1   Come to the balanced rocks and small caves of Indian Rocks. Go around the rocks and begin to descend through a tunnel of mountain laurel.

.2   Arrive back at the parking lot.

**Mile 51.5. Appalachian Trail (and access to the trails of
George Washington National Forest).** See Chapter
3.

Mile 55.1. White Oak Flats Trail [BRP 12]

Length: .1 mile, one way

Difficulty: easy leg stretcher

The White Oak Flats walk begins at the picnic tables and follows a small stream through a bottomland forest of white oaks, azalea, and mountain laurel. (The unmaintained trail across the creek ends in .25 mile at a gated Forest Service road.)

Mile 60.8. Otter Creek Trail [BRP 13]

Length: 3.4 miles, one way

Difficulty: moderate

The trail begins right next to the campground, so if you are staying there, this makes a nice before-breakfast or after-dinner walk. Except for one steep ascent and descent, the pathway follows gradually descending Otter Creek as it winds its way to the James River at BRP mile 63.6. You will pass through a grand variety of vegetations and terrain – hemlock, oak, mountain laurel, rhododendron, and galax line the stream, which has quite a number of inviting wading pools. The trail also crosses hillsides and wide, flat bottomlands.

This trail is worth walking any time of the year. Spring provides an abundance of wildflowers; the creek offers flat rocks for sunbathing and cooling water in the summer; Otter Lake reflects the dazzling fall colors; and icicles sparkle on the hanging rocks in winter.

Since Otter Creek Trail crosses the BRP or comes close to overlooks quite a number of times, you can make this walk as long or as short as you wish. (This can be a good activity to calm down an active group of young campers – send them on the trail and then follow on the Parkway to meet them at prearranged spots.)

.0 Begin the hike in the parking lot downstream from the restaurant.

.02 Side trail to the campground.

.1 Cross Otter Creek on large concrete stepping blocks.

.2 A side trail to the campground comes in from the left. There are a couple of nice pools to cool your feet in here.

.3 Cross under an eye-pleasing stone overpass of the BRP.

.4 Amid a cool hemlock grove, large, flat rocks in the creek are suitable for resting and sunbathing.

.6 Come to steps leading to Terrapin Hill Overlook (BRP mile 61.4). Hemlocks are dominant here. Soon pass under the BRP.

.7 Go under VA RT 130 in a concrete tunnel and immediately cross Otter Creek. The imposing, fern-covered rock cliff is worth a moment's study.

.8 Cross the creek again, walk below the rock cliff, but soon ascend on a fern-lined trail through an evergreen forest.

1 The ascent steepens. (The Park Service has thoughtfully provided a bench to rest upon.) The hillside brings a new environment with it – mountain laurel, galax, and pine trees.

1.2 Begin a very rapid and steep ascent.

1.3 Cross a creek on a hand-railed footbridge; descend gradually to cross a spur ridge. Soon pass a graffiti-abused beech tree.

1.4 Take time to explore and enjoy the quiet coolness of the natural cave to the left. Just beyond, descend quite steeply. (Be careful!)

1.5 Return to Otter Creek.

1.6 Cross a side stream that in times of high water has some very pretty, small cascades.

1.9 Come to some picnic tables, cross Otter Creek on a footbridge, pass by the Lower Otter Creek Overlook, and continue downstream next to the BRP.

2 Once again cross Otter Creek, this time on large boulders. The trail now meanders through a wide bottomland and soon enters an old pine plantation forest.

2.4 Junction with the Otter Lake Loop Trail [BRP 14] (.6 mile to the left leads to the Otter Lake Overlook; see BRP mile 63.1). Turn right to continue on Otter Creek Trail; cross a ditch and a creek on footbridges.

2.5 Come to Otter Lake Overlook, BRP mile 63.1, and continue to walk downstream next to the BRP.

2.7 Pass by the dam, go down the steps, cross Otter Creek on concrete stepping stones, and turn right. (To the left is the Otter Lake Loop Trail [BRP 14].)

2.8 Cross a side stream and walk onto an old railroad bed.

2.9 Turn right and leave the railroad bed.

3.0   Cross Otter Creek, which has some very inviting deep pools here.

3.1   Walk along a stone wall directly below the BRP. Honeysuckle is abundant, but so are greenbrier and poison ivy!

3.4   Arrive at the James River Visitor Center at mile 63.6. This is the lowest point on the BRP.

Mile 63.1. Otter Lake Loop Trail [BRP 14]

Length: 1 mile, round-trip (includes the .2 mile that must be walked along the BRP)

Difficulty: moderate

The Otter Lake Loop Trail has only one extended ascent and descent and offers glimpses of life in and around the lake. Results of the beavers' industrious lifestyle can be seen in quite a number of places, trout and carp inhabit the lake, and water snakes may be spotted slithering along through the underbrush. The normally calm waters of the lake reflect the surrounding hillsides.

.0   Begin at the south end of the parking lot. Descend the steps below the dam, cross Otter Creek on concrete stepping stones, and ascend, rather steeply, to the left. (To the right is Otter Creek Trail [BRP 13].)

.1   You are now directly above the dam, where the downed trees are evidence of a rather active beaver population.

.15   Come around a bend for the first good view of the lake from this trail.

.2   Veer away from the lake and cross a small stream. Traffic noise from the BRP is muted as you ascend around the side of a knoll.

.3   A bench is on top of the ridge line. Turn right. (To obtain an outstanding panoramic view of the lake, follow the trail to the left for 150 feet.)

.45   Come to another bench and begin the descent between two ridges.

.5   Cross a creek and wind through vine-choked bottomland. Soon cross a second creek.

.6   Pass by the ruins of an old homestead and intersect the Otter Creek Trail [BRP 13]. (To the right is the Otter Creek campground restaurant [2.4 miles].) Continue by bearing left and crossing two footbridges.

.8 Reach the BRP and the Otter Lake Overlook. (Your automobile is still some steps away – the parking lot is .2 mile long!)

Trails of the James River Water Gap, Blue Ridge Parkway Mile 63.6

The water gap of the James River is a significant geological formation of the Blue Ridge Mountains. The following two trails offer excellent opportunities to comprehend the force and power of a river that can carve out such a channel for itself through these mountains. (A plaque on the Trail of Trees explains this geological phenomenon in layman's terms.)

Both of these short walks are highly recommended, for the information learned here will increase your knowledge and enjoyment of the surroundings when you walk on some of the BRP's other trails. A trip through the visitor center is also worthwhile.

Mile 63.6. Trail of Trees Self-Guiding Trail [BRP 15]

Length: .4 mile, round-trip

Difficulty: moderate

Highly recommended

Exhibits and signs along the loop trail explain the life cycles and interrelationships of more than forty identified plants and trees.

.0 Begin at the visitor center, drop to the footbridge across the James River, but do not cross it. Instead, continue by ascending the steps straight ahead.

.06 Keep to the left and descend for a commanding view of the James River; eventually descend almost to the river.

.15 Cross a footbridge and ascend next to a large rock outcropping.

.2 Another good viewpoint of the river. This one has an exhibit explaining the formation of a water gap. Soon cross another footbridge and come to a bench. Ascend on steps.

.25 Arrive at a cool, shaded spot (courtesy of a large red maple tree). You'll also find a bench for resting here.

.4 Descend the steps back to the beginning of the trail and return to the visitor center.

Mile 63.6. James River Self-Guiding Trail [BRP 16]

Length: .2 mile, one way

Difficulty: easy

Highly recommended

In the 1800s, a system of canals and locks was built that turned the James River into a vital link between the civilization of the east and the newer settlements west of the Blue Ridge Mountains. The coming of the railroads brought about the decline of the canals, but exhibits and a well-preserved lock on the James River Trail bring those bygone days back to life.

.0 Begin at the visitor center, and in 200 feet turn left onto a concrete footbridge over the James River.

.1 The bridge ends; descend the steps and walk through an open field, enjoying your closeness to the river. Be on the lookout for signs of muskrat.

.15 Arrive at the canal, lock, and exhibits, which explain the history and workings of this nineteenth-century method of transporting people and goods across and through the mountains.

.2 The trail ends overlooking the river.

Mile 71. Glenwood Horse Trail

The Glenwood Horse Trail, a network of well over 50 miles of pathways, is a cooperative effort between the U.S. Forest Service and local equestrian groups. The trail system comes in contact with the BRP at miles 71, 80.5, and 93.1. Information on trailheads, distances, and conditions of the trails may be obtained by contacting the Glenwood Ranger District at P.O. Box 10, Natural Bridge Station, VA 24579.

Mile 71.1. Appalachian Trail (and access to the trails of the James River Face Wilderness Area). See Chapter 3 (mile 51.5 for the wilderness area trails).

Mile 74.7. Thunder Ridge Trail [BRP 17]

Length: .1 mile

Difficulty: easy

Mile 74.7. Thunder Ridge Trail [BRP 17]

Length: .1 mile

Difficulty: easy

This walk through a rocky mountaintop environment of rhododendron and hardwoods brings you to a view of Arnold Valley. The Thunder Ridge Trail and the Appalachian Trail are one and the same here, and if you start at one end of the parking lot and come around to the other, you can brag to your friends that you have now walked a portion of the famous 2,000 mile-long trail!

Mile 74.7. Appalachian Trail. See Chapter 3.

Mile 74.9. Hunting Creek Trail [FS 3]

Length: 2 miles, one way

Difficulty: moderate

Markings: blue paint blazes

This is an extremely pleasant walk as the trail descends via gentle switchbacks through 2 miles of almost continual rhododendron tunnels. It is most delightful in late spring and early summer, when the rhododendron are in full bloom. Although campsites are few and far between, camping is allowed anywhere along this trail.

.0 Walk on the Appalachian Trail just south of the Thunder Ridge Overlook (BRP mile 74.7).

.05 Turn left onto the Hunting Creek Trail.

.2 Enter a large rhododendron thicket.

.3 The rhododendron begins to form tunnels.

.4 The rhododendron is not quite so thick here, which allows great wintertime views into the valley. In the summer, you can behold the rhododendron in all of its magnificent glory.

.6 Switch back to the left as mountain laurel becomes mixed in with the rhododendron.

.7 Switch back to the right. A nice spot to watch the rising sun in the morning.

1   Leave the rhododendron and cross a rock field.

1.2 Reenter rhododendron tunnels.

1.3 As the vegetation changes to towering hemlocks, switch back to the left.

1.4 Switch back to the right.

1.5 Begin to parallel a creek lined by moss-covered rocks, hemlock, and rhododendron.

1.7 After two dry gullies switch back to the right in a rock field. Trail becomes somewhat indistinct. Keep looking for the blue blazes; soon the trail begins to follow a very old road.

1.9 Follow a grassy woods road.

2 Cross a creek and arrive at FSR 45. This trailhead may be reached by automobile by following FSR 951 from the BRP to NC RT 602, which turns into FSR 45.

Mile 76.3. Appalachian Trail. See Chapter 3.

Mile 78.4. Appalachian Trail. See Chapter 3.

Mile 78.7. Apple Orchard Falls Trail [BRP 18 and FS 17]

Length: 3.6 miles, one way

Difficulty: strenuous

The Apple Orchard Falls Trail drops nearly 2,000 feet as it passes by the 150-foot falls and goes through a wonderfully isolated mountain valley. After .2 mile, the trail enters Jefferson National Forest. (Camping is allowed. However, this is a very popular trail, so please use common sense in setting up camp. Try to camp a good distance away from the pathway and avoid setting up in any overused areas.)

Many people simply go down to the falls and then retrace their steps back to Sunset Field Overlook, a round-trip of 2.4 miles. Regaining the 1,000 feet in elevation makes this a strenuous hike.

However, if a car shuttle can be arranged, it is possible to make this a one-way, all-downhill trip. Take FSR 812, which begins at the north end of the Sunset Field Overlook (BRP mile 78.7). This dirt road has only one lane but is well graded and has frequent turnouts. Follow it down the side of Wildcat Mountain to a major intersection with FSR 768. Turn left onto FSR 768 and continue to FSR 59. A left turn onto FSR 59 will lead to the Apple Orchard Falls and Cornelius Creek trailheads [FS 18].

.0 Begin a gradual descent from the Sunset Field Overlook.

.2   Cross the Appalachian Trail and begin a series of long switchbacks.

.6   Come to an old roadway.

.8   Cross a wide, old road (to the left leads to Cornelius Creek Trail [FS 18]).

1   The trail enters a hemlock forest and parallels the creek.

1.1 Pass below a large rock outcropping. Soon descend steeply through rhododendron, and cross the creek on a footbridge, enjoying the small cascades upstream. The trail now veers away from the creek and soon descends steeply.

1.2 Arrive at Apple Orchard Falls, which drops about 150 feet over a stone facing that is surrounded by a moss- and lichen-covered rocky grove. Hemlock trees tower above everything. The water takes many paths down the rocks, so be sure to walk around to get a number of different perspectives of the falls. The trail beyond is rocky, and footing is unsure; it is obvious that many people end their hike at the falls.

1.35 The trail switches back to the left – keep watching for the paint blazes.

1.55 Cross a creek.

1.7 The trail has been relocated to avoid a very steep incline; be on the lookout for the switchback to the right.

2.1 The continued descent becomes much more gradual. If you are on an overnight hike, you should notice that good campsites begin to appear.

2.7 You'll have an even better choice of campsites as the valley floor becomes flatter, wider, and more open with less underbrush.

3.6 Arrive at FSR 59 and the trailhead for the Cornelius Creek Trail. The Forest Service has reconstructed the bridge across Cornelius Creek to make it handicapped accessible. The bridge also now has platforms to enable people in wheelchairs to take advantage of the reportedly good native trout fishing available in the creek.

•   The Apple Orchard Falls Trail may be combined with the Appalachian Trail and the blazed Cornelius Creek Trail [FS 18] for an enjoyable 8.2-mile circuit hike. After reaching FSR 59 via the Apple Orchard Falls Trail, turn left and ascend along the Cornelius

Creek Trail (traversing Backbone Ridge and gaining 1,700 feet in elevation) for about 3 miles to intersect the Appalachian Trail. Turn left on the Appalachian Trail for 1.3 miles to return to the Apple Orchard Falls Trail, where a right turn will lead, in .2 mile, back to the Sunset Field Overlook. Because of the extensive loss and regain of elevation, this should be considered a strenuous hike. Camping is permitted on the Apple Orchard Falls Trail as well as on the Cornelius Creek and Appalachian trails.

Mile 79.7. Onion Mountain Loop Trail [BRP 19]

Length: .1 mile, round-trip

Difficulty: easy

This loop trail winds through a maze of rhododendron and mountain laurel. It is an especially worthwhile walk in early summer when the pink, purple, and white blossoms are putting on their dazzling display.

Trails of the Peaks of Otter Area, Blue Ridge Parkway Miles 83.1–86

Archaeological evidence suggests the Peaks of Otter area was used as a hunting and camping grounds more than 8,000 years ago. Closer to our time, the Algonquian, Cherokee, Iroquois, and Sioux Indians visited the area in search of its abundant and diverse wildlife. Buffalo, elk, and deer once roamed these mountains in numbers large enough to establish well-worn and easily followed pathways across the ridge lines.

Settlers began to move in sometime after the Revolutionary War; around 1830 the first inn was established. By 1860 the Peaks of Otter was a popular resort for flatlanders wishing to enjoy the beauty of the mountains and seeking respite from hot summer temperatures. By the time the Park Service acquired the property in the 1930s, more than twenty families lived on the mountainsides and in the valleys bounded by the three Peaks of Otter – Sharp Top, Flat Top, and Harkening Hill.

The trails here are diverse and interesting enough to keep you occupied for quite some time. One drops quickly and steeply into a small gorge to arrive at a series of cascading waterfalls. Another gradually climbs to the 4,001-foot summit of Flat Top, the tallest of the three peaks. Other trails wind their way through open meadows and old, overgrown orchards and into a forest that is now reclaiming former farmlands. In addition to a moderately easy self-guided nature walk, the most famous excursion of the peaks area is a three-mile climb that leads to the summit of Sharp Top, which affords commanding views of the surrounding countryside.

This area can be enjoyed year-round. Spring arrives with hummingbirds, warblers, and woodpeckers seeking sustenance from the reawakening natural world. Wildflowers, such as mayapple, bloodroot, and foam flower emerge from the slowly warming soil. In summer, an early evening's stroll may be rewarded with a sighting of an opossum beginning its nightly foray or a quickly moving bobcat dashing into the underbrush.

The changing leaf colors of the hickory, birch, oak, and maple brighten the hillsides around Abbot Lake and announce the coming cooler weather. In winter, the Peaks of Otter Lodge, with its picture-windowed sun room, is a pleasant place to sip a cup of coffee and warm yourself after tracking a gray fox along one of the area's snow-covered pathways.

Peaks of Otter has a Park Service visitor center, picnic area, campground, camp store, gas station, snack bar, gift shop, and the Peaks of Otter Lodge. The lodge is open all year. A special tour bus to the summit of Sharp Top operates during the heaviest tourist months.

Mile 83.1. Fallingwater Cascades Trail [BRP 20]

Length: 1.6 miles, round-trip

Difficulty: moderate

This is a true year-round trail, each season offering its own rewards. Snow melt and spring rains swell the amount of water rushing over the falls as the sound is echoed within the narrow confines of the gorge. Tunnels of mountain laurel and rhododendron (in full bloom) provide a welcomed coolness and relief from summer heat, while the intense colors of changing leaves on the surrounding mountainsides are an eye-pleasing sight in the fall. The stillness and isolation of winter is accented by snow-covered branches and thirty-foot icicles growing on the rocks of the cascades.

In conjunction with the Flat Top Trail [BRP 21], the

Fallingwater Cascades Trail was named a National Recreation Trail in 1982.

The loss and gain in elevation classify this hike as a moderate one.

.0   As you leave the parking lot, turn right, descending through tunnels of rhododendron and mountain laurel.

.1   Come to a bench with views of the nearby mountainsides. Descend steeply on stone steps, but in 100 feet level off onto a rough and rocky pathway. In spring and periods of heavy rain, the sounds of crashing water will soon be heard.

.3   Cross hemlock-lined Fallingwater Creek on a footbridge, and arrive at the beginning of the cascades.

.4   Drop steeply on natural stone steps and come to a bench. A few feet further is another bench; switch back to the left. To the left is a good view of the cascading waters; turn to the right to continue on the loop trail.

.5   To the left is an even better view of the cascades – also a large, inviting pool near the base of the falls. Continue on the loop trail to the right.

.6   Cross the creek on a footbridge, enjoying the feeling of isolation here, for most people turn back once they have reached the bottom of the cascades. Begin the climb back to the BRP, and in a few feet come to a bench overlooking the steep, narrow confines of the creek gorge.

.9   A rock slide opens up additional views through the vegetation.

1   Come to a bench situated in a stand of hardwoods.

1.1 The trail to the right leads to the Flat Top parking area (200 feet). Turn left and continue to ascend.

1.2 Pass by a maple tree gigantic in stature.

1.3 Reach the top of the knoll, where there is an old bench. Begin to descend.

1.6 Arrive back at the Fallingwater Cascades Overlook.

Mile 83.5. Flat Top Trail [BRP 21]

Length: 4.5 miles, one way

Difficulty: moderate

Along with the Fallingwater Cascades Trail [BRP 20], the Flat Top Trail was named a National Recreation Trail in 1982. The pathway follows the ridge line of the mountain to the summit, gaining 1,500 feet of elevation along the way, before dropping to the Peaks of Otter picnic area. (A car shuttle can reach the picnic area by turning left onto VA RT 43 directly across from the Peaks of Otter Visitor Center – mile 85.9. Follow VA RT 43 for about half a mile to the picnic area entrance.)

Except for a few spots, most of the ascents and descents are gradual. The reward for doing the full length is the quiet and solitude you will experience compared to the mobs of people that would be encountered on Sharp Top in the summer and fall. It is suggested that you pass up the Cross Rocks Trail at the 2.2 mile mark. It is a narrow and slippery path, and the views are basically the same as those obtained at the summit.

.0 Begin the ascent along the ridge line.

.3 Cross through a gap.

.6 Come to a bench, switch back to the left, and wind around the hillside.

.9 Switch back to the right on a hillside covered with a profusion of ferns.

1.1 Begin to pass through mountain laurel and rhododendron. Here is a good wintertime view of the open fields of Johnson Farm on Harkening Hill. Through the trees the summit of Flat Top can be seen, still almost 1,000 feet above you.

1.3 In a rock field switch back to the right.

1.5 Arrive at a bench. The view here shows that you are already higher than many of the surrounding mountains. Continue to ascend with a series of switchbacks, but soon the trail becomes steeper and rockier.

2.1 Come to another bench.

2.2 Come to the intersection with Cross Rocks Trail (which is very steep and slippery). A rock outcropping at this intersection affords a good view of the Federal Communications Commission installation on top of Apple Orchard Mountain to the north. Continue to the right.

2.7 Drop into a small gap, only to rise again and make the final climb among giant boulders.

2.85 Reach the 4,001-foot summit of Flat Top. Rock outcroppings give commanding views – the Piedmont to the east; Sharp Top to the south; and Harkening

Hill, Chestnut Mountain, and Jennings Creek to the
west. Begin the descent from the summit.

3   A pleasant open area has a good view of Sharp Top;
continue to descend.

3.4 Cross over a ridge line, switch back to the right, and
continue on a now wider pathway.

3.6 Cross another ridge line and descend rapidly. Abbot
Lake is now visible through the vegetation.

4   Swing around to the southeast side of the mountain.

4.1 Enter a laurel thicket and begin a series of
switchbacks.

4.5 Arrive at the Peaks of Otter picnic area parking lot.
(The Peaks of Otter Lodge is .6 mile to the left via
[BRP 22] and [BRP 23].)

Mile 85.7. Abbot Lake Loop Trail [BRP 22]

Length: 1 mile, round-trip

Difficulty: easy

This is a pleasant stroll (also a good place to walk off
a little bit of the delicious Sunday brunch served in the
lodge). The trail goes completely around the lake, offering
possible glimpses of snapping turtles, water snakes, and
beaver. In fact, beaver activity is very abundant about
halfway through the trail. A portion of the forest above the
lake has almost been decimated by the ambitious beavers.

Sunrise and sunset are optimal times to do this walk,
as the glow of the sun may be softly reflected by the lake.

.0   Begin at the steps leading to the sun porch of the
dining lodge; turn right, toward the BRP. Soon the
pavement ends.

.1   The trail to the right leads to the Harkening Hill and
Johnson Farm trails and the visitor center. Bear left,
cross the creek, and walk next to the water's edge.
Tree stumps show recent beaver activity. Hawks and
buzzards are often spotted soaring overhead.

.3   Cross the inlet stream on a wooden footbridge, bear
right, and make a slight ascent into the woods.

.55 The trail coming in from the right leads to the Peaks
of Otter campground.

.6   As you begin to cross the dam, note there is a bench
on a little knoll from which to enjoy the view.

.7   Trail intersection. (A right turn onto Peaks of Otter
Picnic Area Trail [BRP 23; see below] will lead to
Polly Woods Ordinary, Peaks of Otter picnic area,

and the Flat Top Trail [BRP 21].) Bear left onto the pavement to return to the lodge.

.8   Cross a small inlet on an elevated footbridge, and go around the point on the lake. The benches there provide a fine view of Sharp Top directly across the lake.

1   Arrive back at the dining lodge.

Mile 85.7. Peaks of Otter Picnic Area Trail [BRP 23]

(Abbot Lake to Flat Top Trail Head in Picnic Area)

Length: .35 mile, one way; add another .3 mile if you are walking down from the lodge

Difficulty: easy

This short trail is most often used by those who wish to walk from the lodge to the Flat Top Trail. Along the way is the Polly Woods Ordinary, a traveler's inn from the 1800s. Living-history demonstrations are presented during the tourist season; check with the visitor center for dates and times.

.0   Having followed the Abbot Lake Loop Trail from the lodge, begin at the dam and soon reach Polly Woods Ordinary. Pass the cabin, go down steps, and follow the road.

.2   Enter the woods directly across from the rest rooms.

.3   Emerge from the trees. Pass by Big Spring, which has been running for at least 400 years.

.35   Reach the parking lot and the Flat Top Trailhead.

Mile 85.9. Elk Run Self-Guiding Trail [BRP 24]

Length: .8 mile, round-trip

Difficulty: moderately easy

Recommended

Signs identify plants and animals of the forest and explain their interdependence. The pathway is moderately easy, especially if done in the direction described – this allows you to ascend rather gradually and to descend on the only short, steep section of the trail.

Like all the self-guided trails on the BRP, this walk will give you an increased awareness and understanding of your surroundings on some of the other trails.

.0   Begin in the breezeway of the visitor center, and in 10 feet bear left at the intersection.

.05 Cross and then parallel a creek; ascend gradually.

.1 Cross the creek and come to a bench.

.15 Turn right onto an old road, but be alert because the trail turns off the road, to the right, in 150 feet.

.2 Arrive at bench among a jumble of rocks; ascend the hillside.

.4 Come to another bench and cross the creek; continue the ascent.

.5 Arrive at a bench on top of the ridge. The trail bears to the left and begins a rapid descent.

.7 At an old cemetery is another bench. Abbot Lake can be seen through the vegetation.

.8 Arrive back at the visitor center.

Mile 85.9. Johnson Farm Loop Trail [BRP 25]

Length: 2.1 miles, round-trip

Difficulty: moderate

Highly recommended

The Johnson Farm Loop Trail is one of the most fun excursions to be taken on the BRP. In addition to a pleasant walk through a mixed-hardwood forest of the Southern Appalachian Mountains, there is the reward of visiting the Johnson Farm. The farm was occupied from 1854 to the mid-1940s, and the Park Service has done an excellent job of restoring the buildings and land as they would have appeared around 1930.

A great variety of living-history demonstrations are presented on a regular basis (check with the visitor center for times and dates). The audience is usually invited to join in on these activities. Among other things you may find yourself planting or harvesting a garden, stirring some simmering apple butter, or making a patchwork quilt. This trip back into time provides insight into the recent human culture and history of the mountains you are exploring while on the BRP.

(The Johnson Farm Loop and Harkening Hill [BRP 26] trails make use of the same pathway near the end of this walk.)

.0 Begin at the north end of the visitor center parking lot; walk on the pathway toward the Peaks of Otter Lodge.

.1 At the top of a small rise, note the maple tree that is riddled with yellow-bellied-sapsucker holes. (A number of trees nearby have also been visited by the woodpeckers.)

.25 Come to a couple of trail intersections. Go past the first trail to the left – you will return from the Johnson Farm on this pathway. Take the second trail to the left (the one to the right leads .1 mile to the Peaks of Otter Lodge). Cross a creek and come into an open field that has an excellent view of the rock formations on Flat Top Mountain. Continue on a pathway through the field.

.5 Cross a creek, leave the field, and slab a hillside through the woods.

.7 Ascend in a gully between two ridge lines, then switch back to the right onto the hillside.

.8 Turn left onto a dirt road – avoid using the unauthorized trail that continues straight ahead.

.9 Come to the Johnson Farm site – barn, house, other buildings, and gardens. Be sure to take advantage of the hard work of the Park Service and volunteers who have helped to restore the farm. Join in on some of the living-history demonstrations that are presented. Swing around the farmhouse and garden and ascend the hillside.

1 Come to a bench overlooking the farm; enter the woods.

1.25 Arrive at an intersection. (The visitor center may be reached in 2.6 miles by turning right and following the Harkening Hill Trail [BRP 26].) The Johnson Farm Loop Trail bears left and descends.

1.35 Enter the first mountain laurel thicket on this trail.

1.45 Cross over a large-bouldered stream.

1.6 Cross a small side stream.

1.8 Arrive back at the trail intersections you passed earlier. The visitor center is .3 mile to the right; the Peaks of Otter Lodge is .5 mile to the left.

Mile 85.9. Harkening Hill Trail [BRP 26]

Length: 3.3 miles, round-trip

Difficulty: mildly strenuous

Recommended

The Harkening Hill Trail, with its short sections of steep ascents and descents, offers yet another chance to become aware of the human and natural history of the

Balance Rock, just off the Harkening Hill Trail. (Courtesy of the National Park Service, Blue Ridge Parkway)

Blue Ridge Mountains. The Harkening Hill area was used as farmland until the 1940s, as evidenced by the old fruit trees and open meadows (now kept cleared by the Park Service).

The hardwood trees in the wooded areas are young, showing that much of Harkening Hill was open farmland not too long ago; they show, too, that nature can, more or less, return an area back to its original state once left alone.

(The Harkening Hill and Johnson Farm Loop [BRP 25] trails make use of the same pathway near the end of this walk.)

.0   Begin in the breezeway of the visitor center and turn left to the amphitheater. Quickly ascend a series of switchbacks through a deciduous forest of poplar, dogwood, and oak.

.5   Reach the top of a spur ridge – obviously the site of an old orchard.

.75   Attain the summit of a minor knob; there is a limited view from the rocks to the left. Descend to a gap on a narrow ridge line, and resume the ascent on a gentler grade through more old fruit trees.

1   There should be plentiful blackberries and raspberries in season here!

1.1   Note the large boulder perched on two smaller rocks.

1.2   Begin to ascend steeply; wind around the mountainside.

1.5   A rock outcropping gives a good view to the southwest.

1.6   Ascend wooden steps between two giant boulders; walk the ridge line, where the mountainside drops off steeply to the left.

1.8   Attain the summit of Harkening Hill – 3,364 feet. There are good views to the northwest. The rocks make a nice lunch spot and a place to enjoy the antics of the scampering chipmunks. Begin the descent.

1.9   A 300-foot side trail leads to Balance Rock, a large boulder balanced on a much smaller one.

2.1   Pass through a high, open meadow with excellent views of the Federal Communications Commission installation on Apple Orchard Mountain to the northeast. The Allegheny Mountains to the west may be seen on clear days.

2.3   Some flat rocks make it possible to see the summit of Flat Top. The meadows of the Johnson Farm are directly below.

2.4   Come to an old road; follow it for only 200 feet before turning right.

2.6   A trail intersection. (To the left is the Johnson Farm Loop Trail [BRP 25], which leads to the Johnson Farm [.25 mile] and the visitor center [.9 mile beyond the farm].) The Harkening Hill Trail continues to the right – a wide pathway through azalea and mountain laurel.

2.75 Cross a water run.

2.9   Cross a small side creek.

3.1   A trail intersection. (To the left is the beginning of the Johnson Farm Loop Trail [BRP 25]; the other pathway leads to the Peaks of Otter Lodge [.1 mile].) Turn right to continue on the Harkening Hill Trail.

3.2   At the top of a small rise, notice the maple tree that is riddled with yellow-bellied sapsucker holes. (A number of trees nearby have also been visited by the woodpeckers.)

3.3   Return to the visitor center.

Mile 86. Sharp Top Trail [BRP 27]

Length: 1.5 miles, one way

Difficulty: strenuous

Recommended

The Sharp Top Trail, despite its ascent of 1,400 feet in only 1.5 miles, has been one of most popular recreation trails in the country since the nineteenth century. Thousands of people continue to make this pilgrimage every year.

The sweat and strain of the ascent is compensated by mountain laurel, azaleas, chipmunks, and, especially, the views from the bare-rocked summit. The Piedmont lies to the east, while the Allegheny Mountains rise to the west. Most impressive, however, are the long views to the north and south of the BRP snaking its way along the backbone of the Blue Ridge Mountains.

You may want to take this walk in early spring or late fall in order to avoid the hordes of people making use of the trail during the usual tourist season. (During the season a tourist bus is operated that will deliver you to within a few feet of the summit, allowing you to be lazy if you wish to get the view without really putting forth any effort. However, you miss the exercise and joy of reaching the mountaintop under your own power. Check at the camp store, visitor center, or Peaks of Otter Lodge for rates, times, and dates of the bus.)

.0   Begin at the Sharp Top parking lot, close to the camp store. Climb steps and begin the ascent.

.1   The trail becomes paved for a short distance.

.2   Cross the bus road.

.3   Walk through the first mountain laurel on this trail.

.5   Cross a rock field in a draw. In a few hundred feet ascend steeply on rock steps.

.75 Ascend steps set in a rock facing and switch back to the left. There is a good view to the southwest.

1.2 Come onto the ridge line and reach a trail intersection. (A side trail to the right leads, in about .4 mile, to Buzzard's Roost for a grandstand view to the east, south, and west.) To continue to Sharp Top, turn left and ascend.

1.3 Climb steps so steep that the Park Service has provided handrails.

1.45 Cross side trails to the bus loading area.

1.5 Attain the summit of Sharp Top with its superb 360-

degree view! To the east is the Piedmont and the town of Bedford; to the west is Harkening Hill and Harveys Knob, with the James River Valley just beyond. Wheat's Valley, Flat Top Mountain, and Thunder Ridge are to the north, the rocks of Buzzard's Roost to the south, and beautiful Abbot Lake is shimmering almost 1,600 feet directly below.

Mile 90.9. Appalachian Trail. See Chapter 3.

Mile 92.5. Appalachian Trail. See Chapter 3.

Mile 93.1. Appalachian Trail. See Chapter 3.

Mile 95.3. Appalachian Trail. See Chapter 3.

Mile 95.9. Appalachian Trail. See Chapter 3.

Mile 96. Spec Mine Trail [FS 28]

Length: 2.9 miles, one way

Difficulty: moderately strenuous (round-trip), moderate (one way with car shuttle)

The blue-blazed Spec Mine Trail drops from the crest of the Blue Ridge Mountains to the floor of Back Creek Valley. Most of the time it travels either narrow ridge lines or deeply wooded mountainsides, providing an excellent feeling of isolation. Except for the first few hundred feet, this trail is on Jefferson National Forest land, meaning camping is allowed. The best spot to leave your automobile is at the Montvale Overlook, about 200 feet north of the trailhead.

If you hike the trail in the direction described, the walk will be a gradual descent of the mountain. However, to return you must regain nearly 1,400 feet in less than 3 miles, making the hike a moderately strenuous one.

A car shuttle could be arranged by driving north on the BRP to Bear Wallow Gap at mile 90.9. Take VA RT 43 to Buchanan, south on US RT 11, left onto VA RT 640 for 4.5 miles, and make another left onto VA RT 645. In .5 mile arrive at the Spec Mine Trailhead directly across the road from a duck pond. The trail sign is often obscured by overgrown vegetation, so be on the lookout for a trailer on the right side of the road and the duck pond on the left.

.0 Begin at the trail sign a couple of hundred feet south of the Montvale Overlook at mile 95.9. Drop down a narrow ridge line.

.1 Passing through mountain laurel, slab to the left of a high knob. There are good views back to the BRP.

.4 With galax and running cedar lining the pathway, swing around to the west side of a knob.

.6 Cross a spur ridge and continue to descend.

1.1 Come onto a ridge line and ascend a knob; head in a westerly direction following the ups and downs of the narrow ridge line.

1.5 Cross through a rock outcropping to move from the left to the right side of the ridge line. Descend more steeply.

1.7 Switch back to the right, leave the ridge line, and walk on a hillside.

1.9 A small field on the left is a possible good campsite (no water); come onto an old road.

2 Cross FSR 634 (Hammond Hollow Trail [FS 27] may be reached by following FSR 634 to the right for approximately 3 miles.) Proceed straight ahead to continue on the Spec Mine Trail.

2.2 Cross an old road, but continue straight.

2.3 Swing to the right and avoid the faint trail to the left.

2.6 Cross a small water run and walk beside an overgrown field. The trail may be faint but soon becomes an obvious old roadbed again. The forest here is being overtaken by vines.

2.9 Arrive at VA RT 645.

• An adventurous and somewhat strenuous circuit hike may be accomplished by following the Spec Mine Trail for 2 miles, turning right onto FSR 634 for about 3 miles to arrive at the Hammond Hollow Trail [FS 27]. Turn right onto this pathway and ascend rather quickly, gaining about 1,000 feet in approximately 2 miles. Intersect the Appalachian Trail, turn right, and follow the AT as it parallels the BRP for 3 miles. Both will return to the Montvale Overlook. (Camping is allowed along FSR 634 and the Spec Mine and Hammond Hollow trails.)

Full length of this circuit hike is almost 11 miles.

Mile 97. Appalachian Trail. See Chapter 3.

Mile 97.7. Appalachian Trail. See Chapter 3.

Mile 110.6. Stewarts Knob Trail [BRP 28]

Length: .05 mile, one way

Difficulty: easy leg stretcher

This short walk leads to a viewpoint overlooking downtown Roanoke. The trail begins at the far end of the parking lot and makes a short rise through dogwood trees and poison ivy. In less than a minute it levels out. (Do not take the badly eroded trail uphill to the left.) Continue level for another minute and then drop slightly to the viewpoint and a bench on which to relax. Look for persimmons in the fall.

Roanoke Valley Horse Trail, Blue Ridge Parkway Miles 110.6–121.4

The impetus for the Roanoke Valley Horse Trail was provided by equestrians of the area. Forced in by encroaching developments, the trail is almost always within shouting distance of the BRP. Small portions offer a bit of isolation, but every section comes into close contact with housing developments, paved roadways, and private property.

The route is maintained by individual volunteers with the Park Service lending a hand whenever possible. Some sections are well used, while others are becoming overgrown and hard to follow. Be prepared, on the heavily traveled parts, for muddy, churned-up trails peppered with horse droppings. The overgrown portions will require you to negotiate pathways choked by weeds and briers.

The horse trail parallels the BRP on miles 110.6–121.4. One section has yet to be built, however; its completion remains stalled by the logistical problems of providing a horse crossing over the Roanoke River and a loading and unloading area on BRP property. Therefore, the trail does not exist on miles 114.7–116.4.

The Chestnut Ridge Trail [BRP 35] is also considered part of the Roanoke Valley Horse Trail. Of all of the sections, it offers the most wooded, and probably the most rewarding, hiking experience.

Mile 110.6. Roanoke Valley Horse Trail – Stewarts Knob Overlook to Parkway Maintenance Garage, BRP mile 112 [BRP 29]

Length: 1.5 miles, one way

Difficulty: moderate

The initial section of the horse trail rises from the overlook for a short distance before dropping into a pleasantly wooded area. It then passes by several housing developments before ending at the Parkway maintenance area.

.0   Begin on the Stewarts Knob Trail [BRP 28] and ascend slightly.

.05 Turn left uphill on an eroded pathway. The Stewarts Knob Trail continues to the right.

.1   Be alert! At an old fence line, make a hard turn to the right onto an overgrown pathway. Do not follow the unauthorized trail that continues up hill.

.2   Cross under a utility line as the forest becomes more open and the trail a little better defined. Soon, however, the weeds close in again.

.3   Follow the trail downhill as houses become visible to the left.

.6   Wind around in the woods below the houses.

.75 The trail becomes faint as briers overtake the pathway.

1.1 Pass through briers, vines, and brambles to arrive at VA RT 651. Follow the road to the south for a few feet before turning right onto an obscure trail toward the BRP. In a few more feet begin walking next to the Parkway, soon entering a wooded area.

1.2 Cross a small water run.

1.25 Emerge onto an overgrown field where there is no real defined route. Descend.

1.3 Cross another small water run. Ascend and parallel an old fence.

1.4 Reach the top of a knob just behind a house.

1.5 Arrive at the maintenance area.

Mile 112. Roanoke Valley Horse Trail – Maintenance Area to Roanoke River, BRP mile 114.7 [BRP 30]

Length: 3.6 miles, one way

Difficulty: moderate

The first third of this part of the horse trail is either a road walk or hiking right next to houses. The second third is a pleasant walk through suburban farms and open cattle pastures. The final third is in a forest of hardwood and mountain laurel as the land drops to the Roanoke River.

.0 Walk through the woods in front of the maintenance area and come onto a paved trail.

.1 Leave the pavement and follow a fence line that parallels the BRP.

.3 In the corner of the field bear left to come to a BRP entrance access road. Follow the road downhill to VA RT 24 and follow it to the east.

.35 Cross four-laned VA RT 24, and follow VA RT 1033 (Chestnut Mountain Road) for 100 feet. Be alert! Turn onto the trail entering the woods to your right. Remain in the woods.

.6 Walk between the Parkway and Chestnut Mountain Road.

.8 Pass by the private gravesites of Abram and Allie Baker. Make a series of ascents and descents in the woods next to several houses.

1 Veer away from the homes.

1.2 Cross a small water run and switch back to the left. Be alert! Do not continue to go straight; switch back to the right and begin a series of switchbacks to the top of a knob. The trail is now in pleasantly open woods.

1.4 Be alert! At the park border do not follow the boundary line downhill. Rise slightly uphill to walk just below a few houses.

1.5 Descend to cross a small water run, and move away from the houses.

1.7 Pass to the left of a small tree-farm plot and turn right to descend. Be alert! When power lines become visible, look for a faint trail to the left and follow it under the power lines. (Do not go downhill with the power lines.) The trail is obscure here but becomes more defined as it slowly descends to the BRP.

2.1   Parallel the BRP on a brier-covered pathway with houses visible again.

2.3   Cross VA RT 634 (Hardy Drive) and ascend on Hammond Drive.

2.6   Be alert! Turn right into the woods following a utility line right-of-way. Pass by a horse corral and into briers.

2.7   Be alert! Veer away from the utility lines and enjoy the rich aroma of a cattle pasture.

2.9   Walk along a fence line, savoring the bucolic scenery.

3.2   Enter the woods on a wide, soft, and pleasant pathway. Mountain laurel lines the trail.

3.4   The route narrows as it begins to descend.

3.6   The trail ends underneath the Roanoke River Bridge. You must scramble uphill to reach the Parkway. (The Roanoke Valley Horse Trail picks up again at BRP mile 116.4. See Chapter 4.)

3

The Appalachian Trail

From Springer Mountain in Georgia, the Appalachian Trail follows the crest of the Appalachian Mountains through fourteen states and covers more than 2,100 miles on its way to the summit of Mount Katahdin in Maine's Baxter State Park. Every year approximately 200 hearty, boot-clad souls complete the full length in four to six months, but the majority of people make use of the trail for much shorter periods of time – a few hours, a day, a weekend, or possibly a week. Trailside shelters, plenty of easy access points, an extensive network of side trails, and ideal campsites on George Washington and Jefferson National Forest lands are what draw many of these hikers to the AT along the BRP.

Virginia contains over 500 miles of the AT, about one-quarter of its total distance. Of that, a little more than 100 miles parallel the BRP from Rockfish Gap (mile 0) to Black Horse Gap (mile 97.7), where the trail swings to the west and leaves the main crest of the Blue Ridge Mountains. Construction of the Parkway on the original route of the AT south of Black Horse Gap necessitated a major relocation in the 1940s and 1950s. Before that time the trail had continued in the direction the BRP now follows – crossing Rocky Knob and the Peaks of Dan before entering North Carolina near Galax, Virginia.

The AT is the result of one man's vision and many people's hard work. Benton McKaye foresaw the growth of population in the eastern United States. He also recognized the human need to be able to step back from civilization for a while to become refreshed and renewed by the peace and beauty of the natural world. His 1921 proposal for an extended footpath in the Appalachian Mountains resulted in volunteers building the first few miles of the AT in New York in 1922. Sixteen years later the final link in the AT was completed on a ridgetop in central Maine. Volunteers (and some federal and state employees) continue to relocate, build, and maintain America's premier National Scenic Trail.

If you want to spend some energetic but rewarding days filled with the camaraderie of the trail, contact one of the local clubs and join them on a workhike to maintain a section of the AT along the BRP:

Maintains the AT on BRP miles 0–13.6:
    Old Dominion Appalachian Trail Club
    P.O. Box 25283
    Richmond, VA 23260
Maintains the AT on BRP miles 13.6–27.2:
    Tidewater Appalachian Trail Club
    P.O. Box 8246
    Norfolk, VA 23503
Maintains the AT on BRP miles 27.2–97.7:
    Natural Bridge Appalachian Trail Club
    P.O. Box 3012
    Lynchburg, VA 24503
Maintains the section of the AT south of BRP mile 97.7:
    Roanoke Appalachian Trail Club
    P.O. Box 12282
    Roanoke, VA 24024

The following AT descriptions are somewhat brief but should give you enough information to plan and successfully complete a trip on the trail. All distances are measured as a one-way hike, and descriptions are arranged in a north-to-south direction. The AT is well marked and usually well maintained. For a complete description of the AT along the BRP, consult the *Appalachian Trail Guide to Central Virginia*. This and other AT guidebooks and additional information about the trail are available from:

    The Appalachian Trail Conference
    P.O. Box 807
    Harpers Ferry, WV 25425
    304-535-6331

Mile 0

> Length: 7.3 miles
>
> Difficulty: moderately strenuous
>
> Shelter: mile point 4.8

This initial section of the Appalachian Trail to parallel the BRP is quite enjoyable as it contours around the mountainsides and past several small water runs. The walking is made even more pleasurable by the fact that the route uses portions of old roadways that were once important transportation links for numerous inhabitants of the central Blue Ridge Mountains. When not following these roadbeds, you'll be on superbly constructed pathways built by volunteers of the Old Dominion Appalachian Trail Club and of the Appalachian Trail Conference's Konnarock Crew. In addition, the isolation in Mill Creek Valley allows you to forget that you are so close to the BRP.

There are plans to relocate a portion of this section of the AT. Contact the Appalachian Trail Conference or Old Dominion Appalachian Trail Club for current information.

.0   At the very start of the BRP in Rockfish Gap, the AT drops to the east of the Parkway and begins a gradual descent along an old woods road.

.5   Cross a small trickle of water; rise for a distance only to drop back down again.

.9   A small moss- and fern-lined creek makes a nice resting spot before you start to rise again – this time at a little more rapid rate.

1.3   As you level out in an area of large grapevines, be alert! The AT leaves the old road and ascends on a footpath to the right, soon merging onto a roadbed to continue its traverse of the mountainside.

1.6   Be alert! The trail veers to the left onto a wide and well-built footpath, soon crossing a creek valley and ascending to a long stretch of minor ups and downs.

3.2   Ascend quickly for a short distance only to begin a long downward trend.

3.8   Pass through an area of previous mountain farm use (as evidenced by an old decaying structure and piles of stones that were removed from the earth to enable the ground to be put to agricultural use) and ascend on old woods road.

4   Be alert! The AT bears left to leave the overgrown roadbed and begin its long switchbacked descent into Mill Creek Valley.

4.8   Arrive at uniquely built Wolfe Shelter and its distinctive privy. Enjoy the peace and solitude of this small and isolated mountain valley before crossing Mill Creek and rising via a multitude of switchbacks.

5.7   Come to a good view of Rockfish Valley, Rockfish Gap, and mountains in the southern part of Shenandoah National Park.

6.2   Be alert! The AT swings left to begin following an old road around the side of Dobie Mountain. (The blue-blazed trail to the right follows the former route of the AT and is an alternate pathway to the end of this section.)

7.1   Begin to descend just after the blue-blazed trail rejoins your route.

7.3   Arrive at the Humpback Gap parking area. Northward for .2 mile on the BRP would lead to the Humpback Rocks Visitor Center (water and rest rooms) and Mountain Farm Trail [BRP 1].

Mile 6

(same walk as [BRP 2] in Chapter 2)

Length: 3.75 miles (plus an additional .3 mile side trail to the Humpback Rocks picnic area)

Difficulty: strenuous

Views to the west from Humpback Rocks make this a nice walk in the evening, while the eastward views on Humpback Mountain might lure you for a sunrise hike. Abundant springtime trillium, evidences of former inhabitants, remote ridge line walking, and possible deer sightings are additional attractions. The hike is strenuous due to the climb up to Humpback Rocks.

A relocation is planned for this section. Contact the Appalachian Trail Conference or the Old Dominion Appalachian Trail Club for the most recent information.

Camping is not permitted on this section.

.0   Begin by ascending from the Humpback Gap parking area along open meadows known as a "deadening."

.5   Do not take the old, eroded trail to the left; continue straight and soon begin a series of switchbacks.

.9   The trail to the left leads 800 feet to Humpback Rocks and grand views of Back Creek Valley and Pine Ridge. Bear right at the intersection to continue on the AT, here with small ups and downs and several viewpoints.

2   Attain the summit of Humpback Mountain. Rock outcroppings allow views of Rockfish Gap and Shenandoah National Park to the north, Shenandoah Valley to the west, and Rockfish Valley to the east. Begin to descend.

3   The view to the south is of Wintergreen Resort.

3.75 Take the blue-blazed trail (same as [BRP 3] in Chapter 2) to the right for .3 mile to arrive at Humpback Rocks picnic area (BRP mile 8.5).

Mile 8.4

Length: 1.6 miles

Difficulty: moderate

After ascending the .3 mile approach trail, this AT section is almost all downhill. Perhaps its most significant feature is at the end of the section – a delicious, cool drink from Dripping Rocks Spring.

Camping is not permitted on this section.

.0   At the far end of the Humpback Rocks picnic area parking lot, follow the blue-blazed trail uphill (marked with an AT symbol – [BRP 3] in Chapter 2.)

.3   Trail intersection. Turn right onto the AT and descend, passing by Laurel Springs (unreliable) and ascending to come close to the Wintergreen Resort.

1.6   Arrive at Dripping Rocks Spring parking area (BRP mile 9.6).

Mile 9.6

Length: 4.3 miles

Difficulty: moderate

A fairly recent AT relocation, this short excursion is worthwhile because of the abundant spring wildflowers, a steeply plunging stream, and two views. One is along a grassy ridge, and the other is from a prominent outcropping.

Except for the areas near the road crossings, camping is allowed anywhere along this section of the AT.

.0   From the Dripping Rocks Spring parking area, cross the BRP and descend.

.5   There are good views of Shenandoah Valley and

Torry Ridge from an open ledge.

1.2   A .1 mile side trail leads to a westward view from a rock outcropping.

2.1   Cross a bubbling, gurgling, rushing stream making its way down the steeply sloping mountainside; continue with ascents and descents.

4.3   Arrive at the Three Ridges Overlook (BRP mile 13.1).

Mile 13.1

Length: .5 mile

Difficulty: moderately easy

Spring and fall flowers will draw you into the open meadows, while the short ascent and descent will help awaken your legs after driving in a car all day.

.0   From the Three Ridges Overlook ascend into the woods and emerge onto an open field.

.2   Reach a wooded knoll; descend through a Park Service–maintained field.

.5   Arrive at VA RT 664 in Reeds Gap. Three hundred feet to the right is the BRP (mile 13.7).

Mile 13.7

Length: 44.8 miles (does not include any of the side trails)

Difficulty: strenuous

Shelters: mile points 1.6, 7.4, 14.8, 21.8, 31.4, and 36.8

Highly recommended

This long stretch of the AT contains just about everything that makes hiking in central Virginia worthwhile – magnificent views, rhododendron- and hemlock-lined mountain streams filled with native trout, remote virgin forests contrasting with cattle-dotted grazing lands, wildflowers by the thousands, and ample opportunities for quiet, isolated, and scenic campsites.

As the BRP makes a wide arc to the west around the Tye River Valley, the AT stays to the east, leaving the Parkway and traversing some of the highest mountains and lowest valleys of the Blue Ridge Mountains in Virginia. The wildly fluctuating elevations turn these 45 miles into some of the best hiking to be found along the BRP.

The trail leaves the Parkway to ascend the 3,970-

foot summit of Three Ridges, then plummets almost 3,000 feet to the Tye River, only to climb even higher in a little over 4 miles to the top of The Priest (4,063 feet).

The next 18 miles of trail never drop below 3,200 feet and actually pass over three additional summits of more than 4,000 feet in elevation each. The up-and-down effort this altitude requires is rewarded with grand views from short side trails, rock outcroppings, and wide, open fields. The trail again drops below 1,000 feet – this time to follow a rhododendron- and hemlock-lined stream to a stand of virgin timber – before rising again to meet the BRP at mile 51.5.

This route has six AT shelters; in fact, camping is allowed almost anywhere along it. (Exceptions are noted in the trail description.) Side trails (also noted) and plentiful automobile access points open up a number of circuit-hike possibilities and the opportunity to spend quite a few days camping, exploring, and hiking in the Blue Ridge Mountains of central Virginia.

.0   Leave the parking area in Reeds Gap on VA RT 664 and ascend.

.8   Come to a viewpoint to the west; descend.

1.6 Turn left onto an old road to continue on the AT. Straight ahead is the Maupin Field shelter and spring.

•   Directly behind the shelter is the Mau-Har Trail [FS 303], an excellent alternative to the long climb of the AT over Three Ridges. The Mau-Har drops steadily, paralleling Maupin Creek and passing by numerous waterfalls – one over 40 feet high. This 3-mile side trail rejoins the AT at the 8.2 mile point, .8 mile south of Harpers Creek shelter.

1.7 Leave the roadway and turn left onto a pathway going uphill to begin a long, steady climb.

2   Arrive at the summit of Bee Mountain; descend slightly only to rise again.

3.6 The rock outcropping to the right provides a view of The Priest.

4.2 Attain the highest point on Three Ridges and begin to descend via switchbacks.

5.7 Pass Chimney Rocks.

6   Arrive at another view of The Priest.

7.4 Come onto an old road and turn left. (Harpers

Creek shelter and water are .1 mile to the right.)

8.2 At the intersection with the Mau-Har Trail [BRP 303], bear left.

• A right turn onto Mau-Har will lead back to the Maupin Field shelter in 3 miles.

10 Cross the Tye River on a cable-suspension bridge and arrive at VA RT 56. The BRP (mile 27.2) is 11.5 miles to the right on VA RT 56. Cross the paved road to continue on the AT, and begin the 4-mile, switch-backed climb to the summit of The Priest.

12.7 A rock outcropping overlooks the Tye River Valley.

14.5 The wooded summit of The Priest offers no views, but .2 mile beyond, a short side trail leads to a panorama of Pinnacle Ridge to the west and Three Ridges to the north. Descend.

14.8 Trail intersection. One-tenth mile to the left is The Priest shelter and spring. Bear right to continue on the AT, where camping is prohibited for the next .3 mile.

15.6 Come to VA RT 826, a dirt road passable by automobile. It descends .5 mile to the Forest Service's Crabtree Meadows campground (water available) and the Crabtree Falls Trail before continuing on about another 4 miles to VA RT 56 near Montebello.

• The 3-mile Crabtree Falls Trail [FS 526] descends along Crabtree Creek passing by five major falls areas and numerous smaller cascades before arriving at VA RT 56 a few miles east of Montebello.

Continue on the AT by crossing VA RT 826 and ascending into the woods.

16.1 Reach the top of the ascent and descend.

16.5 Cross Cash Hollow Road (impassable by car) and gradually ascend for the next 1.5 miles.

17.9 Views of the Little Priest, The Friar, High Peak of Tobacco Row, and the Cardinal are obtained from Cash Hollow Rock.

18.7 Attain the 4,040-foot top of Maintop Mountain, where there are no views due to its wooded summit.

19 Trail intersection.

- The side trail to the left goes .1 mile to Spy Rock for a 360-degree view unequaled anywhere else in the area. Maintop Mountain is due north, while the whole Religious Range – The Priest, Little Priest, The Friar, Little Friar, and The Cardinal are visible to the northeast, east, and south. Whetstone Ridge and Fork Mountain are to the west. Don't pass up the chance to enjoy this wonderful vista.

19.5 Cross Fish Hatchery Road. (VA RT 56 near Montebello is 1.5 miles to the right.) Ascend.

20.3 Reach the highest point on the ridge line and descend to cross a dirt road.

21.4 The Twin Springs (one to the left, the other to the right) make this an inviting campsite.

- The blue-blazed Lovingston Spring Trail [FS 731] bears right onto an old road, arrives at another good campsite next to Lovingston Spring in 2.2 miles, and, .9 mile beyond, rejoins the AT at mile point 25.4.

  Cross the dirt road to continue on the AT south of Twin Springs.

21.8 The trail to the left goes to the Seely-Woodworth shelter and spring in .1 mile. Bear right to continue on the AT.

24.5 A rock outcropping affords a view of The Priest.

25.4 Cross Greasy Spring Road and the junction with Lovingston Spring Trail [FS 731].

26 Cross FSR 246.

27.2 Arrive at FSR 63, an automobile access point. (To the right, via FSR 63 and VA RT 634, is US RT 60 [7 miles], about 3 miles east of the BRP [mile 45.6] in Humphrey Gap. Cross FSR 63 to continue on the AT.)

28 Continue to ascend in an open field as a better vista unfolds with every step you take.

28.7 Arrive at the summit of Tar Jacket Ridge. Gaze northward to marvel at what you have traversed so far – Elk Pond Mountain, Maintop Mountain, and The Priest. Turn 180 degrees to see where you are going – over Cole Mountain and Bald Knob. Descend on an old road.

29.2 Come into Hog Camp Gap. (FSR 48 is passable by automobile and goes to Wiggins Spring and a good campsite .5 mile to the right. The spring is a true joy, as it bubbles forth gallons of cool, clear water every hour. US RT 60 is less than 4 miles beyond Wiggins Spring via VA RTS 755 and 634.)

• One-half mile to the left in Hog Camp Gap is a nice diversion – the 5.5-mile Pompey Mountain Loop Trail [FS 702]. It just misses the summit of Pompey Mountain but does lead to a .4-mile side trail [FS 701] to the top of Mount Pleasant for good views of the surrounding countryside. A spring and campsite are located about midway on the loop.

Cross FSR 48 and begin the ascent of Cole Mountain to continue on the AT from Hog Camp Gap. Watch the blazes closely as the AT follows a maze of dirt roads and trails.

30.6 Arrive at the 4,022-foot summit of Cole Mountain. Enjoy this final 360-degree grandstand view. Tar Jacket Ridge and Elk Pond Mountain are almost due north, while the Religious Range is to the northeast. Your route over Bald Mountain lies to the south. Descend.

31.4 Come into Cow Camp Gap and cross a roadbed. The Cow Camp Gap shelter and spring are .6 mile to the left along this old road.

32.2 Attain the wooded summit of Bald Knob (4,049 feet) and begin a long, gradual descent – eventually dropping below 3,000 feet for the first time in more than 18 miles.

35 Come into the Long Mountain Wayside picnic area on US RT 60 (4 miles east of BRP mile 45.6). Cross the highway, bear right, and descend via switchbacks.

36 Cross and begin to parallel Brown Mountain Creek, passing by old foundations and other remnants of former settlements.

36.8 Arrive at the Brown Mountain Creek shelter and spring. Cross the creek on a footbridge.

38.8 Cross FSR 38 (passable by automobile), which leads, to the left, to US RT 60 at Long Mountain Wayside (3.5 miles).

39.4 Come to the first view of Pedlar Lake, which is the

reservoir for the city of Lynchburg. Camping is prohibited for the next 2 miles. The trail continues around the lake on a rough, up-and-down treadway.

41   Cross Pedlar River just below Pedlar Dam. The AT crosses the field and passes through a gate onto a paved road.

41.4 Turn right onto FSR 39. Be alert! In less than 200 feet, the trail leaves the road to the left and crosses a creek on a footbridge. Camping is allowed from here to the end of this section of the AT. Begin a long ascent.

41.9 Pass by a 4.5-acre virgin forest.

42.2 Cross a dirt road.

43.8 Cross a second dirt road. Continue with several small ups and downs.

44.3 Cross VA RT 607.

44.8 Arrive at the parking area on the BRP (mile 51.5).

Mile 51.5

Length: 21.9 miles (does not include any side trails)

Difficulty: strenuous

Shelters: mile points .4, 9.2, and 14.1

The AT again swings away from the BRP, this time to the west. Rising to 3,372-foot Bluff Mountain, the trail then follows a narrow, rocky ridge line to impressive views overlooking the James River Water Gap. Thousands of years of erosion have allowed Virginia's longest river to punch its way through the Blue Ridge Mountains as it flows eastward to the Chesapeake Bay.

Water seems to be the focal point of this AT segment. Johns Hollow shelter is located in a wide, flat valley created by a stream descending the steep slopes of Little Rocky Row. Crossing the James River, the trail enters the James River Face Wilderness Area and comes to the narrow confines of a gorge built by Matts Creek. Large pools, close to Matts Creek shelter, are hard to resist on warm summer days.

The trail then climbs steadily to Highcock Knob (3,073 feet) before arriving at the end of the section in Petites Gap (BRP mile 71.1).

Except for the road walk along the James River and on BRP land near Petites Gap, camping is allowed throughout this section. Three side trails north of the

James River offer circuit-hike opportunities. The James River Face Wilderness Area has a network of trails interconnecting with the AT, allowing a number of extended backpacking excursions. Road access is at the beginning, middle, and end of the section.

.0   From the parking area at mile 51.5, cross the BRP and ascend.

.4   Come onto an old road and turn left. The road to the right descends 1,000 feet to the Punchbowl shelter and spring next to a small pond.

.6   Leave the roadbed and continue to ascend on a worn pathway.

1   Attain the summit of Punchbowl Mountain, descend slightly, but soon resume climbing via switchbacks.

2   The wooded summit of Bluff Mountain precludes any good views; descend.

2.5   Pass a viewpoint.

3.6   Trail intersection.

•   The blue-blazed trail [FS 511] to the right descends 4.5 miles through Belle Cove Valley to reach US RT 501 a couple of miles north of Glasgow.

     Bear left to continue on the AT.

4.6   Trail intersection.

•   Blue-blazed Saddle Gap Trail [FS 703] drops 2.5 miles to FSR 36 about 3 miles north of US RT 501.

     Bear right and ascend out of the gap to continue on the AT.

6.1   Reach the high point on the ridge line and descend, only to begin another climb.

7   A short path to the left leads to Fullers Rocks. The impressive view is of the James River cutting through the Blue Ridge Mountains and of the steep mountainsides south of the river in the James River Face Wilderness Area.

7.2   Trail intersection.

•   To the right, blue-blazed Little Rocky Row Trail [FS 512] goes down almost 3 miles to US RT 501, about 2.5 miles west of where the AT crosses US RT 501 at mile 11.1.

To continue on the AT, make a hard left. Descend steeply, sometimes on switchbacks, sometimes not. Also, cross several dirt roads.

9.2 Johns Hollow shelter and spring are just to the left of the AT. Soon, cross and follow FSR 36 and other dirt roads. Watch closely for the blazes.

11.1 Reach US RT 501. (BRP mile 63.7 is 3 miles to the left; Glasgow is almost 3 miles to the right.) Turn left along the highway and cross the James River on a bridge just in front of the dam and hydroelectric plant. Continue to follow US RT 501.

11.5 Turn right into the woods, ascend, and enter the James River Face Wilderness Area on an old road.

13.1 Reach a ridge line and begin to descend, passing by a good spring.

14.1 Cross Matts Creek and soon come to Matts Creek shelter on the opposite bank. The water supply is from the stream, so be sure to treat before using. Leave the creek and begin a long, long ascent.

14.8 Come to series of views overlooking the James River.

16.9 Reach a ridge line and trail intersection. The AT bears to the left and ascends.

• The Balcony Falls Trail [FS 7], a portion of which some maps and guidebooks identify as an extension of the Sulphur Spring Trail, bears right. It gradually descends for 5.5 miles, passing a couple of views of the James River, to reach VA RT 782. An automobile can reach this trailhead by following FSR 35 (which becomes VA RT 781) from Petites Gap (BRP mile 71.1) for 3 miles to VA RT 759. (Along the way pass trailheads for the Sulphur Spring Trail [FS 7; same as Balcony Falls Trail], 1 mile from the BRP, and the Belfast Creek Trail [FS 9], 2 miles from the BRP.) Turn right onto VA RT 759 and follow it for 3 miles to VA RT 782. (About 1.5 miles from the junction of VA RT 781 and VA RT 759 is the Gunter Ridge Trailhead [FS 8], .3 mile beyond the Glenwood Iron Furnace.) A right turn onto VA RT 782 for another 1.5 miles will bring you to the Balcony Falls Trailhead [FS 7].

17.4 Trail intersection. The AT makes a hard left and continues to ascend.

- The Belfast Creek Trail [FS 9] goes right for .4 mile to an intersection with the Gunter Ridge Trail [FS 8] then bears left for 1.5 miles to Devils Marbleyard, a large area of giant boulders. It then descends Belfast Creek for another mile to VA RT 781. (See trailhead directions in the mile point 16.9 description above.)

  The Gunter Ridge Trail [FS 8] bears right from the intersection and uses switchbacks through a profuse growth of mountain laurel to reach VA RT 781 in 4.5 miles. (These trailhead directions may also be found in the mile point 16.9 description above.)

19.2 Trail intersection. Cross to continue to gradually ascend on the AT.

- To the left, the Sulphur Spring Trail [FS 7] descends 2 miles to the AT and Balcony Falls Trail [FS 7] intersection (mile point 16.9). To the right, the Sulphur Spring Trail passes the Piney Ridge Trail [FS 2] in 1.5 miles and continues to follow the old road another 2.5 miles to Sulphur Spring and FSR 35. (See the mile point 16.9 description above for trailhead directions.)

  The Piney Ridge Trail [FS 2] bears left from the Sulphur Spring Trail to gradually descend the ridge line for 3.5 miles to FSR 54. This trailhead may be reached by leaving the BRP at mile 63.7, following US RT 501 west for .5 mile, and turning left onto FSR 54. The trail begins about a half mile up this road.

19.8 Marble Spring campsite. The spring is .1 mile to the right. Continue on the AT with ascents, steeply at times.

20.7 Attain Highcock Knob (no views) and descend quickly.

21.9 Arrive at Petites Gap and FSR 35. The BRP (mile 71.1) is less than 500 feet to the left.

Mile 71.1

Length: 3.4 miles

Difficulty: strenuous

Passing through the Thunder Ridge Wilderness Area, the AT climbs more than 1,300 feet in less than 2 miles. Late spring wildflowers are especially plentiful on the ascent. A second climb is rewarded by a view of the James River and the distant Allegheny Mountains to the west.

Except in the areas around Petites Gap and the Thunder Ridge Overlook, camping is permitted along this entire section.

.0   Cross FSR 35 in Petites Gap (.1 west of BRP) and ascend on an old road into the Thunder Ridge Wilderness Area.

.4   Be alert! The trail turns left from the old road onto a footpath.

1   Pass a view to the right.

2   Arrive at the summit of Thunder Ridge (no views). Descend, only to rise again.

3.3 Trail intersection. To the left is the Thunder Ridge Overlook parking lot (BRP mile 74.7). Bear right and come to the view overlooking the James River and Allegheny Mountains. Continue beyond the view and, in .1 mile, leave the AT to reach the parking lot via a side trail to the left.

Mile 74.7

Length: 1.7 miles

Difficulty: moderately easy

Shelter: mile point 1.4

This short segment is most notable for the easy access it provides to the Thunder Hill shelter and accompanying spring. Columbine and trillium line the pathway in May and June.

Camping is allowed on the entire section except in the areas around the Thunder Ridge Overlook and the BRP crossings. Hunting Creek Trail [FS 3] also provides a few isolated campsites.

.0   Park at the Thunder Ridge Overlook, take the approach trail to the AT, and turn left.

.3   Cross the BRP (mile 74.9).

.4   Trail intersection.

- Blue-blazed Hunting Creek Trail [FS 3] descends, by way of switchbacks and rhododendron tunnels, for 2 miles to FSR 45. (See Chapter 2, mile 74.7, for a detailed description of this trail and directions to the trailhead on FSR 45.)

  To continue on the AT, bear right on a gently ascending pathway.
1.4 Come to the Thunder Hill shelter and spring.
1.7 Arrive at the BRP (mile 76.3).

Mile 76.3

Length: 2.6 miles

Difficulty: moderately strenuous

A superb relocation by volunteers of the Natural Bridge Appalachian Trail Club and the Appalachian Trail Conference's Konnarock Crew permits the AT to cross the top of Apple Orchard Mountain as it once did in the 1930s. Camping is prohibited near the BRP road crossings and on the summit of the mountain.

.0 Park at the Apple Orchard Overlook (BRP mile 76.5) and walk back to the AT crossing at mile 76.3. Turn left onto the AT in a level area; soon begin to ascend.
.6 Rock steps enable you to pass under The Guillotine, a most interesting rock formation.
.9 Rocks on the summit of Apple Orchard Mountain permit a more than 250-degree view of the surrounding mountains.
2.3 Come to FSR 812, and in less than .1 mile turn left onto a side trail to Sunset Field Overlook.
2.6 Arrive at Sunset Field Overlook (BRP mile 78.4) and a grand view into the Great Valley of Virginia.

Mile 78.4

Length: 17.4 miles (does not include side trails)

Difficulty: strenuous

Shelters: mile points 2.9 and 14.5

Leaving the main crest of the Blue Ridge Mountains, the AT heads west to cross a couple of relatively level ridge lines before losing nearly 2,000 feet to descend to VA RT 714. From this road it makes more than ten ascents and descents (one of over 1,000 feet) before rejoining the BRP in Bear Wallow Gap (mile 90.9).

Springtime travelers of this challenging part of the AT will be compensated by a profuse array of blooming wildflowers. Mayapple is one of the first to appear in late March, quickly followed by bloodroot and trillium in April. Azalea and wild geranium burst forth in May, while rhododendron and mountain laurel line the trail in late May and early June.

A 7.5-mile circuit, via the Apple Orchard Falls [FS 17] and Cornelius Creek [FS 18] trails, offers a chance to view the falls, do some isolated ridge-line walking, and find plenty of flat campsites. Additional side trails present other options.

Except for areas near the road crossings, camping is permitted throughout the section and on the side trails.

.o   Begin at the Sunset Field Overlook and descend on the Apple Orchard Falls Trail.

.2   Trail intersection; turn left to continue on the AT.

- The Apple Orchard Falls Trail [FS 17] goes straight ahead for 1 mile to the falls and 3.4 miles more to FSR 59 and the intersection with the Cornelius Creek Trail [FS 18]. (See Chapter 2, mile 74.8, for a detailed description and trailhead directions.)

.9   Reach the ridge line and descend.

1.4   Trail intersection; the AT bears to the left.

- The Cornelius Creek Trail to the right traverses Backbone Ridge and Cornelius Creek for 3 miles to arrive at FSR 59 and an intersection with the Apple Orchard Falls Trail.

2.9   Trail intersection; bear right to continue on the AT.

- The short blue-blazed trail to the left goes to the Cornelius Creek shelter and water. (The BRP [mile 80.4] may be reached by following the unblazed trail behind the shelter for .1 mile to a dirt road. Turn left on the road to reach the BRP in 1,000 feet.)

4   Come to a view of the Federal Communications Commission installation atop Apple Orchard Mountain. Continue with minor ups and downs on the ridge line. Eventually begin a long descent.

7.5   Follow a dirt road to the right. Be alert! In less than

.1 mile the trail turns to the left and descends along a creek.

7.9 Come onto a dirt road littered with hundreds of buttons. Pay attention to the blazes as the trail follows different roads through a series of intersections.

8.3 Cross VA RT 714 and ascend.

9.6 Reach the ridge line and continue with very minor ups and downs. However, eventually begin a long descent with occasional views.

11.3 Come onto VA RT 614, turn right, cross the bridge, and in less than 500 feet turn left uphill into the woods.

• This point may be reached by driving VA RT 619 from the BRP in Powell's Gap (mile 89.1) to the intersection with VA RT 614. Turn left and stay on VA RT 614 to pass by the Little Cove Mountain Trailhead and, .9 mile beyond that, arrive at the AT crossing. Little Cove Mountain Trail [FS 25] ascends for nearly 3 miles to join the AT at mile point 15.8 (below).

12.7 Trail intersection; the AT bears to the left and begins a long series of ups and downs on the ridge line.

• The Cove Mountain Trail [FS 23] drops to the right 2 miles to reach VA RT 622 about .2 mile from VA RT 614 in Arcadia. One-tenth of a mile down the Cove Mountain Trail, the Buchanan Trail [FS 24] bears left and descends for 3 miles, via trail and dirt roads, to reach VA RT 43 about 1 mile south of Buchanan.

14.5 A short side trail to the left goes to Cove Mountain shelter (water not readily available).

15.8 Fork in the trail.

• The Little Cove Mountain Trail [FS 25] turns to the left to reach VA RT 614 in about 3 miles.

Bear right to continue on the AT.

17.4 Arrive at VA RT 43. The BRP (mile 90.9) is less than 500 feet to the left.

Mile 90.9

Length: 1.7 miles

Difficulty: moderately easy

From the parking area on VA RT 43, walk uphill, under the BRP, and, in .1 mile, turn into the woods on an old road. For the next 1.7 miles the AT meanders with slight ups and downs through a mostly hardwood forest. Changing leaf colors make this an exceptionally pretty walk in the fall. The section ends at the Sharp Top Overlook (BRP mile 92.5).

Camping is not permitted on this section.

Mile 92.5

Length: .6 mile

Difficulty: easy

Crossing the BRP from the Sharp Top Overlook, the AT stays close to the Parkway and experiences almost no change in elevation. FSR 4008 is reached in .6 mile. Follow the old road to the left to arrive at the Bobblets Gap Overlook (BRP mile 93.1).

Camping is prohibited on the entire section.

Mile 93.1

Length: 2.4 miles (does not include side trails)

Difficulty: moderate

Shelter: mile point .1

Continuing on the narrow, main crest of the Blue Ridge Mountains, the AT crosses a couple of wooded knobs and passes by Bobblets Gap shelter. Side trails present options for extended hikes and/or campsites.

Camping is prohibited on the AT here, but allowed on the side trails and along Forest Service roads.

.0 Follow the woods road to the right of Bobblets Gap Overlook. In 300 feet cross FSR 4008 and turn left onto the AT.

.1 The blue-blazed trail to right leads 1,000 feet to the Bobblets Gap shelter and spring.

.9 Trail intersection.

• Blue-blazed Hammond Hollow Trail [FS 27] to the right descends about 2 miles to FSR 634. Combining the Hammond Hollow Trail with FSR 634, FSR 4008, and/or the Spec Mine Trail [FS 28] (BRP mile 96) makes for a couple of nice circuit hikes.

Bear left to continue on the AT.

2.1   Come onto a woods road.

2.4   Cross the BRP (mile 95.3) and come to the Harvey's Knob Overlook.

Mile 95.3

Length: .7 mile

Difficulty: moderate

The AT leaves Harvey's Knob Overlook (good views of Flat Top and Sharp Top), ascends a small knob, and descends to the Montvale Overlook at BRP mile 95.9.

Camping is not permitted on this section.

Mile 95.9

Length: 1 mile

Difficulty: moderate

The AT ascends from the Montvale Overlook, passes over a ridge line, and quickly descends to cross the BRP at Taylor's Mountain Overlook (BRP mile 97).

•   The Spec Mine Trail [FS 28] leaves the BRP 200 feet south of the Montvale Overlook. (A detailed description and trailhead information may be found in Chapter 2, mile 95.9.) This trail may be combined with FSR 634, FSR 186, the AT, and/or the Hammond Hollow Trail [FS 27] for two pleasant circuit hikes.

Camping is permitted along the side trails and the Forest Service roads, but not on the AT.

.0   Ascend into the woods from the Montvale Overlook.

.7   Attain the highest point of the knob and descend.

1   Cross the BRP and arrive at Taylor's Mountain Overlook (BRP mile 97).

Mile 97

Length: .7 mile

Difficulty: moderate

This is the final section of the AT that completely parallels the BRP. It ascends from the Taylor's Mountain

Overlook and crosses two low knolls before descending to FSR 634 (an old roadway that was once a vital link between eastern and western Virginia) in Black Horse Gap (BRP mile 97.7).

Camping is prohibited on this section.

Mile 97.7

The route of the AT, having been displaced by the construction of the Parkway, now takes its leave of the BRP. It crosses several ridges to reach the Wilson Creek shelter and water in 2.5 miles before continuing 3 more miles to arrive at FSR 191, the final easy access to the BRP. A left on FSR 191 will lead to BRP mile 101.5 in Curry Gap (1.1 miles). From FSR 191, the trail gradually descends to Troutville, Virginia, in about 6 miles. The AT then continues for 700 more miles to its southern terminus atop Springer Mountain in northern Georgia.

4

The Roanoke River to

Julian Price Memorial Park

BLUE RIDGE PARKWAY MILES 114.9–296.9

Just south of the Roanoke River the land takes a very marked and noticeable change. No longer steep and narrow, the Blue Ridge Mountains spread out onto a broad and rolling plateau. The Parkway meanders through the bucolic scenery and farmlands of rural Virginia. Open meadows, grazing cattle, fields of waving tobacco leaves, and rows of rustling cornstalks line the BRP.

Roanoke, a growing metropolis in the Great Valley of Virginia, dominates many of the views along the northern portion of this section. Suburban developments are surprisingly close to the Parkway in many places. Private land, not national forests, line both sides of the BRP.

Less public land and fewer BRP trails mean there are not as many opportunities for extended overnight hikes as in the previous section. However, Rocky Knob Recreation Area and Doughton Park have systems of interconnecting trails leading to isolated backcountry campsites on BRP land.

Trails may be fewer in number per mile of BRP in this section, but you are compensated by their quality. Pathways are no longer confined to the single, narrow ridge line and steep hillsides. Many (BRP miles 169 and 238.5) wander over high, open meadows. These grazing lands provide 360-degree views, and the gently rolling fields make for easy walking. Other trails (BRP miles 217.6 and 241) take advantage of dramatic views provided by rocky bluffs that drop steeply to the east.

As stated, human impact is more prevalent on this

portion of the BRP. Moses H. Cone built more than twenty-five miles of Carriage Roads (BRP mile 294) on his estate, which is now a part of the Parkway's property. What had been intended as a retreat for employees of a private company has now become the Julian Price Memorial Park (BRP mile 295.9), complete with campground and three superb hiking paths. Rugged trails (BRP miles 167.1 and 243.7) drop into isolated valleys to pass by decaying remnants of former homesteads. Shorter trails (BRP miles 154.5 and 176.2) lead to reconstructed mountain homes and communities. Still others (BRP miles 116.4 and 294) come into contact with the backyards of present-day housing developments.

Mile 114.9. Roanoke River Self-Guiding Trail [BRP 31]

Length: .6 mile, round-trip (not including the two side trails, each .2 mile, round-trip)

Difficulty: moderate (the first side trail is strenuous, the second, easy)

There are actually three different routes contained in this one trail. The main route is a self-guided nature trail with signs identifying particularly interesting spots and plants along the way. The short side trails lead to the banks of the Roanoke River and out to a viewpoint overlooking the slow-moving waters of the stream.

.0   Begin at the parking lot and descend gradually.

.1   A side trail drops rather steeply to the rocks along the river, giving access to a reportedly good fishing spot below the hydroelectric generating plant. To continue on the self-guiding trail, go straight, cross under the BRP, and arrive at another side trail to the left. This is an easy, gradually descending walk that leads to a view of the river. Bear to the right to continue on the self-guiding trail. The terrain here drops steeply down the sides of the Roanoke River canyon wall, but the pathway remains wide and well constructed.

.2   Come to a bench allowing you to rest under the coolness of a large hemlock tree. In a few feet begin a loop trail by turning right, ascending slightly, and coming to another bench. Note the sharp contrast between the many evergreens on one side of the trail and the dominant deciduous trees on the other.

.3   Begin to loop back by turning to the left and going

down a few steps. A few more feet leads to a bench
with good wintertime views of the river canyon.

.4 Return to the beginning of the loop trail. The parking lot is .2 mile from here.

Mile 115.5. East on Rutrough Road (VA RT 658) is
Explore Park, offering a reconstructed mountain
community, multiple trails, camping, interpretive
programs, and more. (Future plans call for direct
access from BRP mile 15.2.)

Mile 116.4. Roanoke Valley Horse Trail [BRP 32]

(See Chapter 2, mile 110.6, for more information on
the Roanoke Valley Horse Trail.)

Length: 2 miles, one way

Difficulty: moderate

Alternating between woods and fields, this section
of the horse trail is almost never out of sight of one house
or another. Exit the Parkway at mile 115.5, turn right onto
Rutrough Road (VA RT 658), go under the Parkway, and
stop at the first dirt road – the beginning of this section.

.0 Ascend the road, which is actually a driveway to a
private home.

.2 Leave the dirt road to the right and follow a woods
road next to a house.

.6 Enter an open field.

.7 Begin to follow graveled VA RT 712.

.9 Cross VA RT 616; walk beside driveway.

1.1 In an open field, walk next to the BRP. You are almost
walking in someone's backyard. Ascend and descend
through honeysuckle.

1.5 Cross VA RT 116 (Jae Valley Road) and walk in the
open field.

1.7 Reenter the woods for a short time, then come back
out into the open.

1.8 Cross two creeks. Ascend via switchbacks in the
woods.

1.9 Reach the top of a pine-covered knob next to a horse
pasture; descend.

2 Arrive at BRP mile 118 (no parking or pull-off area).

Mile 118. Roanoke Valley Horse Trail [BRP 33]

(See Chapter 2, mile 110.6, for more information on the Roanoke Valley Horse Trail.)

Length: 4.5 miles, one way

Difficulty: moderate

This is by far the most wooded section of the horse trail to parallel the Parkway. There are a number of pleasant spots along the route – possibly the most notable being a wooded stretch within sight of the small hamlet of Gum Spring. The trail comes back to the BRP in a couple of places, allowing you to decide on the length of your walk.

Also, this final section of the horse trail provides access to the Chestnut Ridge Trail [BRP 35], considered a part of the Roanoke Valley Horse Trail.

.0 At BRP mile 118, ascend into the woods on the western side of the Parkway.

.2 Negotiate a set of switchbacks, cross a creek, and ascend.

.4 At the top of the knob swing around a large dead tree.

.5 Almost touch the BRP, but abruptly swing away into a bottomland trail of honeysuckle, briers, mud, and muck.

.6 Ascend behind a subdivision.

.8 Cross paved VA RT 666 (Bandy Road); enter a pine forest next to the BRP. Soon you must be sure to avoid the path to the right, which goes into the subdivision.

1 Walk in another bottomland of muck, mud, and briers. Ascend through even more muck.

1.1 Turn left onto a wide pathway at the top of a knob.

1.2 In an open field of briers and weeds ascend next to the BRP.

1.3 Begin to descend into an overgrown forest.

1.5 Cross paved VA RT 668 (Yellow Mountain Road). Ascend, for a short distance, on a brier-covered rocky trail. Come almost to the Parkway and descend.

1.7 Near the corner of a parking lot turn left and ascend to walk the hillside above the little settlement of Gum Spring. Continue via a series of ups and downs, enjoying the shade of the woods.

2.9 Be alert! Do not take the road that goes uphill to the Parkway. Continue on a smaller pathway.

3.1 Walk below the Gum Spring Overlook. (This overlook is at mile .1 on the Mill Mountain Spur Road, which is connected to the Parkway at BRP mile 120.5.)

3.15 Cross Mill Mountain Spur Road and ascend into the woods.

3.25 Intersection. The trail to the right is a short connector pathway to the Chestnut Ridge Trail [BRP 35], considered a part of the Roanoke Valley Horse Trail. Bear left uphill to continue to follow the main route.

3.9 Cross the Parkway (BRP mile 120.7, no parking or pull-off area), and begin to descend. The sounds of the rock crusher at the Rockydale Quarries will become very evident.

4 Avoid the cross trails and switchback to the BRP. Walk along a fence next to the Parkway.

4.3 Swing to the left of an open field and next to a house and garden.

4.5 Arrive at VA RT 766 (Stable Road) and the end of the Roanoke Valley Horse Trail.

Mile 120.4. Roanoke Mountain Summit Trail [BRP 34]

Length: .3 mile, round-trip

Difficulty: moderate

Follow the narrow, winding side road off of the BRP (3.7-mile loop) to reach this pathway. The parking lots near the summit offer commanding views of the Roanoke Valley to the west and Back Creek Valley to the east. This is also a popular area for watching sunsets and launching hang gliders.

The loop trail leads to the top of Roanoke Mountain. The view from the summit is limited, but the rewards of this walk are worth it. It leads to the highest point of the mountain, where you can enjoy intimate contact with a mountaintop environment of evergreens, mountain laurels, and rock formations.

.0 Begin at the far end of the parking lot and immediately descend a set of stone steps with wooden handrails. In about 200 feet begin an ascent on more stone steps.

.1 Arrive at the summit of Roanoke Mountain, which offers good wintertime views; continue forward with a gradual descent while slabbing around the top of the mountain through mountain laurel.

.3   With a deep bear wallow on the right, begin a quick ascent, of less than 300 feet, to the parking lot.

Mile 120.5: Chestnut Ridge Trail [BRP 35]

Length: 5.3 miles, round-trip

Difficulty: moderate

Part of the Roanoke Valley Horse Trail (see Chapter 2, mile 110.6, for more information on the Roanoke Valley Horse Trail), the Chestnut Ridge Trail basically encircles the Roanoke Mountain campground. Leave the BRP at mile 120.5 and follow Mill Mountain Spur Road for 1.1 miles to the Chestnut Ridge Overlook to reach the trailhead. (The campground is about .2 mile past the overlook.) The pathway, lined with galax, mountain laurel, and rhododendron is wide and well graded for most of the way.

The trail crosses Mill Mountain Spur Road twice and passes by quite a number of short side trails to the campground, so this walk can be made about as long or short as you wish. The last 1.5 miles are not as well maintained or quite as scenic as the rest of the hike. Also, you may be sharing the path with horseback riders – be careful where you step.

This is a recommended early-morning or -evening hike for those who wish to escape the hustle, bustle, and noise of a crowded campground.

.0   Begin at the Chestnut Ridge Overlook. Immediately come to a trail junction. One-tenth mile to the left is the Roanoke Mountain campground. Bear right and descend slightly through dogwood and maple. In less than 200 feet come to the red-blazed Chestnut Ridge Trail and turn left onto a wide pathway with little change in elevation. You'll find good wintertime views of the small community of Gum Spring here.

.15   Round a spur ridge and begin a series of small ascents and descents.

.6   With Mill Mountain Spur Road less than 100 yards to the left, switch back to the right and descend.

.8   Switch back to the left and continue to descend.

1   Cross a culvert and begin an almost unnoticeable rise in elevation.

1.4   Round another spur ridge and descend.

1.5   A side trail to the right goes about 100 feet to VA RT 669. Keep left, ascend a short distance, and come to Mill Mountain Spur Road. Along the road it is .4 mile left to the Roanoke Mountain Campground and .6 mile to Chestnut Ridge Overlook. To continue on the Chestnut Ridge Trail, cross the road and reenter the woods. In a few feet a trail leading to VA RT 669 comes in from the right. Bear left and begin to rise gradually.

1.6 Cross under a small utility line. Continue the gradual ascent on a forest floor that is conspicuously free of much undergrowth.

1.9 Cross under and parallel the utility line for 100 feet. The pungent smell of galax permeates the air.

2.1 To the left is a campsite, picnic table, and water fountain. The trail now begins a long loop around the campground. In a few hundred feet cross a trail which, to the left, leads to the campground. Soon, cross a spur ridge and another short trail to the campground. Begin a descent and, at the switchback, veer away from the campground.

2.3 Avoid the unauthorized trail to the right; switch back to the left on a more gradual descent.

2.5 Descend steeply to cross a gully. You may be close to the campground, but this spot offers quiet solitude.

2.7 Make a hard left and follow the trail into a narrow gully between two small ridge lines. Rise gradually.

2.9 Switch back to the right (straight ahead leads to the campground amphitheater). Ascend and follow an old roadbed.

3.1 Switch back to the left (there is another side trail to the campground).

3.2 Reach the top of a spur ridge. Campsites are immediately to the left.

3.5 Note the many mine diggings next to the trail. The pathway here is making use of an old narrow gauge railroad bed. These railroads used to lace the Blue Ridge Mountains, bringing the area's rich natural resources out to mills and processing plants.

3.6 A signed trail to the left leads .2 mile to the RV section of the campground.

3.8 Begin to ascend with many dogwood trees lining the trail. Soon there are open views across a trailer park to the Rockydale Quarry and surrounding mountains. The character of the trail changes markedly. It becomes narrower and sometimes overgrown with thorns, briers, and poison ivy. Descend.

4.1　Descend steeply.

4.3　Cross under some large utility lines. The trail may be indistinct, but continue straight and reenter the woods.

4.4　Cross the utility lines and then parallel them for 200 feet before descending to the left into the woods.

4.5　Come to VA RT 672. Directly across the road is a short spur trail to a main portion of the Roanoke Valley Horse Trail [BRP 33]. To continue on the Chestnut Ridge Trail turn left onto VA RT 672, cross under Mill Mountain Spur Road, and reenter the woods to the left. The trail is almost in the backyards of some Gum Spring homes.

4.6　Pass under utility lines as the pathway becomes wider and finally regains a sense of isolation. Begin to climb as you enter the deeper woods.

5.3　Return to the starting point of the trail; the Chestnut Ridge Overlook is 150 feet to the left.

Mile 123.2. Buck Mountain Trail [BRP 36]

Length: .5 mile

Difficulty: moderately strenuous

This trail climbs steadily to obtain good views of the mountains surrounding the southern Roanoke Valley. Because of its close proximity to the city, the area receives an inordinate amount of use and abuse. There are quite a number of unauthorized trails leading off of the main trail. Please stay on the main pathway to help preserve the beauty of this place.

.0　Follow blacktop for the first 200 feet. The great diversity of deciduous trees on the mountainside put on a very vibrant and colorful display in the fall. The well-used pathway, with concrete and wood water bars, makes a series of short, quick rises interspersed with some level spots.

.3　Come to a bench overlooking Fort Lewis Mountain. From here the trail become steeper and rockier.

.5　At the summit of the knob turn left, where you will find a bench and views of the Roanoke Valley. McAfee's Knob and Tinker Mountain dominate the distant skyline. Continue around the small loop trail to look down upon the BRP and Rockydale Quarry.

Mile 154.5. Smart View Loop Trail [BRP 37]

Length: 3 miles, round-trip

Difficulty: easy to moderate

A fern-lined pathway, open meadows, abundant wildflowers, an old mountain cabin, and superb views are awaiting those who walk the Smart View Loop Trail. Large stately oaks testify that this area was once open farmland, giving the trees the room needed to grow to such magnificent proportions.

.0 Begin at the fence in the parking lot outside of the picnic area. Cross through the fence stile and walk in an open meadow.

.1 Arrive at a bench and enter the woods.

.2 The side trail to the right leads to the picnic area.

.4 Come to another bench. The trail to the left leads, in a few hundred feet, to the Smart View Overlook. Bear right and descend on a fern-lined pathway.

.5 Switch back under utility lines and cross the creek on a log footbridge. The trail continues to descend into a hollow.

.6 Begin to ascend through a rhododendron thicket.

.7 Ascend steeply on rock steps and come to a bench. The wildflowers are especially plentiful here.

1 A water fountain and rest rooms are to the right; continue straight.

1.1 The trail to the right goes to the picnic area; bear left and descend.

1.2 Arrive at a cabin built by the Trails family in the 1890s. You'll also find a bench and a splendid view of the flatlands of the Piedmont to the east.

1.3 Cross a small creek on a stone bridge and switch back to the left to ascend a knob. (The parking lot at the beginning of the trail may be reached by following the path to the right.)

1.5 Come to a bench with another good view of the Piedmont.

1.9 Begin to descend through an evergreen forest.

2.1 Switch back to the right.

2.6 Another bench – this one in the cool shade of a deep forest.

3 The trail to the right will take you back to the picnic area. Turn left and arrive at the starting point.

Mile 162.4 Rakes Mill Pond Overlook [BRP 38]

Length: .05 mile, round-trip

Difficulty: easy leg stretcher

This short walk will bring you down stone steps to a pleasant view of a mill dam built in the 1800s and a rhododendron-lined pond and stream. A very pleasant and peaceful spot.

Trails of the Rocky Knob and Rock Castle Gorge Area, Blue Ridge Parkway Miles 167.1–169

Rock Castle Gorge, contained in the 4,500-acre Rocky Knob Recreation Area, is a significant feature of the Blue Ridge. Millions of years of stream erosion have carved a deep, narrow, and impressive valley. Views from the BRP and the upper portions of the Rock Castle Gorge [BRP 39] and Black Ridge [BRP 42] trails can be quite breathtaking. The gorge's terrain drops steeply, almost vertically in some places, with a high point of 3,572 feet on Rocky Knob to a low of 1,700 feet at Rock Castle Creek.

This great difference in elevation allows you to experience two seasons in just one walk. By mid-March bloodroot may be blooming near the creek, while winter snows could still be falling on Rocky Knob and Grassy Knoll. If the fall weather is a bit too chilly, camp in the Gorge to prolong summer's warmer temperatures.

Until the 1920s, a complex mountain community existed within the confines of this rugged topography. Farmers scratched out a living while the rushing waters of Rock Castle Creek powered a thriving industry of sawmills and gristmills. In its heyday, more than seventy families lived in the area. Many reminders of these days will be encountered along the trails.

The recreation area contains a Park Service visitor center, campground, rustic cabins for rent, picnic grounds, and backcountry camping.

Mile 167.1. Rock Castle Gorge Trail [BRP 39]

(includes the Hardwood Cove Self-Guiding Nature Trail)

Length: 10.6 miles, round-trip

Difficulty: strenuous

Markings: white paint blazes

Highly recommended

Rock Castle Gorge Trail was named a National Recreation Trail in 1984 because of its geographical and historical significance. Included within its full length are the Hardwood Cove Self-Guiding Nature Trail and a portion of the Black Ridge Loop Trail [BRP 42]. The nature trail is self-guiding; brochures explaining plant life along the trail may be obtained from the contact station in the campground or from a ranger.

Backcountry camping is allowed (one of only two such places on BRP land) on a site next to Rock Castle Creek – about 3.5 miles from the beginning of the trail. Required permits (free) can be obtained at the Rocky Knob Visitor Center (mile 169) or the ranger station (mile 167) near the campground. Vehicle access to within .25 mile of the campsite is possible by leaving the BRP at mile 165.3 to follow VA RT 8 to the east. In 6 miles turn right onto VA RT 605, and in a little more than .5 mile arrive at a gated fire road. The campsite is .25 mile up the fire road.

High open meadows, precipitous views, tumbling cascades, historical sites, and free backcountry camping make this a hike you shouldn't miss. Trout fishing is also said to be good on both Rock Castle and Little Rock Castle creeks.

The full length of this hike should not be undertaken lightly. Steep and narrow descents and arduous ascents definitely classify Rock Castle Gorge Trail as strenuous.

.0   At the entrance to the Rocky Knob campground, cross the BRP and pass through the fence stile. Turn left and descend through open meadow.

.1   Arrive at a bench, enter the woods, and cross a fence.

.3   Switch back and cross a rhododendron-lined water run (actually the headwaters of Little Rock Castle Creek). Soon turn left and cross a damp area on a log bridge; the trail descends gradually through a pleasant hardwood forest.

.5   Come to another bench. In a couple of hundred feet begin a gradual ascent of an old road.

.8   Switch back to the right on the old road.

Rock Castle Creek along the Rock Castle Gorge Trail. (Courtesy of the National Park Service, Blue Ridge Parkway)

.9   There is a bench here at the ridge line. Begin to descend.

1.1   Arrive at a bench overlooking an area that was obviously settled at one time. Look around and perhaps discover the foundation of a decayed cabin or the remains of an old orchard. Cross the creek on a log bridge as the trail begins a gradual climb.

1.5   Another bench sitting atop another ridge line. Descend.

1.6   Even though the hillside has become very steep, the trail remains well built.

1.8   Come to a bench at the start of a steep descent.

1.9   Another bench; continue to descend steeply.

2.3   Arrive at a bench in a draw. The descent becomes more relaxed.

2.5   At another bench begin to parallel Little Rock Castle Creek in an open valley.

2.7   The inviting pools will make you want to cool your feet in the creek. You'll also find yet another bench. Soon cross a small side stream on a log bridge.

3   Arrive at the fire road and turn right to continue on Rock Castle Gorge Trail. VA RT 605 is 250 feet to the left.

3.25   Arrive at the backcountry camping area, site of a former Civilian Conservation Corps camp. From 1937 to 1942, corps workers helped build the BRP and structures contained within the Rocky Knob Recreation Area. All that remains of the CCC camp are old foundations, but benches, fire grates, and pit toilets are available for the modern-day camper.

3.4 A bench next to the creek affords a cool place to rest during hot summer days.

3.7 The road swings away from the creek and follows along the base of a mountain.

4.2 Cross the creek on a log bridge.

4.5 Arrive at the White House, built in 1916. The former residence of a well-to-do citizen of the Rock Castle community, this property is still in private hands – be sure to treat it with respect so that others may continue to enjoy this portion of the Rock Castle Trail. The road continues up the creek as the valley begins to narrow.

4.7 Cross the creek on a log bridge.

4.8 Recross the creek, which descends a number of one- and two-foot waterfalls. Ascend steeply through rhododendron.

5.1 The road is now high above the creek, which has a series of beautiful waterfalls rushing through moss- and lichen-covered boulders.

5.3 Arrive at a bench overlooking the creek gorge.

5.4 Level out for a short distance as you pass by a vertical rock facing that turns into a 100-foot waterfall during spring rains.

5.6 Be alert! The trail leaves the road to the right, drops down, passes a bench, and crosses Rock Castle Creek on a log bridge. This is the beginning of the Hardwood Cove Self-Guiding Nature Trail. A pamphlet containing information that corresponds to the numbered signs along the nature trail is available from the contact station at the Rocky Knob campground or from a ranger. (The pamphlets box at the beginning of the nature trail is often empty; it is thus best to get the pamphlet before starting your hike.)

5.7 Pass by an old house site.

5.8 Come to a bench and soon cross through a jumble of boulders known as Bare Rocks. While the small caves and holes are tempting to inspect and explore, please be aware that many animals may make their homes here – including copperheads and rattlesnakes.

6.2 Come to the end of the Hardwood Cove Nature

Trail. Continue the ascent through rhododendron tunnels. Soon ascend more steeply.

6.4 The creek to the right tumbles down in a lovely series of cascades.

6.5 Cross the creek and continue with a more gradual ascent through mountain laurel and rhododendron.

6.6 Begin an ascent on a series of short switchbacks.

6.8 Come to a bench in a gap where the trail levels out for a short distance.

7 Arrive at a bench overlooking a rhododendron-surrounded water run. Soon cross over a fence and enter a cattle-grazing area.

7.1 Come onto Grassy Knoll and follow arrowed posts through the pastureland.

7.3 Just before entering the woods, you'll find a bench amid the bucolic surroundings.

7.5 Cross a fence and walk under some microwave towers.

7.6 Emerge onto the open meadows and reap the rewards for all of your hard huffing and puffing climbing out of Rock Castle Gorge. The high, open pastures afford grand 360-degree views, and the gently sloping land makes for easy and relaxing walking. Bear right and descend along the fence line. (The gravel road to the left is part of the Black Ridge Trail [BRP 42], which joins the Rock Castle Gorge Trail at this point.)

7.7 Uplifted stones make some interesting formations. The views seem to get better with every step you take. This area is very reminiscent of the Bald Mountains in central North Carolina.

8 Cross a fence and enter into the woods as the descent quickens.

8.2 Arrive at a bench with limited views into Rock Castle Gorge. Come out of the woods and onto open meadows for more superb views.

8.3 Enter some woods to ascend around a knob.

8.5 Do not follow the red boundary markers at the top of the knob. Continue straight ahead and descend for another great view.

8.7 The Black Ridge Trail [BRP 42] turns left and goes uphill through the field to arrive at the Rocky Knob Visitor Center in .1 mile. (Water and sanitary facilities are available near the visitor center.) Bear right to continue on the Rock Castle Gorge Trail and come to another view into the gorge.

8.8 Begin a series of small ups and downs through mountain laurel.

9 Pass by the Rock Castle Gorge Overlook (BRP mile 168.7).

9.1 Reenter the woods and make a short, steep ascent.

9.2 Ascend on rock steps and walk on a narrow, precipitous trail for a short distance.

9.3 Pass by a side trail to the left that leads to the picnic area in .25 mile. Begin the ascent of Rocky Knob.

9.4 Two trail options here. The trail straight ahead goes to the Saddle Overlook in about .5 mile of fairly level walking, making it possible to bypass the climb to the top of Rocky Knob. Rock Castle Gorge Trail bears to the right, switching back through mountain laurel, and goes to the knob and then down to the Saddle Overlook. The rest of this trail description follows that route.

9.7 Attain the ridge line, which has limited views; follow it next to a steep drop-off.

9.8 Arrive at the summit of Rocky Knob, the highest point of the Rock Castle Gorge Trail. An old shelter allows good views into the gorge. Bear right and descend steeply. (The red-blazed trail to the left simply goes down to the optional pathway to the Saddle Overlook.)

10 The trail coming in from the left is the optional pathway. (Taking it would lead back to the picnic area in .6 mile.) Bear right and pass by the Saddle Overlook (BRP mile 168). Ascend into the woods.

10.2 Cross over the top of a knob.

10.3 Pass through a fence stile and come into an open pasture for the final stretch of great views. Follow vehicle tracks for a few hundred feet and then veer left onto a pathway. Pass by fenced-in spring boxes and follow arrowed posts through the field. Go through a small, old orchard.

10.5 Begin to closely parallel the BRP.

10.6 Cross through the fence stile to the left to arrive back at the Rocky Knob campground.

Mile 169. Rocky Knob Picnic Loop Trail [BRP 40]

Length: 1.3 miles, round-trip

Difficulty: moderately easy

Markings: yellow paint blazes

This trail is an enjoyable diversion from the picnic area, which, during the summer months and on holidays, may be overflowing with visitors. The path stays within shouting distance of the picnic area yet, passing through a hardwood-, rhododendron-, and hemlock-crowded forest, allows the walker to become detached from civilization for a while.

.0   Begin at the trail sign to the left and behind the Rocky Knob Visitor Center.

.05   The trail to the left is the Black Ridge Trail [BRP 42], which leads to the Rock Castle Gorge Trail [BRP 39]. Bear right to continue on the Rocky Knob Picnic Loop Trail and descend through a pleasant hardwood forest.

.2   The trail to the left is another part of the Black Ridge Trail; stay to the right to continue on the yellow-blazed Picnic Loop Trail.

.3   With a nice feeling of isolation the trail descends through a towering hardwood and hemlock forest, which is made all the more appealing in late spring when the abundant rhododendron are in full bloom.

.5   Cross a small water run and begin a series of small ups and downs through rhododendron tunnels.

.7   Emerge from the rhododendron into open forest and ascend; the trail to the right goes back to the picnic area.

.8   Switch back to the right, avoiding the unauthorized trail that continues straight ahead.

.9   The trail to the left [BRP 41] leads to Rocky Knob and the Saddle Overlook. Bear right and come into the picnic area, where there are a number of confusing side trails. Continue to follow the yellow-blazed path. Pass by a large picnic shelter, walk through the parking lot, reenter the woods, and ascend.

1.2   Pass by a large fallen tree that has been burned at the core by lightning.

1.3   Arrive back at the visitor center.

Mile 169. Woodland Trail [BRP 41]

Length: .8 mile, one way

Difficulty: easy

Markings: red blazes

This is a short, easy connector trail between the Rocky Knob picnic area and the Saddle Overlook (BRP mile 168). It offers nothing particularly exciting, but it does open up a number of options to connect with the other trails in the Rocky Knob Recreation Area.

The trailhead may be reached by driving into the picnic area to the large parking lot and picnic shelter. The red-blazed pathway begins at the trail sign.

.0   Begin at the large parking lot in the picnic area and ascend gradually.

.2   Cross the BRP and ascend into the woods.

.25   Meet Rock Castle Gorge Trail [BRP 39]; turn to the left.

.3   The Rock Castle Gorge Trail switches back to the right to begin its ascent of Rocky Knob. Continue straight on the well-built, red-blazed Woodland Trail, passing through mountain laurel and paralleling the BRP.

.7   The trail to the right makes a steep ascent to the summit of Rocky Knob. Bear to the left and rejoin the Rock Castle Gorge Trail. Bear left again.

.8   Arrive at the Saddle Overlook for a good view into Rock Castle Gorge.

Mile 169. Black Ridge Trail [BRP 42]

Length: 3 miles, round-trip

Difficulty: moderate

Markings: blue paint blazes

Highly recommended

Bucolic mountain farms, rhododendron and mountain laurel thickets, and relaxing walking in high, open meadows make the walker feel on top of the world. If time restraints prohibit you from walking the full trail, at least take the time to enjoy the views along the open pastures (from mile point 1.6 to the end of the trail), which are reminiscent of the Bald Mountains in central North Carolina.

.o   Begin to the left and behind the Rocky Knob Visitor Center.

.05 The trail to the left leads to the Twelve O'Clock Knob Overlook and Rock Castle Gorge Trail [BRP 39]. (You will return via the latter trail.) Bear to the right.

.2   The trail to the right is the Picnic Loop Trail [BRP 40]. Bear to the left and continue to descend on the blue-blazed Black Ridge Trail.

.3   Turn right to follow a utility-line right-of-way.

.4   At an old cabin site turn left, cross a creek, and ascend on an old, fern-lined woods road.

.7   The road is beside open meadows – enjoy the farmland views to the west.

1   Swing away from the fields and continue the ascent, now through mountain laurel and rhododendron.

1.1 Level out and parallel the BRP; soon begin to ascend gradually.

1.5 Be alert! Turn left from the road, cross a fence, and enter open fields.

1.6 Cross the BRP; pass through a fence; ascend in a cow pasture on the gravel road.

1.8 At the top of the ridge, make a hard left (to the right is the Rock Castle Gorge Trail [BRP 39]), and follow the fence line down the open meadow.

1.9 Gradually descend and pass by an interesting rock formation. This stretch of the trail is absolutely superb. The walking is gently sloping downhill, the views are 360 degrees, and the constant winds will cool you down even on the hottest of days. Walking and hiking just doesn't get much better than this.

2.2 Cross a fence and enter the woods, descending a little more quickly.

2.5 Arrive at a bench with limited views into Rock Castle Gorge. Soon come back to open meadows with better views.

2.6 Reenter woods and ascend around a knob.

2.7 Do not follow the red-paint boundary markers at the top of the knob. Continue straight and descend for one final grand view.

2.9 The Rock Castle Gorge Trail [BRP 39] continues straight ahead. Turn left through an open field, cross the BRP, ascend some stone steps, and come back to the beginning of this trail. Turn right.

3   Arrive at the Rocky Knob Visitor Center.

Mile 176.2. Mountain Industry Trail (Mabry Mill) [BRP 43]

Length: .4 mile, round-trip

Difficulty: easy

Highly recommended

E. B. Mabry operated a gristmill and blacksmith shop on this site from 1910 to 1935. The Park Service has reconstructed the mill and other structures to recreate a typical Blue Ridge Mountain community of the early 1900s. Various displays, devices, and live demonstrations on gristmilling, blacksmithing, and other mountain crafts bring these bygone days back to life.

During the fall, parking (and walking space) is often minimal, as large crowds arrive to watch the annual apple butter– and sorghum molasses–making demonstrations. (Check with the visitor center at Rocky Knob for times and dates of all demonstrations.)

As with the other interpretive trails of the BRP, this simple walk is highly recommended because the information learned here will enhance your appreciation of sights encountered on future trail hikes.

Also, be on the lookout for turtles, ducks, muskrats, and other aquatic life in and around the pond.

Mabry Mill may be the most photographed scene on the entire BRP. The best time to photograph the mill is probably early evening, when the glow of the setting sun is reflected in the pond.

.0   Begin north of the restaurant, enjoy the view of the mill across the pond, and in a couple of hundred feet bear left at the intersection and cross the flume that brings water to power the mill. Come to the mill and visit with the miller (during tourist season). Continue on the paved pathway.

.1   Pass by millstones, a lumber-drying rack, a log cart, a bark mill for obtaining tannin, and Matthews Cabin.

.15 Study the whiskey still and sorghum-making display.

.2   Turn left and walk through the shed of the black-smith shop, where you can discover what an important role the blacksmith played in the daily life of mountain communities. A soap-making display is next.

.25 Rest on a bench overlooking the Mabry Mill community.

.3   Cross over the flume, go down some steps, and cross the creek.

.4   Arrive back at the parking lot.

Mile 179.2. Round Meadow Creek Trail [BRP 44]

Length: .4 mile, round-trip

Difficulty: moderately easy

The narrow gorge of Round Meadow Creek is a wonderful spot on hot, summer afternoons; you can actually feel the temperature drop as you descend. Cool hemlock groves, a gurgling stream, flowering rhododendron, and towering pines are this trail's attractions.

.0   Begin the trail by descending through a grand display of rhododendron.

.1   Reach the creek, which is lined with hemlock and rhododendron. Turn left, walking along the stream and under the BRP.

.2   Be alert! The trail leaves the old road and ascends to the left through lofty hemlocks and pines.

.4   Cross under the BRP and arrive back at the Round Meadow Overlook.

Mile 188.8. Groundhog Mountain Picnic Area Observation Tower [BRP 45]

Length: less than 200 feet

Difficulty: easy leg stretcher

A short walk of less than one minute leads to the tower for a commanding view of the quartzite peak of Pilot Mountain, the Dan River Valley, and surrounding scenery. A great payoff for so little effort!

The picnic area is surrounded by fences displaying different construction styles.

Mile 189.9. Puckett Cabin Walk [BRP 46]

Length: less than 75 feet

Difficulty: easy leg stretcher

A thirty-second walk brings you to the log home of Mrs. Orleans Hawks Puckett. A midwife from 1865 to 1939, she is credited with assisting in hundreds of births in remote mountain cabins.

Mile 216.9. The BRP enters North Carolina.

Trails of the Cumberland Knob Recreation Area,
Blue Ridge Parkway Mile 217.5

The Cumberland Knob Recreation Area, the Parkway's first recreation area, was built in 1936 by the Civilian Conservation Corps. A common theory is that the area received its name from William Augustus, the duke of Cumberland and son of King George III. The duke was commander of the British forces in their victory against the army of Bonnie Prince Charlie in the Battle of Culloden in April of 1746.

The 1,000-acre recreation area has a picnic grounds, rest-room facilities, and a visitor center. The picnic area is almost always full on sunny summer weekends and holidays.

Mile 217.5. Gully Creek Trail [BRP 47]

Length: 2.5 miles, round-trip

Difficulty: moderately strenuous

Recommended

The small, bubbling cascades of Gully Creek lead you into a cool, narrow canyon lined with abundant ferns, pungent galax, and extensive mountain laurel and rhododendron thickets. Although it begins and ends at the Cumberland Knob picnic area, the trail travels quite some distance and, at its farthest point, gives the impression that not many people bother to walk its full length. Therefore, Gully Creek is a recommended outing for those who wish to enjoy the serenity of quiet surroundings and lightly traveled pathways. However, be forewarned – the climb out of the Gully Creek canyon makes this a moderately strenuous excursion.

.0   Begin behind and to the left of the visitor center. Descend rather quickly.

.2   Begin a series of switchbacks through mountain laurel and rhododendron.

.4   Cross a small water run.

.5   Switch back and parallel the creek.

.8   Come to a small set of cascades as the unmistakable smell of galax fills the air. Cross the creek.

.9   The creek makes some nice, small waterfalls in this area. For the next .3 mile cross the creek at least seven more times.

1.2   Begin the ascent on fern-lined switchbacks.

1.4   Reenter thick stands of rhododendron and mountain laurel.

2.2   Cumberland Knob Trail [BRP 48], to the left, leads .2 mile to Cumberland Knob and .4 mile to the picnic area. Bear right to remain on the Gully Creek Trail.

2.4   The trail to the left is another portion of the Cumberland Knob Trail. Come into the picnic area.

2.5   Arrive back at the visitor center.

Mile 217.5. Cumberland Knob Trail [BRP 48]

Length: .6 mile, round-trip

Difficulty: easy leg stretcher

This nice, extended leg stretcher affords a chance to escape the crowds and noise of the picnic area. Wildflowers seem to be everywhere. So does poison ivy. A shelter and open area on top of the knob may provide a quieter place for a picnic.

The Cumberland Knob Trail makes use of a short section of the Gully Creek Trail [BRP 47].

.0   Follow the trail to the right of the visitor center, passing by several picnic tables.

.1   Enter the woods, where the smell of galax becomes immediately apparent. Flame azalea and rhododendron blossoms line the trail in the spring. Be on the lookout for blueberries in late summer and early fall.

.3   Arrive at the shelter and a somewhat obstructed view. A connector trail to the Gully Creek Trail [BRP 47] bears right. Swing left around the shelter and descend to continue on the Cumberland Knob Trail. The azalea is particularly thick here.

.4   Just before entering the field, swing around to the right, staying on the edge of the woods. Beware! That wonderful garden of lush green leaves next to the pathway is actually a profuse array of poison ivy.

.5   Trail intersection. The Gully Creek Trail is to the right. Turn left to continue on the Cumberland Knob Trail, and in a few feet come onto a paved pathway next to the field.

.6   Arrive back at the visitor center.

Mile 218.6. Fox Hunter's Paradise Trail [BRP 49]

Length: less than .2 mile, round-trip

Difficulty: easy

A paved pathway through a mountaintop forest extends to a grand view overlooking a valley and the flatter Piedmont lands to the east. Fox hunters used to sit on this spur ridge listening to the baying of their hounds echoing off of the surrounding mountainsides.

Mile 230.1. Little Glade Mill Pond Trail [BRP 50]

Length: .2 mile, round-trip

Difficulty: easy

An easy loop around the pond offers possible glimpses of aquatic life – newts, snapping turtles, frogs, dragon flies, and a good variety of fish. Rhododendron lines the creek, and rose hips adorn bushes in the fall.

Several picnic tables overlook the pond.

Trails of Doughton Park,
Blue Ridge Parkway Miles 238.5–244.7

Doughton Park was originally known as "The Bluffs," called so for the precipitous cliffs overlooking Basin Cove. In 1951 the area was named in honor of Robert Lee Doughton, a North Carolina congressman and staunch supporter of the BRP.

Like the Rocky Knob Recreation Area and Rock Castle Gorge, the mountains, valleys, and hollows of Doughton Park were once home to a number of inhabitants. However, whereas Rock Castle Gorge supported several communities, the population here was much sparser. People were more isolated from one another. Martin Brinegar's family lived near the summits of the Blue Ridge, while Martin Caudill's numerous offspring were spread out on the upper reaches of Basin Creek. A few other families scratched out a living along the banks of Cove Creek. Cabins, old foundations, and other reminders of these tenacious people, who inhabited the area until the 1920s and 1930s, will be encountered on many trails in the park.

With more than 30 miles of pathways, Doughton Park trails traverse a variety of terrain and pass through several different vegetation zones. The gently undulating meadows make strolling rather easy while you enjoy stirring views of far-away peaks and nearby valleys. Rocky, rugged, and narrow ridge lines are natural pathways from the meadows into forests, crowded with rhododendron and mountain laurel. The warmer environs of Basin and Cove creeks are home to towering hemlocks, luxuriant ferns, and carpets of running cedar. Often in the spring these valley floors are bursting forth with flowers while the mountain summits of Doughton are still covered with snow.

The eastern edge of the park is bordered by the Thurmon Chatham Game Land. This certainly increases your chances of catching a glimpse of a deer, rabbit, squirrel, raccoon, fox, or maybe even a bobcat or bear.

A primitive backcountry campsite, which can only be reached by foot travel, is located in the valley where Basin and Cove creeks meet. Free camping permits may be obtained from the Doughton Park campground contact station or the ranger station at BRP mile 245.4.

In addition to the primitive campsite, Doughton Park also contains a Park Service campground, a camp store, gift shop, gasoline station, picnic area, and the Bluffs Lodge.

QUICKEST ROUTE TO NC RT 1730 AND THE PRIMITIVE CAMPSITE

Drive south on the Parkway from Doughton Park to BRP mile 248. Head east on NC RT 18 for 6 miles, turn left onto NC RT 1728 for 4 miles, and then make another left onto unpaved NC RT 1730. Watch carefully for a small parking area on the right, 3 miles beyond this intersection at a bridged stream. To the left is the end of the Grassy Gap Fire Road [BRP 58]; walk 1.7 miles on this road to reach the campsite.

Mile 238.5. Brinegar Cabin Walk [BRP 51]

Length: .1 mile, one way

Difficulty: easy leg stretcher

Martin Brinegar built this log cabin in the 1880s. His family lived here until the 1930s, when the property was purchased by the Park Service. A short walk brings you to the cabin and down to a spring house that once served as the "refrigerator" for the Brinegar family. Exhibits and special interpretive demonstrations are presented during the tourist season.

Mile 238.5. Cedar Ridge Trail [BRP 52]

Length: 4.5 miles, one way

Difficulty: moderately strenuous from BRP to Grassy Gap Fire Road; strenuous if hiked in the opposite direction

Markings: orange paint blazes

The Cedar Ridge Trail is a longer and possibly more enjoyable route into Basin Cove than the Bluff Ridge Trail [BRP 56]. Its pathway is certainly gentler, as it spends more than 4 miles descending from the BRP to the Grassy Gap Fire Road at NC RT 1730 near Abshers, North Carolina.

Abundant spring flowers, such as cinquefoil and fire pink, make up for the relatively few scenic overlooks. The purple and pink flowers of rhododendron and mountain laurel accompany late May and early June hikers almost the entire distance of the trail.

.0   Ascend on the Bluff Mountain Trail [BRP 53] from the Brinegar Cabin parking lot. Soon enter a meadow of cinquefoil and wild strawberries.

.1   Reach the top of the rise and descend.

.2   Intersection. The Bluff Mountain Trail goes to the right. Turn left and pass through the fence stile to continue on the Cedar Ridge Trail.

.3   Enter a thick rhododendron tunnel.

.6   Begin a series of switchbacks.

1.1   Go out of and back into national park lands. Ascend slightly over a small knob and resume your descent.

1.4   Begin to walk right on top of the ridge line, which has become narrower. Soon rock outcroppings to the right allow some limited views into the basin.

1.8   Ascend and then descend on switchbacks. There is another small rock outcropping on the right.

2.3   Ascend for 300 feet and then resume the descent, sometimes on switchbacks. Take note that as the rhododendron begins to fade, the forest floor becomes more open.

3.7   At a switchback, a slight break in the vegetation gives another limited view into the valley. The mountain laurel becomes much heavier.

3.9   Take note of the well-crafted stone wall along the pathway. The builders of this trail have insured that it will be here for some time to come.

4.4   Fire pinks are quite abundant as you pass through a fence stile.

4.5   Arrive at the Grassy Gap Fire Road [BRP 58]. The parking area on NC RT 1730 is 300 feet to the left. (See page 99 for directions to this parking area.)

Mile 238.5. Bluff Mountain Trail [BRP 53]

Length: 7.5 miles, one way

Difficulty: moderate, with some long easy stretches

Markings: yellow paint blazes

Highly recommended

A soft pathway of pine needles and grass. Open meadows with views to wave after wave of Blue Ridge Mountain summits. Towering pine groves contrasted with wind-stunted trees. Precipitous cliffs overlooking Caudill Cabin, nestled in the upper reaches of Basin Cove. All of these turn Bluff Mountain Trail into some of the best walking to be found along the BRP. In other words, do not miss this one!

The full length of the trail parallels the Parkway and comes into contact with a number of parking areas. With a car shuttle you can make this walk as long or as short as you wish. The picnic area and campground provide water and rest rooms, while the coffee shop might be the perfect spot to take a lunch break.

.0   Begin at the trail sign in the Brinegar Cabin parking lot and ascend.

.1   Good view back onto Brinegar Cabin and the valleys below. Continue through the small field and descend.

.2   Trail intersection. The pathway to the left is the Cedar Ridge Trail [BRP 52]. Bear right to continue on the Bluff Mountain Trail.

.4   Slab to the left of a knob. (Follow the trail and not the roadway.) The pathway widens as you enter open fields with good views of the surrounding mountains.

.7   Cross through a fence stile, enter an old pine grove, and continue with gradual ups and downs.

1.1   Slab to the left of a knob and ascend into the RV portion of the campground. (Water is available here.) Cross the parking lots and bear to the right, leaving the RV campground.

1.3   Cross the BRP and ascend.

1.4 Come to a trail-map poster in the main part of the campground. Walk just below the campground road and descend gradually past several campsites. (Water and rest rooms are available in the campground.)

1.7 Leave the campground and continue to descend through a hardwood forest and rhododendron tunnels.

1.9 Cross the BRP in Low Notch (mile 239.9), where there is a view of mountain summits stretching as far as you can see. Ascend through a heavy forest.

2 Cross through a fence stile.

2.1 Ascend into an open field and walk along the fence line, passing by a livestock loading pen.

2.3 Cross through a fence stile and continue to ascend.

2.4 Pass by an overlook parking lot, enjoying the views from the open meadows.

2.5 Top the knoll and begin to descend.

2.6 Cross the BRP and walk along the fence.

2.7 Arrive at the Doughton Park Coffee Shop, BRP mile 241.1. (Rest rooms available.) The trail continues at the far end of the parking lot. Descend the steps and enter woods.

2.8 Diagonally cross the BRP to your left and ascend into woods and rhododendron. The trail here becomes a little indistinct, but cross the picnic area road, bear right (avoiding the trail that goes left to the Bluffs Lodge), and continue to ascend.

3.0 The views begin to open up as you climb and reach the top of a knob. Rest rooms and water are to your right.

3.2 Pass through a fence stile and continue to enjoy the wonderful views, especially to the south and west. Make sure that you follow the trail and not the old roadway.

3.6 Reach the top of the knob for the best views yet. Begin to descend.

3.8 Pass through a fence stile and walk on the sidewalk next to the parking area.

4.0 Cross through another fence stile and ascend once again in the open field.

4.2 Intersection. The Bluff Ridge Trail [BRP 56] takes off to the left. Bear right to continue on the Bluff Mountain Trail.

4.3 Pass through another fence stile and walk along the

edge of a rocky cliff. The view is truly breathtaking, with the BRP and steep mountain walls dropping into Cove Creek Valley directly below you. Descend first through wind-stunted evergreens and then on steep switchbacks in a dense forest.

4.5 Switchbacks begin to level out.

4.7 The Alligator Back Overlook (BRP mile 242.4) is on your right. Continue straight on the yellow-blazed Bluff Mountain Trail and in a few feet come to a stone-walled overlook. The view here is into Cove Creek Basin. Continue to parallel the BRP.

4.9 The rocks to the right provide another viewpoint.

5 Walk directly below the BRP. Wildflowers, thorn bushes, and poison ivy are abundant. Look back to see the rugged Bluff Mountain ridge line that you descended. Soon slab to the left of a knob, staying almost level in a pleasantly wooded area.

5.6 Cross a small water run in a draw and return to walking just below the BRP, where you will find good views from the open field.

5.8 Pass by the steps to the Bluff Mountain Overlook (BRP mile 243.4). Continue straight and go through a fence stile. The grassy pathway is made even softer by needles dropped from the lofty evergreens lining the trail.

6 Leave the evergreens behind and enter a hardwood forest.

6.3 Do not take the steep trail up to the old road! Instead, bear left and follow the pathway below the roadbed.

6.4 Cross Grassy Gap Fire Road [BRP 58] and continue through an open meadow.

6.6 Swing around the ridge and into the woods. There is very little elevation change from here to the end of the trail.

6.9 Open fields provide an opportunity to look out across Basin Cove. Soon slab to the right of a knob and enter woods on a pine needle–softened pathway.

7.4 Trail intersection. The Flat Rock Ridge Trail [BRP 60] goes off to the left. Bear right to continue on the Bluff Mountain Trail.

7.5 Pass through a fence stile and ascend the steps to the Basin Cove Overlook (BRP mile 244.7) for a grandstand view of Stone Mountain to the northeast.

Mile 241. Fodder Stack Trail [BRP 54]

Length: 1 mile, round-trip

Difficulty: moderate

Markings: brown paint blazes

As it snakes its way to the rock jumbles of Fodder Stack, the trail is a narrow path passing by aspen trees and superb views of the sheer walls of Basin Cove. The views to the east are unobstructed; early risers can watch the day begin in peace and solitude. The trail's close proximity to the picnic area, lodge, and campground make it very popular at other times of the day.

.0   The trail begins at the far end of Bluff Lodge's upper parking area. Drop steeply; you'll get wonderful views into Basin Cove.

.07   Come to a bench with a vantage point of Caudill Cabin almost directly below.

.2   Arrive at another bench with equally breathtaking views.

.3   Begin to ascend, soon coming to yet another dramatic view from the rock outcropping to the right. Continue on a narrow ridge line.

.4   Come to a bench with a view to the northwest. The trail levels out somewhat.

.5   Bear to the left and climb up on a rock-obstructed pathway as you begin to circle around Fodder Stack. (Do not take the dangerous, unauthorized trail that goes steeply downhill.) Soon arrive at a bench just below the summit.

Mile 241. Wildcat Rocks Trail [BRP 55]

Length: .1 mile, round-trip

Difficulty: easy

Recommended

This trail, recommended for its ease and impressive view, also begins at the far end of Bluff Lodge's upper parking lot. Bear to the right to begin. The trail extends to views overlooking Caudill Cabin and the expanse of Basin Cove. It then loops back to the parking lot via rhododendron tunnels and the lodge's manicured lawn.

Please note: Do not attempt to reach the Caudill Cabin by hiking directly down the mountainside from Wildcat Rock. The rough terrain is extremely hazardous, and the steep slopes are easily eroded by foot traffic. See the Basin Creek Trail [BRP 57] for access to the cabin.

Mile 241. Bluff Ridge Trail [BRP 56]

Length: 2.8 miles, one way

Difficulty: moderately strenuous from BRP to Cove Creek; very strenuous if hiking in the opposite direction

Markings: red paint blazes

A steep journey, the Bluff Ridge Trail is the shortest route from the BRP to the backcountry campsite on Cove Creek. The trail offers excellent views near the Parkway but soon enters heavy woods as it quickly drops 2,000 feet in less than 3 miles.

Easiest access to the trailhead is to follow the picnic area road to its turnaround. Leave your car here and follow the trail markers uphill through the open field.

.0 Follow the trail markers from the parking area uphill through the open meadow.

.2 Trail intersection. The Bluff Mountain Trail [BRP 53] goes to the right. Enjoy the magnificent setting here before bearing left to continue on the Bluff Ridge Trail. Soon cross through a fence stile and come to a shelter with an outstanding view to the southeast of Cove Creek Valley and innumerable ridge lines of the Blue Ridge Mountains stretching off into the distance. A wonderful place to be for sunrise. Descend and cross through another fence stile.

.3 The rocks to the right afford a limited view into the upper reaches of Cove Creek Valley. Descend steeply.

.6 Come into a gap with a trail sign pointing the way. Ascend steeply through mountain laurel.

.9 Reach the top of the ascent and descend at a more moderate pace. Soon rise gradually.

1.2 Reach the top of another knoll; descend gradually on the narrower ridge line. Soon, however, begin to climb again.

1.7 Attain the top of a knoll.

1.8 Reach the top of another knoll and descend steeply. Level out somewhat as you enter a mountain laurel thicket.

2.3   Turn to the left, onto a newly built switchback. (This avoids a vegetation recovery area.)

2.4   Come back to the original trail.

2.6   Drop into a small gap, but continue with a steep descent following the backbone of the ridge line on switchbacks.

2.8   Arrive at the backcountry campsite on Cove Creek. (Camping permits are available from the Doughton Park campground contact station or the ranger station near mile 245.4.) A right turn onto Grassy Gap Fire Road [BRP 58] will lead back to the Parkway in 5 miles. To the left, just a few feet, is the beginning of Basin Creek Trail [BRP 57]. Following Grassy Gap Fire Road to the left will bring you to NC RT 1730 in 1.7 miles. (See page 99 for auto access to NC RT 1730.)

Mile 243.7. Basin Creek Trail [BRP 57]

Length: 3.3 miles, one way

Difficulty: moderately strenuous

Markings: dark blue paint blazes

Ascending the tumbling waters of Basin Creek, the trail passes by many artifacts and reminders that these mountain hollows were heavily populated at one time. The numerous members of the Caudill family lived in and farmed the hidden reaches around Basin Creek. The main family cabin, located at the end of the trail, sits nestled between Fodder Stack and Bluff Ridge. The isolation of this homesite demanded that the Caudills be an independent and self-reliant family.

The Basin Creek Trail is reached only by hiking one of Doughton Park's other trails to the backcountry campsite on Cove Creek. Easiest access would be to walk 1.7 miles from the end of Grassy Gap Fire Road [BRP 58] at NC RT 1730. (See page 99 for vehicle access to NC RT 1730.)

Basin Creek is also well known for some of the best native brook trout fishing in the area.

.0   Begin the trail next to the backcountry campsite, at the intersection of Grassy Gap Fire Road [BRP 58], Bluff Ridge Trail [BRP 56], and Basin Creek Trail [BRP 57].

.05   Walk through rhododendron on an old roadway.

There are some inviting large pools in the creek next to you. Continue to ascend through hemlock.

.6   All that remains of this old cabin is the chimney.

.7   Cross Basin Creek and follow the blue-blazed pathway past a deteriorating rail fence. Running cedar lines the trail. Soon come back to the old roadbed.

1   The creek makes a few pretty cascades – also, some pools that would be hard to resist on hot summer days.

1.1 Cross Basin Creek. You are now almost constantly passing through tunnels of rhododendron and mountain laurel.

1.2 Cross Basin Creek again, and then recross it near some small waterfalls. Ascend rather steeply for a short while.

1.3 Come to a limited view of a thirty-foot waterfall and descend back to the creek.

1.4 Cross a creek and walk through a forest that at one time was obviously pastureland.

1.5 Cross another creek and continue to parallel Basin Creek on the old road.

1.8 Cross Basin Creek.

1.9 Pass by another chimney and cross the creek where there are some great swimming holes.

2   Cross the creek. Again ascend somewhat steeply and enter more former grazing lands. The old roadway more or less disappears. Continue with small ascents and descents.

2.2 Step over a side stream and pass by another cabin site. Cross Basin Creek.

2.4 Enjoy the thirty-foot waterfall. Cross Basin Creek.

2.6 Cross Basin Creek again and ascend on a narrow path.

2.8 Cross the creek here and in 200 feet.

3   Cross Basin Creek for the final time. Ascend steeply, avoiding the old road and staying close to the creek.

3.3 Arrive at the reconstructed but deteriorating Caudill Cabin. Fodder Stack, Wildcat Rocks, and Bluff Ridge are almost directly above you.

Mile 243.7. Grassy Gap Fire Road [BRP 58]

Length: 6.5 miles, one way

Difficulty: moderate

Markings: green paint blazes

By far the gentlest route into Basin Cove, the Grassy Gap Fire Road takes 6.5 miles to descend 1,800 feet from the BRP, pass by the backcountry campsite, and arrive at NC RT 1730 near Abshers, North Carolina. Along the way are a couple of chances to explore the homesites of former inhabitants of the Basin Cove area. Also, the headwaters of Cove Creek, which the road parallels much of the way, are known to carry a large number of native brook trout.

For an easy half-day walk, arrange a car shuttle to meet you at NC RT 1730 (see page 99 for directions).

.0   The trailhead for Grassy Gap Fire Road is not marked well. Be on the lookout for a gated road about .5 mile south of the Bluff Mountain Overlook (BRP mile 243.4). The overlook is the closest parking area to the Grassy Gap Fire Road. Begin the walk by passing through a fence stile.

.1   Cross the Bluff Mountain Trail [BRP 53] and go through a fence. Be sure to shut the gate behind you. Enter the woods and begin your long, gradual descent.

.4   Cross over a spur ridge and enter a rhododendron thicket.

.6   Emerge from the rhododendron and make a wide, arching switchback.

.9   Do not take the side road that comes in from the right.

1   In periods of wet weather there should be a small spring on the left.

1.2   The road cuts across the ridge line and swings to the opposite side.

1.8   Now in a wider, flatter area, pass by some reminders of the former human inhabitants of this area. Explore a little and you may find rusted barrel hoops, old tools, and maybe the foundation of a now nonexistent cabin. Cross the creek on a stone and metal culvert.

2.2   Cross a well-constructed stone bridge and begin to closely parallel the creek.

2.4   Where another creek comes in from the left, arrive in an open valley littered with artifacts from the days when mountain people tried to make a living along these creeks.

2.6   Cross the creek as it descends in a series of small cascades. Rhododendron and hemlock ensure that the trail will be lined with green vegetation throughout the year.

2.8   Cross the creek and begin a gradual ascent.

3.4   Resume your gradual descent.

4.2   There is a nice wading pool here as Grassy Gap Fire Road once again crosses the creek.

4.4   A small wooden bridge precedes your arrival into the wide Basin Cove Valley.

4.8   Arrive at the intersections with Bluff Ridge [BRP 56] and Basin Creek [BRP 57] trails. The primitive backcountry campsite is on your right along the banks of Cove Creek. (Free camping permits may be obtained from the Doughton Park campground contact station or the ranger station at BRP mile 245.4.) Cross Basin Creek and continue to follow Grassy Gap Fire Road.

4.9   Reach the top of a small rise and begin to gradually descend.

5.4   Cross a small side stream on a wooden bridge. The rhododendron, hemlock, ferns, and running cedar give this valley a lush, green look even in winter.

6   A stone wall lines the roadway where there is one final good view back upstream.

6.5   Arrive at the intersections with Cedar Ridge [BRP 52] and Flat Rock Ridge [BRP 59] trails. A few feet beyond is the parking area on NC RT 1730.

Mile 244.7. Flat Rock Ridge Trail [BRP 59]

Length: 5 miles, one way

Difficulty: moderately strenuous from BRP to Grassy Gap Fire Road; strenuous if hiking in the opposite direction

Markings: light blue paint blazes

The Flat Rock Ridge Trail is a more rugged, and therefore possibly a more rewarding, hike into Basin Cove than the Cedar Ridge Trail [BRP 52]. Worthwhile views into Basin Cove open up on soaring rock outcroppings as rhododendron and mountain laurel appear to line almost every inch of the trail. Be on the lookout for deer, turkey, and maybe even a black bear.

Although the narrow ridge line that the pathway follows eventually descends into the valley, it seems to have more than its share of small knobs and knolls. The trail, of course, goes up and over almost every one of them. Switchbacks and excellent trail-building techniques (take note of the superbly constructed stone walls used to stabilize the trail) make these ups and downs a little easier to negotiate.

.0   From the Basin Cove Overlook pass through a fence stile and descend.

.1   Trail intersection. The Bluff Mountain Trail [BRP 53] bears to the left. Turn right to follow the Flat Rock Ridge Trail, pass through another stile, and descend via switchbacks. The flame azalea is especially beautiful here.

.4   Gradually descend through rhododendron and mountain laurel.

.5   Reach the top of a rise and begin to descend through rhododendron tunnels that are almost unbelievably colorful in late May and early June.

.7   A break in the vegetation allows a view into Basin Cove. Descend on a series of switchbacks, taking note of the stone walls lining the pathway.

1.2   Come to the game land boundary. The ridge line here is now quite narrow. Soon come into a gap and begin to ascend.

1.7   Reach the top of the rise, where a rock outcropping gives a limited view of Bluff and Cedar ridges. In a few feet the view to the east gives you the feeling that you are high above any of the surrounding lands.

1.9   A grandstand view into Basin Cove! Continue to descend via switchbacks in rhododendron.

2.5   Come out of the rhododendron and onto a narrow ridge line. The rhododendron has evidently come to the limit of its environment, as there is almost a definite line here – the rhododendron now disappears and mountain laurel takes its place as the dominant understory in the forest.

2.8   Begin a gradual rise.

3   Resume the descent.

3.2   Be alert! The trail turns to the left and descends along the side of the mountain. Do not continue straight by following the game land boundary line.

3.4   Return to the ridge line and the boundary markers.

3.5   Begin an ascent.

3.6   Resume descent.

3.8 Ascend again.

4.0 Descend.

4.4 Breaks in the vegetation reveal the fact that you are much, much lower than you were the last time you had a good view.

4.8 Cove Creek becomes audible below you.

5   Cross the creek and arrive at Grassy Gap Fire Road [BRP 58] and Cedar Ridge Trail [BRP 52]. Left on Grassy Gap Fire Road for 1.7 miles will lead to the primitive campsite and the intersections with Bluff Ridge [BRP 56] and Basin Creek [BRP 57] trails. The parking area on NC RT 1730 is just a few feet to the right. See page 99 for vehicle access to this parking area.

Mile 260.3. Jumpinoff Rocks Trail [BRP 60]

Length: 1 mile, round-trip

Difficulty: easy

Recommended

Lined with galax, pepperbush, and trailing arbutus, this path is a nice break from riding in an automobile. The viewpoint at the end of the walk is quiet and secluded from the Parkway – a favorable location to enjoy a sunrise or have an afternoon snack.

.0   Begin by rising through rhododendron thickets.

.1   Come into a small gap where a break in the vegetation permits a view into the deep valley below.

.15 A bench on which to rest.

.25 Level off and then begin to descend through mountain laurel.

.3   Arrive at another bench.

.4   Galax becomes abundant and lines both sides of the trail.

.5   Arrive at the view looking out across the valley to prominent Stone Mountain in the distance.

Mile 264.4. The Lump Trail [BRP 61]

Length: .2–.3 mile (the trail is actually a field area)

Difficulty: moderately easy

Highly recommended

There is no real trail here, but what an appropriate name for the area! This high, open meadow is just a large "lump" of land that ascends quickly from the Parkway.

There are excellent views from the top into Yadkin Valley and out across the multitude of ridges that rise to meet the horizon in all directions.

Walk through the fence and wander around on The Lump, enjoying the views and, in season, possibly a wild strawberry or two. This windswept knob might be a good location for a cool yet sunny spot for a lazy summer afternoon of sunbathing.

Trails of the E. B. Jeffress Park Area, Blue Ridge Parkway Miles 271.9–272.5

This small recreation area was named in honor of E. B. Jeffress, chairman of the North Carolina State Highway and Public Works Commission in 1933. In addition to being an enthusiastic supporter of the BRP project, he lead the fight to keep the Parkway from becoming a toll road.

The park contains picnic tables and rest rooms.

Mile 271.9. Cascades Trail [BRP 62]

Length: .9 mile, round-trip

Difficulty: moderate

Recommended

The Park Service has placed signs along the Cascades Trail identifying much of the plant life to be found in the Blue Ridge Mountains. As with other signed, self-guiding trails, this short walk is recommended because it offers knowledge that will enrich your additional excursions along the BRP.

Dropping quickly off the ridge line, the pathway follows Falls Creek to the cascades. The rushing, roiling falls of fifty or sixty feet will be most impressive after a hard spring rain.

The climb back up from the cascades gives this trail a moderate rating (and possibly moderately strenuous if you are a little out of shape).

.0   Begin on the paved trail next to the rest rooms.

.05   Bear to the right at the loop-trail intersection and pass by several large Solomon's seal plants. Begin to descend.

.1   There is a bench next to bountiful flame azalea that put on a very colorful display here in mid- to late May. The cascades soon become audible as you quickly descend through mountain laurel and rhododendron.

.3 Cross Falls Creek on a log bridge and bear right at the loop-trail junction.

.4 Arrive at the upper viewing platform at the top of the cascades.

.45 Come to the lower viewing platform, which brings you even closer to the rushing waters of the falls. Retrace your steps to return.

.5 Bear right at the loop-trail junction and enjoy the attractive bell-shaped dog hobble flowers. Follow the small cascades of the creek upstream.

.6 Arrive at a bench under a birch tree.

.7 Another bench.

.9 Bear right at the loop-trail intersection, and in a few feet return to the parking lot.

Mile 272.5. Tompkins Knob Trail [BRP 63]

Length: .6 mile, one way

Difficulty: easy

The Tompkins Knob Trail is a connector trail between the Tompkins Knob parking lot and the E. B. Jeffress Park picnic area. Along the way this easy route passes by Jesse Brown's Cabin, occupied in the late 1800s. The trail also goes by the Cool Spring Baptist Church, a log structure noteworthy not only for its historical significance but also for its rib-pole roof construction.

.0 Descend on the trail from the northern end of the Tompkins Knob parking lot.

.1 Pass by Jesse Brown's Cabin, which was moved to this site sometime near the turn of the century to be closer to Cool Spring. In a few feet go by the Cool Spring Baptist Church. The building itself was actually used only during inclement weather; most of the religious services were held out of doors. Continue past the church on a level trail and into an old orchard.

.2 Descend rather quickly.

.25 As the descent levels out a little, arrive at a bench in a hardwood forest. A few sassafras trees are scattered about, but Solomon's seal and mayapple are plentiful.

.35 Enter a stand of pine trees whose dropped needles help soften the pathway.

.5   Come to another bench.

.6   Arrive at the picnic area in E. B. Jeffress Park. Rest
       rooms and water are just across the parking lot.

Trails of Moses H. Cone Memorial Park, Blue Ridge Parkway Miles 294–295.4

Around the turn of the century, having insured his personal wealth as the "Denim King," Moses H. Cone purchased this property near Blowing Rock, North Carolina, to develop as his personal estate.

Moses and his wife, Bertha, not only appreciated the natural beauty of the mountains but sought to enrich its diversity. Cone imported a variety of apple trees that would mature from June into November. Aided by Gifford Pinchot, the "Father of American Forestry," the Cones landscaped the estate with extensive plantings of white pine, hemlock, sugar maple, and rhododendron. Meadows were created not only for sheep and cattle, but they and the apple orchards were placed so as to be pleasing to the eye when viewed from the Manor House.

For the walker and hiker, the most outstanding changes Moses Cone made to the landscape were to build more than 25 miles of carriage trails that twist, wind, and meander into every part of the estate. All of the trails are interconnected; most walks begin at the Manor House. Numerous possibilities exist for extensive day-long hikes through the property without ever retracing your steps. Because these roads were built for horses pulling carriages, they rise and fall at gentle grades. The most difficult trail in this park receives no more than a moderate rating.

Some of the carriage roads are popular with the local population. Expect to share a part of your day with other walkers, picnickers, joggers, horseback riders, and, in winter, cross-country skiers.

A craft shop is operated in the Manor House by the Southern Highland Handicraft Guild, and during the tourist months artisans demonstrate their skills on the front porch. Recommended tours of the Manor House are held on an irregular basis. Check at the information desk for dates and times.

Mile 294. Rich Mountain Carriage Trail [BRP 64]

Length: 5.1 miles, one way

Difficulty: moderate

Recommended

The Rich Mountain Carriage Trail is one of only two trails that ascend instead of descend from the Manor House. On the way to the summit of Rich Mountain, for excellent views of the estate and surrounding countryside, the trail goes through open fields and into rhododendron-thick forests, circles by small Trout Lake and old building foundations, and passes other reminders that the Cones worked every part of their estate.

Rich Mountain Carriage Trail is one of the longest trails in the park and thus is one of the least used. This ensures a peaceful and relaxing walk.

Although the one-way length is 5.1 miles, there are a couple of options to make your walk a little shorter:

You could begin or end the walk where the trail intersects Flannery Fork Road .9 mile from the Manor House. Auto access to this point may be obtained by following the Parkway south from the Manor House to BRP mile 294.6 in Sandy Flat Gap. Exit the Parkway, turn right, go under the BRP, and bear right onto Flannery Fork Road. Be aware that there is not a parking area at the point where the Rich Mountain Carriage Trail crosses Flannery Fork Road.

A second option for shortening the walk to the summit of Rich Mountain is to make use of the Shulls Mill Road Extension [BRP 76] of the Rich Mountain Carriage Trail.

The Mountains to Sea Trail (see Appendix G) makes use of a portion of the Rich Mountain Carriage Trail.

.0   From the parking area next to the Manor House descend the steps leading to the Carriage Barn and turn left onto a gravel road.

.1   Cross under the BRP and arrive at an intersection. To the right is Flat Top Carriage Trail [BRP 65]. Bear left to continue on the Rich Mountain Carriage Trail and enter woods thick with magnolia trees.

.35   Switch back to the right.

.45   Switch back to the left.

.6   Switch back to the right.

.7   Cross a small stream on a culvert.

.9   Pass by a stock loading pen and cross Flannery Fork Road. Continue to descend along the rhododendron-lined road. Trout Lake can be seen through the vegetation.

1.1   Come to the intersection with Trout Lake Trail [BRP 75]. Continue straight and begin to walk beside the lake.

1.3   Cross over the dam and outlet stream. Begin a gradual rise.

1.5   Trail intersection. The Trout Lake Trail is to the left. Make a hard right to continue on the Rich Mountain Carriage Trail.

1.7   Magnolias are plentiful along the trail.

2.3   Switch back to the left.

2.7   The field you are heading for can be seen through the vegetation.

2.8   Pass through a gate (be sure to close it after you) and come into open pastureland.

3.1   Arrive at another stock loading pen and a trail intersection. The Shulls Mill Road Extension [BRP 76] of Rich Mountain Carriage Trail bears to the left. Switch back right and continue to ascend on the road. (Please do not add to the erosion of this field by following the unauthorized trail straight up the hillside.) There are good views of Grandfather Mountain from here. Wind your way around the mountain, leaving the meadow and entering a rhododendron and hardwood forest.

3.7   Pass by a fence stile where the Mountains to Sea Trail (see Appendix G) leaves the road and descends to the left.

4.2   Reenter the meadow. Cone used this area as a deer park.

4.3   Switch back to the left and begin spiraling around the summit of the mountain. (Please, from here to the end of the trail, do not leave the road and follow the unauthorized trails that go straight uphill through the field. Lazy and uncaring people have established these trails to save themselves a few steps. The damage they are doing to this hillside is evident. Recall that the route was originally a carriage trail, which by its very nature must take this roundabout way to reach the summit.)

4.6   Once again, please stay on the road.

4.9   A final time, avoid the temptation to leave the road.

5.1 Circle back to where the road meets itself. Now you can leave the road and climb the final few feet to the 4,370-foot summit of Rich Mountain. Here are excellent views, especially to the north and west.

Mile 294. Flat Top Mountain Carriage Trail [BRP 65]

Length: 2.8 miles, one way

Difficulty: moderate

Recommended

Like the Rich Mountain Carriage Trail [BRP 64], this path also ascends rather than descends from the Manor House. The grandstand view from the fire tower that Cone built on the summit of Flat Top Mountain is not the only thing that makes this a recommended journey. Wildflowers line much of the trail through a deep maple forest, and broad pastures provide additional vistas. You can even visit Mr. and Mrs. Cone's final resting place to thank them for providing such pleasurable roadways to walk upon.

.0 From the parking area next to the Manor House, descend the steps leading to the Carriage Barn and turn left onto a gravel road.

.1 Cross under the BRP and arrive at an intersection. The Rich Mountain Carriage Trail [BRP 64] goes left. Bear right to continue on the Flat Top Mountain Carriage Trail. Begin to ascend, with a field on one side of you supplying views of Grandfather Mountain, while the sugar maples and magnolias on the other side of the road provide some cool shade from the sun.

.2 Switch back to the right, entering woods. Soon switch back left, where, in May, white trillium fills the forest floor.

.7 Enter an open field.

.75 Make a left at the trail intersection onto a grassy road.

.9 Follow the grassy road around the gravesite of Moses and Bertha Cone and Sophie and Clementine Lindau.

1 Return to the intersection, turn left, and resume your ascent through the perfectly manicured pasture.

1.4 Just before reentering the woods, you will get a couple of good views of Grandfather Mountain and

some views of the development in Blowing Rock,
North Carolina. Begin a series of switchbacks in the
forest, where wildflowers proliferate.

2   Make a quick zigzag where you can see part of the
shopping mall in Blowing Rock. Continue ascending
on switchbacks lined with mayapple, wild mustard,
and chickweed.

2.55 Swing around the final switchback.

2.8   Ascend the fire tower to observe the surrounding
scene: Grandfather Mountain to one side, Blowing
Rock to the other and below, green fields, the Cones'
gravesite, and the road you just walked.

Mile 294. Watkins Carriage Road [BRP 66]

Length: 3.8 miles, one way

Difficulty: moderate

In springtime the Watkins Carriage Road will be the
place for wildflower lovers to walk. The carriage road
switches back at least ten times on its descent from the
Manor House to US RT 221 near Blowing Rock. Nature
has seemingly chosen a special, different wildflower to
grow in the wide, flat area of each switchback. You can expect lousewort, wild geranium, violets, painted trillium,
rhododendron, mountain laurel, and more.

By vehicle, you can access the trailhead near US RT
221 at Blowing Rock by following the Parkway north from
the Manor House and exiting at BRP mile 291.9. Take US
RT 221 toward Blowing Rock for .2 mile to a residential
dirt road on the right. (The New River Inn will be on your
left.) Following the dirt road for .2 mile will bring you to
the Watkins Carriage Road. Be aware that there is no
space for parking your car here.

The Watkins Carriage Road is also a part of the
Mountains to Sea Trail (see Appendix G).

.0   Go down the steps from the front porch of the
Manor House and turn left onto paved Watkins Carriage Road, enjoying the views out across the Cone
estate.

.1   The pavement ends. Cinquefoil, speedwell, white
trillium, wild mustard, and wild strawberries line the
road.

.2   Pass by an old spring house and orchard.

.45 Enter the woods, where the wildflowers become
even more prolific. The forest is carpeted with white

trillium, touch-me-nots, buttercups, purple asters, Solomon's seal, iris, and chickweed.

.55 Intersection. The Deer Park Carriage Road [BRP 69] goes to the right. Bear left and continue to descend on the Watkins Carriage Road. Speedwell and other flowers persist in large numbers.

.9 Lousewort is the special flower of this switchback. Descend as rhododendron begins to close in on the road.

1.1 Wild geranium dominates a switchback to the right.

1.5 Switch back left amid a tract of lousewort.

1.8 This switchback to the right has three flowers in abundance – cinquefoil, wild strawberries, and violets.

2.3 Another switchback with dominant flowers – violets and white trillium.

2.4 Galax and painted trillium prosper on this switchback to the left.

2.5 Lousewort once again prevails.

2.6 One final switchback dominated by lousewort.

2.7 Intersection. To the right is the Black Bottom Carriage Road [BRP 67]. Bear left to continue on Watkins Carriage Road.

3 Walk next to a fence enclosing a field and pond.

3.2 The shopping mall in Blowing Rock is visible in the distance.

3.3 Enter a forest of hemlock and rhododendron.

3.8 Cross over a stream, pass through the gate, and arrive at the end of the Watkins Carriage Road. US RT 221 is .2 mile to the right.

Mile 294. Black Bottom Carriage Road [BRP 67]

Length: .5 mile, one way

Difficulty: easy

The Black Bottom Carriage Road is a short connector trail between Watkins Carriage Road [BRP 66] and the intersection of The Maze [BRP 70] and the Apple Barn Connector Road [BRP 71]. This means that you must first walk one of these roads in order to reach the Black Bottom Carriage Road. A little different from the other carriage roads, this one passes through a moist bottomland rich in ferns and mosses.

.0 At the intersection of Watkins [BRP 66] and Black Bottom [BRP 67] carriage roads (2.7 miles from the

Manor House via the Watkins Carriage Road) bear right to begin walking the Black Bottom Carriage Road. At first you will descend, but soon begin a gradual rise next to a stream. This bottomland forest contains hardwoods, rhododendron, and galax.

.1 Cross the stream and swing to the left into a moist, mossy area of many small water runs.

.2 Cross the stream on a culvert, begin a steady rise, and enter a forest of pines.

.4 The pine trees start to thin out.

.5 Arrive at the junction with The Maze [BRP 70] to the left and the Apple Barn Connector Road [BRP 71] to the right.

Mile 294. Bass Lake Carriage Road [BRP 68]

Length: 1.7 miles, one way

Difficulty: easy

Recommended

Moses Cone built a number of lakes on his estate and stocked them with bass and trout. The largest is Bass Lake, a focal point of the view from the Manor House porch.

Bass Lake Carriage Road is an easy, level route around the lake with good views back up to the Manor House. It begins where the Deer Park [BRP 69] and Apple Barn Connector [BRP 71] carriage roads intersect, quickly drops through a hardwood forest, and then encircles the lake. The road ends at a parking area on US RT 221 near the Blowing Rock Stables.

By vehicle, you may reach the parking area on US RT 221 by following the Parkway south from the Manor House and exiting at BRP mile 294.6. Follow US RT 221 toward Blowing Rock. There is a large, signed parking area on the left soon after passing Laurel Lane (which will be on your right).

.0 From the intersection of the Deer Park [BRP 69] and Apple Barn Connector [BRP 71] carriage roads, walk downhill on the Bass Lake Carriage Road.

.5 Arrive at the intersection with The Maze [BRP 70], which comes in from the left. (Straight ahead will keep you on the Bass Lake Carriage Road, but you would miss the walk around the lake.) Make a hard right and walk next to the lake on a road shaded by stately maple trees.

.6   Pass by the foundation of a former boat house. Purple asters line the road.

.9   Cross an inlet stream. The Manor House is visible uphill.

1   Cross a second inlet stream.

1.1   Cross the third inlet stream.

1.2   Now at the most scenic spot on this walk, you're able to look all the way across the lake and uphill over the estate to the Manor House.

1.3   Intersection. A left would return you from whence you came. Make a right to finish the walk on the Bass Lake Carriage Road.

1.45   Walk uphill through rhododendron and maple.

1.55   Intersection with the Duncan Carriage Road [BRP 72] coming in from the right. Bear left steeply uphill to continue on the Bass Lake Carriage Road.

1.7   Arrive at the parking area on US RT 221.

Mile 294. Deer Park Carriage Road [BRP 69]

Length: .7 mile, one way

Difficulty: moderately easy

With the large number of deer that are seen along the Parkway today, it may be hard to believe that the population at the turn of the century was almost decimated. The local inhabitants' hunting dogs ran down and killed as many, if not more, deer than the inhabitants killed for meat. Loss of habitat due to farming and lumbering added to the pressures put upon the deer.

Moses Cone recognized what was happening to the deer in the Southern Appalachians and imported herds from further north. He kept the herds in "deer parks" (hence, the name of this carriage road) on his estate in the hope that their numbers would grow and could then be released into the wild. Obviously, Cone's experiment was a success.

The Deer Park Carriage Road is a connector trail that descends from Watkins Carriage Road [BRP 66] to join with the Bass Lake Carriage Road [BRP 68]. It more or less follows the fenced-in boundary of the main pasture below the Manor House and is the quickest route from the house to Bass Lake.

.0   To begin this walk, just over half a mile from the Manor House, make a hard right at the intersection with the Watkins Carriage Road [BRP 66], which goes

off to the left. Descend past Solomon's seal in a
mixed forest of maple, magnolia, and poplar.

.2 Walk right next to a fence where dwarf iris bloom.

.4 The rise is so slight as to be almost imperceptible.

.5 Resume the gradual descent through hemlocks.

.7 Arrive at an intersection and the end of the Deer
Park Carriage Road. The Apple Barn Connector
Road [BRP 71] goes off to the left while the Bass
Lake Carriage Road [BRP 68] is to the right.

Mile 294. The Maze [BRP 70]

Length: 2.3 miles, one way

Difficulty: moderate

You could not really become lost on this walk, but
the road certainly does twist, turn, and almost double back
on itself, making you wonder which direction you will be
heading next. Most of the length of the road is in a deep
forest whose dominant trees alternate among oaks, pine,
and magnolias. The mark of Gifford Pinchot, Cone's
friend and landscape architect, is evident in the way many
of the stands of trees are arranged. The thick vegetation
mutes much of the exterior sounds, making this a quieter
walk than some of the other carriage roads.

The Maze begins at the intersection of the Black
Bottom [BRP 67] and Apple Barn Connector [BRP 71] carriage roads and ends at the intersection with Bass Lake
Carriage Road [BRP 68], about .3 mile from the parking
area on US RT 221. See [BRP 68] for directions to the parking area.

.0 Walk uphill from the intersection of the Black Bottom [BRP 67] and Apple Barn Connector [BRP 71]
carriage roads.

.2 The Maze begins to wind around and is just a few
feet below where you are now walking.

.3 Mighty white pines drop their needles on the road.

.5 Switch back to the left.

.6 Take a wide curve to the right among oak trees.
Magnolias are also numerous.

.8 Come back into nice, neat rows of pines.

1.2 Squirrels seem to enjoy this particular spot where
the road makes a switchback to the left.

1.5 Switch back to the right.

1.7 Your peace, isolation, and tranquility are broken.
Come around a bend in the road and encounter a

housing development that has been built right on the border of Moses H. Cone Memorial Park. Watch out for the dogs!

2.1　Finally leave the housing development behind.

2.3　Arrive at an intersection and the end of The Maze. Bass Lake is directly in front of you. A hard right will bring you to the Manor House via the Bass Lake [BRP 68] and Deer Park [BRP 69] carriage roads. A right will allow you to walk around the lake on the Bass Lake Carriage Road. A left turn will bring you to the parking area on US RT 221 in about .3 mile.

Mile 294. Apple Barn Connector Road [BRP 71]

Length: .2 mile, one way

Difficulty: easy

This is a short trail that connects the Black Bottom Carriage Road [BRP 67] and The Maze [BRP 70] with the Deer Park [BRP 69] and Bass Lake [BRP 68] carriage roads.

Mile 294. Duncan Carriage Road [BRP 72]

Length: 2.5 miles, one way

Difficulty: moderate

The collaboration between Cone and Pinchot is also evident on the Duncan Carriage Road. This route passes by stands of planted white pines and several apple orchards as it drops from the Manor House to the parking area on US RT 221. See [BRP 68] for information on vehicle access to this parking area.

.0　Go down the steps from the front porch of the Manor House and turn right, enjoying the view out across the estate.

.2　Enter woods and turn left onto a dirt road. (Straight ahead is just a service road.)

.5　Returning to the edge of the meadow, switch back to the right and walk under a venerable old magnolia tree.

.6　Switch back to the left.

.8　Arrive at an intersection. Rock Creek Bridge Carriage Road [BRP 73] is to the right. Bear left to continue on Duncan Carriage Road. Come back to the meadow, ascend slightly, and proceed beyond one of Cone's old apple orchards.

1   Resume the descent and stroll in a pine forest for a brief stretch.

1.2   Switch back left.

1.4   Come back to the meadow for the final time and switch back right.

1.8   Cross over a stream on a culvert and switch back left.

2.35   Intersection. The Bass Lake Carriage Road [BRP 68] is to the left. Bear right and ascend to continue on Duncan Carriage Road.

2.5   Arrive at the parking area on US RT 221.

Mile 294. Rock Creek Bridge Carriage Road [BRP 73]

Length: 1.7 miles, one way

Difficulty: moderately easy

The Rock Creek Bridge Carriage Road has become, in the last several years, extremely popular with the horseback riders of the Blocking Rock area. If you don't mind a bit of mud, a few droppings, and sharing your walk with the horses, the road can be a pleasant enough venture. It begins at the .9 mile point on Duncan Carriage Road [BRP 72], crosses under US RT 221, and parallels that highway before making a loop around a heavily wooded knob. The trail ends on Laurel Lane.

You may gain vehicle access to the far trailhead by following the Parkway south from the Manor House. Exit the BRP at mile 294.6 in Sandy Flat Gap and follow US RT 221 toward Blowing Rock. At the first right, turn onto Laurel Lane. The trailhead is across from the stables.

.0   Having followed the Duncan Carriage Road [BRP 72] .9 mile from the Manor House, turn right onto the Rock Creek Bridge Carriage Road and descend through the woods.

.5   Break out of the woods.

.6   Go under US RT 221 and ascend.

.7   Swing around a knob and continue to ascend.

.8   Switch back to the right and then to the left.

.1   Turn right to walk the loop around a knob. Ascend where lousewort lines the road.

1.1   Bear right at the loop-trail intersection. Amble in a deep woodland heavily populated by Solomon's seal. There is a limited view into the valley where the road swings around the knob.

1.4   Bear right at the loop-trail intersection.

1.5   Return to the main road and descend in rhododendron.

1.7   Arrive at Laurel Lane.

Mile 294. Figure Eight Trail [BRP 74]

Length: .5 mile, round-trip

Difficulty: easy

Recommended

This self-guiding pathway is the same one the Cones
used for their daily morning walks. The Park Service
keeps the almost level trail under white oak, red maple,
and black cherry in excellent repair. Signs along the way
provide information about the Cones, their estate, and the
trailside plant life.

Besides being a short, pleasurable walk, this recommended trip offers a lot of background information that
will enhance the rest of your walks on the estate.

.0   Go down the first flight of steps from the Manor
House; turn right. Ascend gradually and begin the
trail lined with chickweed, Solomon's seal, and violets. Soon turn left where the trail is bordered by
rhododendron on one side and white trillium on the
other.

.1   Enter a dense rhododendron thicket.

.2   Intersection. Make a hard right and begin the figure
eight. Stay straight at the next two intersections.

.3   Having completed the figure eight, bear right and
gradually descend, passing birch, oak, and sugar
maple.

.5   Arrive back at the Manor House.

Mile 294.6. Trout Lake Trail [BRP 75]

Length: 1 mile, round-trip

Difficulty: easy

Recommended

Since it is almost perfectly level and is exactly 1 mile,
the Trout Lake Trail has become popular with the locals
as a jogging track. The most outstanding feature is a hem-
lock-dominated cove forest. Such forests are quite rare
along the BRP.

See [BRP 76] for information to the Trout Lake Trailhead.

.0   From the road between the two parking lots for the Trout Lake Trail, descend steeply toward the lake. In 100 feet arrive at the main trail, turn left, and walk among violets, rhododendron, and bluets.

.3   Intersection. The Rich Mountain Carriage Trail [BRP 64] goes left for 3.6 miles to the summit of Rich Mountain. Bear right to continue on the Trout Lake Trail. Descend into the magnificent and wonderful hemlock cove forest.

.5   Cross the dam and outlet streams. Continue to circle the lake.

.6   Intersection. The Rich Mountain Carriage Trail [BRP 64] goes 1.1 miles to the left to reach the Manor House. Bear right to progress on the Trout Lake Trail.

.7   Where violets become abundant you will lose sight of the lake.

.9   Come to the Trout Lake parking area road and turn right. Watch for jewelweed and speedwell.

1   Be alert! The trail turns to the right into the woods. In a couple of hundred feet take the trail uphill and arrive back at the point where you started this walk.

Mile 294.6. Shulls Mill Road Extension of the Rich Mountain Carriage Trail [BRP 76]

Length: .5 mile, one way

Difficulty: moderate

This is a shortcut to the summit of Rich Mountain. Be forewarned, though, that like most shortcuts, the extension road ascends the mountain at a steeper grade than most of the other carriage roads. If the road were just a little bit longer, it would be rated a moderately strenuous hike.

The Shulls Mill Road Extension trailhead may be reached by following the BRP south from the Manor House. Exit the Parkway at mile 294.6, double back underneath the BRP, and bear left onto Shulls Mill Road. You will pass two roads to the right that lead to the two parking lots for the Trout Lake Trail [BRP 75]. The trailhead is on the right just past the second intersection. There is just enough room for one automobile to pull off the road here.

.0   From the little parking spot on Shulls Mill Road, cross through a fence stile and ascend rather steeply.

.3   A small spring runs just below the road at a wide curve.

.5   Arrive at the junction with the Rich Mountain Carriage Trail [BRP 64]. A turn to the right will bring you to the Manor House in 3.1 miles. Make a left turn and you can ascend to the summit of Rich Mountain in 2 miles.

Mile 295.4. Sims Creek Trail [BRP 77]

Length: .1 mile, one way

Difficulty: easy

Follow the pathway from the middle of the Sims Viaduct Overlook through a heavy growth of rhododendron. Arrive at the Green Knob Trail [BRP 78] and Sims Creek in .1 mile. Cross the creek on a footbridge to arrive at a bench and a surprisingly splendid little flower garden. Abundant butterflies flutter about, songbirds chirp cheerfully, and the sun brightens the banks of the creek. The variety of wildflowers is phenomenal – violets, white violets, jewelweed, jack-in-the-pulpits, wake robin trillium, Solomon's seal, wild mustard, and clusters of speedwell.

This is certainly a nice spot to take a break from riding in the car.

Trails of Julian Price Memorial Park, Blue Ridge Parkway Miles 295.9–297

As president of Jefferson Standard Life Insurance Company, Julian Price intended for this land to become a recreation spot for the company's employees. Upon his unexpected death in 1946, the company donated the land to the Parkway as a public recreation area.

The park has become one of the most popular areas of the BRP. The campground's close proximity to the populations of Boone, Blowing Rock, and Asheville, North Carolina, almost guarantees that it will stay full during the usual tourist months.

All three of the park's trails are recommended trips. One encircles the lake, where bass and bream are abundant; another goes into a bottomland forest of wildflowers and hardwoods. The longest pathway passes through an ancient lake bed that is surrounded by caves once used for shelter by archaic Indians.

In addition to the campground, Julian Price Memorial Park also has a picnic area and offers boat rentals for those who wish to enjoy the lake to its fullest.

Mile 295.9. Green Knob Trail [BRP 78]

Length: 2 miles, round-trip

Difficulty: moderately strenuous

In a little over 2 miles you will be treated to many of the vegetation zones that occur along the Parkway – lakeside, bottomland forest, rhododendron and mountain laurel thickets, small wildflower meadows, and open pasturelands. As a bonus, the rugged ridge line of Grandfather Mountain may also be seen from the trail.

.0   Descend the steps from the Sims Pond Overlook (the pond was named after Hamp Sims, a former resident of the area). Cross the outlet stream and walk beside the pond, a favorite haunt of zealous anglers. Rhododendron soon hides the pond from view.

.15   You are now beyond the pond. Cross and parallel Sims Creek through a moist and lush bottomland forest.

.3   At a man-made falls begin to ascend as the creek descends via small pools and cascades.

.4   Arrive at a bench and cross the creek, enjoying the impressive showing of rhododendron.

.5   Cross a small side stream and be watching for a few jack-in-the-pulpits.

.6   Ascend to walk directly below the BRP's Sims Creek Viaduct and arrive at an intersection. The Sims Creek Trail [BRP 77] goes uphill for .1 mile to the Sims Creek Viaduct Overlook (BRP mile 295.4). Bear left and cross Sims Creek to continue on the Green Knob Trail. Pass by a bench in a small field crowded with wildflowers.

.7   Cross the creek.

.8   Cross the creek and continue to ascend; birch trees dominate.

1   Pass through a fence stile and enter a verdant meadow. Continue to follow the obvious trail.

1.1   Arrive at a bench under a cool shade tree and amid a serene pastoral landscape. Continue to climb following trail post markers in the field.

1.2   Reenter the woods on an old road. Wild mustard makes up a large part of the undergrowth.

1.3   Come to another bench.

1.4   Bypass the very summit of Green Knob, but break out into the open just long enough to admire the rugged ridge line of Grandfather Mountain in the distance. Cross through a fence stile, reenter the woods, and drop quickly.

1.5   Arrive at another bench, this one overlooking a field of wild strawberries. Descend steeply.

1.7   On this steep descent catch a glimpse of Price Lake with Grandfather Mountain as a backdrop.

1.8   Pass through a fence stile.

2   Cross through another fence stile, descend into a rhododendron thicket, and then diagonally cross the BRP to arrive back at the Sims Pond Overlook.

Mile 296.5. Boone Fork Trail [BRP 79]

Length: 4.9 miles, round-trip

Difficulty: moderately strenuous

Highly recommended

Thanks to the extensive acreage of Julian Price Memorial Park, the Boone Fork Trail is one of those rare BRP trails that may wander quite some distance from the Parkway yet remain within Park boundaries.

This route has so much to enjoy that you should probably allow more than the two to three hours needed to walk it without taking any breaks. Bring a lunch and a book and relax. Soaking up your surroundings here, you can savor one of the most quiet and pleasurable trails the Parkway has to offer. Two major streams are paralleled, allowing ample opportunity to investigate this environment. Beavers have built dams on Boone Fork, and their activity is evident along much of the stream. Wade through one of the cool pools and luxuriate in the warmth of the summer sun as you take a break on one of the large, flat rocks in midstream.

Bloodroot hails the arrival of spring around the second week of April. Mountain laurel and rhododendron bloom along Bee Tree Creek in May or June.

Rock outcroppings make interesting formations that invite further explorations. Open meadows sit almost in the shadow of Grandfather Mountain.

The Mountains to Sea Trail (see Appendix G) makes use of a portion of the Boone Fork Trail.

.0 Cross the bridge behind the rest rooms in the picnic area and in 200 feet turn right onto the loop trail. Parallel Boone Fork (named for a nephew of Daniel Boone), passing picnic tables and a water fountain.

.1 The flat land and bog here are believed to be the site of an ancient lake. Silt deposited by streams filled the lake bed, resulting in a rich soil that supports a wide diversity of plant life including wild mustard, cinquefoil, and wild strawberries. In season enjoy a few blackberries, which also grow well here. Caves in the cliffs surrounding the lake served as shelter for archaic Indians.

.3 Enter the woods and observe the first signs of beaver activity on this trail.

.5 Cross the creek on a footbridge. The beaver activity appears to be even more energetic in this area.

.6 Pass next to a large overhanging boulder that could be used as an emergency rain shelter.

.9 The flat rocks at this small waterfall might entice you to take a short sunbath. Soon the Mountains to Sea Trail comes in from the right, having dropped off Rich Mountain in Moses H. Cone Memorial Park.

1.1 Ascend slightly to an old railroad grade. Note that the creek is much larger and moving more rapidly than when you started your walk.

1.3 Begin walking in heavy rhododendron growth as the creek drops even further below you, making enough noise now to sound like a river.

1.5 Avoid the faint, descending trail to the right.

1.7 Climb the wooden stepladder between two large boulders. Be alert! Three hundred feet after the ladder the trail makes an abrupt hard right (do not continue straight) and descends back down to the banks of Boone Fork. Turn left and follow the creek downstream next to a number of small waterfalls.

1.9 Cross a small side stream on stepping stones.

2 Cross a log footbridge and descend wooden steps. (Do not continue straight.)

2.1 The trail becomes somewhat rough and makes several short ups and downs before gradually descending to the railroad grade.

2.3 Cross Bee Tree Creek, turn left, and ascend following the creek upstream.

2.5 Cross the creek on a log bridge, recross it in 100 feet, and cross again in 150 feet. This isolated creek valley appears to be a favorite spot of numerous songbirds. Stop and listen to the melodies for a little while. As you ascend you will cross the creek eight more times in the next .4 mile, sometimes on a log footbridge, sometimes on stepping stones.

3.1 Step over the creek, which, by this time, is not much more than a trickle of water. Walk in a forest of birch so extensive that you would almost think you were in New England. Soon recross the creek three more times.

3.4 Come to a bench sitting in a rhododendron thicket.

3.5 Pass through a fence stile, walk in an open meadow for just a few feet, make a hard left, and reenter the woods.

3.6 Break out into an open meadow and follow the faint path and road straight ahead.

3.7 Come to a utility line and descend to the left in a field full of cinquefoil.

3.8 Intersection. Bear left as the Tanawha Trail (see Chapter 5) comes in from the right and shares the same pathway with the Boone Fork Trail for a short distance. (This portion of the Mountains to Sea Trail terminates at this junction with the Tanawha Trail, which is not yet a dedicated segment of the Mountains to Sea Trail.) Go through a fence stile and walk in a dense rhododendron tunnel.

4 Intersection. The Tanawha Trail turns to the right. Bear left to continue on Boone Fork Trail. Dwarf iris, chickweed, and wild geranium compete for growing space on the forest floor.

4.1 The trail to the right is a short connector to the campground. Bear left, cross the campground road, and walk by rest rooms and water fountains on a paved trail.

4.3 Cross the campground road again and continue on an unpaved pathway.

4.4 Follow the trail behind the campground contact station (BRP mile 296.9) and make a couple of minor ups and downs.

4.5   Pass by Loops E and F of the campground. Continue to follow the trail and enter a growth of rhododendron.

4.9   Come into an open field and soon arrive back at the rest rooms and picnic area.

Mile 296.9. Price Lake Loop Trail [BRP 80]

Length: 2.5 miles, round-trip

Difficulty: moderately easy

Recommended

The Price Lake Loop Trail is the perfect path for an early morning or early evening stroll.

Dull gray fog curling upward from the lake turns a brilliant pink as the morning sun rises in the east. Be watching for the darting flights of bats when they dive in search of one last insect before retiring for the day. Water snakes begin to wriggle toward open areas to warm themselves in the sun, and snapping turtles may be seen breaking the surface of the lake. Songbirds are especially active around the lake in the early morning hours.

The long shadows of early evening help to hide the homes of muskrats and bog turtles. Birch leaves rustle in the cool breezes. Walking along the far side of the lake, across the water you can see the warm evening camp fires beginning to flicker throughout the campground.

.0   At the southern end of the Boone Fork Overlook, turn left onto a trail bordered with rhododendron. (Boone Fork Overlook is reached by turning into the campground at BRP mile 296.9. Bear right in the campground to reach the overlook.)

.2   Cross Cold Prong on a footbridge. The smooth, slow-moving water of the stream reflects the sunlight and overhanging rhododendron. Walk through a bottomland forest.

.3   Cross wide Boone Fork on a footbridge. Pass by a bench and enter a small birch forest.

.4   Walk out to the waters edge for your first good view of Price Lake. An especially beautiful sunrise spot.

.5   Continue walking next to the water and arrive at a bench where a number of painted trillium bloom.

.6   Reenter the woods and swing away from the lake. Songbirds appear to enjoy this locality, as the volume of their music is greater here than other areas around the lake.

.7   Cross a small water run.

1   Pass over a creek on a footbridge and come to a bench. Ascend slightly for just a short distance.

1.2   Come to another bench.

1.4   Pass by a giant boulder that has trees growing on top of it. The trees have wrapped their roots around the rock, extending themselves into the soil.

1.7   Come onto the BRP and walk over the bridge with a view across Price Lake.

1.1   Walk along the Price Lake Overlook and enter a rhododendron tunnel at the southern end of the overlook. Make several small ups and downs.

2.1   Come into the campground and begin to follow a paved pathway. In a few hundred feet pass by a rest room and Loop A of the campground.

2.4   In a field of Solomon's seal, wild geranium, and mayapple, leave the campground. In a few feet come to an intersection. The trail to the right goes to other sections of the campground and is a connector trail to the Tanawha Trail (see Chapter 5). Bear left and walk through the amphitheater to continue on the Price Lake Loop Trail.

2.5   Return to the Boone Fork Overlook.

5

The Tanawha Trail

Just as the Linn Cove Viaduct is considered a monumental engineering and design achievement, so, too, must the Tanawha Trail. Constructed at a cost of almost three-quarters of a million dollars, the pathway uses innovative and extravagant trail-building techniques. Not content to make use of the usual log footbridges, the Tanawha Trail crosses some streams on high, arching structures of wood and steel, whose lines blend in with the natural surroundings. Boardwalks, some close to 200 feet long, facilitate traversing boulder-strewn hillsides while protecting delicate environments from trampling footsteps. Wooden staircases wind around stone outcroppings, enabling the trail to pass through areas that would have been too rugged to cross had traditional trail-building techniques been employed.

The word Tanawha means "fabulous eagle" or "hawk." Long before European settlers arrived, the Cherokee Indians used the word to describe what is now known as Grandfather Mountain. In fact, more than half the length of the Tanawha Trail is on the southeastern slope of this 5,964-foot summit, the highest of the Blue Ridge Mountains. One of the oldest in the world, Grandfather Mountain contains a myriad of scenic locations to investigate and appreciate. Quartzite outcroppings line cascading streams. Sunlight, filtered through the opulent forest canopy, highlights giant fern fronds and soft beds of moss. One moment you could be walking in dark rhododendron tunnels typical of the Southern Appalachians. Just a short time later the trail will bring you into a spruce, hemlock, and birch forest more reminiscent of the mountains of Maine and New Hampshire. Rock fields and blueberry gardens provide open spots from which you can enjoy soaring vistas.

Once the side of Grandfather Mountain is traversed, the Tanawha Trail drops into a deep, mature forest. But just before ending, it ascends to the bucolic serenity of man-made meadows. Bountiful and colorful wildflowers burst forth from the open fields in both the spring and fall.

A couple of points along the Tanawha Trail provide access to the trails on Grandfather Mountain. These trails are on private property, where a permit and payment of a fee are required before you are allowed to walk on them. Pay attention to this regulation! The trails are regularly patrolled to enforce this policy. (For more information, see the section Trails of Grandfather Mountain in Chapter 6.)

The Mountains to Sea Trail (see Appendix G) will someday make use of almost the full length of the Tanawha Trail.

Please note: In a departure from the way the rest of this guidebook is arranged, the Tanawha Trail is described from its southern BRP mile point to its northern BRP mile point. There are two reasons for this. The Park Service inventory of BRP trails officially lists the Tanawha Trail as beginning at the Beacon Heights parking area (BRP mile 305.2) and ending in Julian Price Memorial Park (BRP mile 297.2). In addition, the walking is generally easier if you hike the Tanawha Trail from south to north.

Also, please keep in mind that the following descriptions include the short access trails going to and from the parking areas and overlooks. Most people just walk a section or two of the Tanawha Trail, and the access-trails information is provided so that they may know exactly how long a section is. If you were to walk the complete Tanawha Trail without going to any of these parking areas or overlooks, its full length would be about .55 mile shorter than if you were to add together the full lengths of all the sections.

Mile 305.2. Tanawha Trail (from Beacon Heights Parking Area to Stack Rock Parking Area at BRP Mile 304.8)

Length: .9 mile, one way

Difficulty: moderate

The beginning section of the Tanawha Trail drops from Beacon Heights to cross US RT 221 and then ascends to the southeastern flank of Grandfather Mountain.

There are only limited views along the way, but wildflower lovers will be delighted to know that this short stretch possesses more than its fair share of colorful blossoms.

The route of the trail across rugged ground – boulder fields and several small stream crossings – is a good introduction not only to the Tanawha Trail but also to the flora and terrain you'll encounter if, once you complete this short section, you continue to follow the trail across the southeastern facing slopes of Grandfather Mountain.

.0   From the Beacon Heights parking area cross the paved service road, bear left, and ascend, on trail, into the woods. Beginning sometime in April, the pathway is lined with the pink, white, and purple petals of painted trillium, galax, and rhododendron, which start to bloom, in turn, about 2 to 4 weeks apart.

.07   Intersection. The Beacon Heights Trail [BRP 83] is to the right. Also, the Mountains to Sea Trail comes in from the right to join up with the Tanawha Trail. Bear left and descend. Spring hikers are likely to notice a number of painted trillium and lily of the valley along the trail. Although these members of the lily family may most often be thought of in association with the Blue Ridge Mountains, both flowers are known to grow as far west and north as Manitoba, Canada, and as far south as the mountains of northern Georgia.

.2   Enter a bottomland forest and walk almost level. Soon make a short ascent and descent.

.35   Cross US RT 221 and ascend to walk between that highway and the Parkway.

.5   Descend through an area of large boulders covered with rock tripe. In a couple of hundred feet come to a wooden footbridge next to a stone foundation of the BRP.

.6   Enter a small but pretty hemlock forest and boulder field.

.75   Emerge from the boulder field and hemlock forest.

.8   Ascend steps.

.9   Bear left (the Tanawha Trail continues to the right) to arrive at the Stack Rock Overlook with its view of the "mile-high" swinging bridge on Grandfather Mountain.

Mile 304.8. Tanawha Trail (from Stack Rock Parking Area to the Linn Cove Visitor Center at BRP Mile 304.4)

Length: .65 mile, one way

Difficulty: moderately strenuous

The falls on Stack Rock Creek and interesting rock formations are the outstanding features of this section. Human handiwork, such as the wooden staircase winding around giant boulders, is almost as interesting as nature's own wonders.

This section – which is rugged, so be forewarned! – ends at the Linn Cove Information Station, where rest rooms and water are available.

.0   Begin at the Stack Rock Parking Area and in 100 feet bear left. (The Tanawha Trail also goes right for .9 mile to the Beacon Heights parking area at BRP mile 305.2.) Descend through an area where galax is the dominant ground cover.

.15   Cross a small water run and ascend a wooden staircase winding around the giant rock formation. There are limited views to the east. Continue with short, steep ups and downs.

.3   Cross Stack Rock Creek with its beautiful falls and cascades. Ascend steeply on forty-nine stone and wooden steps. This is rugged country of giant rock outcroppings and boulders. In fact, the trail even passes through a narrow cleft in one of the rocks.

.35   Cross a small water run and continue with short, steep ups and downs in rhododendron.

.5   Break out of the rhododendron and into a hardwood forest.

.65   Arrive at the Linn Cove Information Station.

Mile 304.4. Tanawha Trail (from Linn Cove Information Station to Wilson Creek Overlook at BRP Mile 303.7)

Length: 1.35 miles, one way

Difficulty: moderately strenuous

Handicap access: first .15 mile

The first .15 mile of this section is paved and leads to a point directly below the Linn Cove Viaduct. There you can closely examine the preset segmented concrete construction of the viaduct that makes it such an engineering marvel.

After the viaduct, the trail, now unpaved, ascends steeply through large boulder fields to level off, somewhat, in a beech and birch forest.

.0   Follow the paved trail from the north end of the parking lot.

.15   Come to the point where you are standing directly below the viaduct. Continue on unpaved pathway. The trail now ascends quite steeply, and in a couple of hundred feet you will be level with the floor of the viaduct. Continue ascending and walk through a tunnel created by leaning boulders. Do not enter a second tunnel; rather, bear to the right of it, ascend on stone steps, and continue to weave around additional boulders.

.4   Cross Linn Cove Branch on a wooden footbridge.

.5   Intersection. The trail to the right leads, in 60 feet, to a view over the viaduct and out to the mountains in the east. Continue on the main pathway, which is edged by galax, painted trillium, and rhododendron.

.7   Descend steeply only to reascend steeply. Repeat this pattern a number of times.

1   Cross a small water run.

1.25   Intersection. (The Tanawha Trail continues to the left.) Bear right to descend to the Wilson Creek Overlook. Walk under the BRP, bear right again, and ascend.

1.35   Arrive at the Wilson Creek Overlook.

Mile 303.7. Tanawha Trail (from Wilson Creek Overlook to Rough Ridge Parking Area at BRP Mile 302.9)

Length: 1.45 miles, one way

Difficulty: moderately strenuous

Without a doubt this is the most spectacular section of the Tanawha Trail. Blueberry fields and heath balds open up 360-degree views unequaled anywhere else along the trail.

Once again, the builders of this trail have done some pretty amazing work. In order to protect the fragile environment yet provide access to this area, a 200-foot-long elevated boardwalk crosses the landscape. Looking down onto the Linn Cove Viaduct from the boardwalk, you will soon recognize the similarity in design philosophies of the two structures.

.0 Descend the steps from the Wilson Creek Overlook, turn left under the BRP, and ascend. (Avoid the un-authorized trail that goes off to the right, back under the BRP.)

.1 Join the Tanawha Trail and bear right. (The Tanawha Trail also goes left for 1.25 miles to the Linn Cove Information Station.) Immediately cross Wilson Creek on a footbridge. The trail is lined with bluets and chickweed before entering a stand of rhododendron.

.2 Descend around large rock outcroppings.

.3 Ascend steeply to pass large boulders.

.6 Pass through a field of fringe phacelia.

.8 Cross a spur ridge covered with lily of the valley.

.9 Arrive at an open rock outcropping for exciting 360-degree views. The ridge line of Grandfather Mountain looms above, and the peaks and ridges to the south rise up from the Parkway. The flatter lands of North Carolina are visible to the east. The board-walk trail may be seen on the mountainside below you. Descend.

1.2 Come onto the boardwalk and continue to enjoy the open views. Mountain laurel and rhododendron in bloom in early spring add to the delights of this spot. Cross over the boardwalk and descend into the woods.

1.4 Use an arching footbridge to cross over the waters of a fork of Little Wilson Creek, which cascade over a flat, tilting rock facing. Come to an intersection and bear right to descend to the Rough Ridge parking area. (The Tanawha Trail continues to the left.)

1.45 Arrive at the Rough Ridge parking area.

Mile 302.9. Tanawha Trail (from Rough Ridge Parking Area to Raven Rocks Overlook at BRP Mile 302.4)

Length: .8 mile, one way

Difficulty: moderate

The Tanawha Trail – what better way to experience the great diversity of Grandfather Mountain? The pre-vious section meandered onto a rhododendron-covered landscape typical of the mountains of North Carolina. This short portion of the trail will seem to transport you

Tanawha Trail at Rough Ridge, overlooking the Linn
Cove Viaduct. (Photograph by William A. Bake)

several hundred miles to the north. The pathway enters a New England–type forest of hemlock, spruce, oak, and birch.

.0   Ascend the steps on the north end of the Rough Ridge parking area.

.05   Intersection. Turn right. (The Tanawha Trail also goes left for 1.4 miles to the Wilson Creek Overlook.) Ascend and watch for red squirrels, which inhabit Grandfather Mountain in significant numbers.

.2   Cross the water run that descends on a large, flat, sloping rock facing. Descend.

.3   Walk level for about 200 feet and then begin a series of small ups and downs.

.7   Intersection. Bear right to descend to the Raven Rocks Overlook. (The Tanawha Trail continues to the left.)

.8   Arrive at Raven Rocks Overlook.

Mile 302.4. Tanawha Trail (from Raven Rocks Overlook to Boone Fork Parking Area at BRP Mile 300)

Length: 3.2 miles, one way

Difficulty: moderate

Still closely paralleling the BRP, this long section of the Tanawha Trail begins in a deep forest, with much of the pathway passing through rhododendron and mountain laurel tunnels. Be prepared for a change of scenery once the trail breaks out of this understory of dense vegetation. The forest floor becomes a jumble of rocks and boulders draped by large fronds of fern and carpeted with soft, thick moss.

This section of the Tanawha Trail also provides access to some of the trails in the Grandfather Mountain system. Permits and payment of a fee are required to walk upon these pathways. (For more information, see the section Trails of Grandfather Mountain in Chapter 6.)

.0   Ascend the trail at the southern end of the overlook.

.1   Intersection. Turn right. (The Tanawha Trail also goes left to reach the Rough Ridge parking area in .7 mile.) Descend for a short distance.

.2   Ascend, passing by wake robin trillium.

.3   Level out for a short distance and then begin a series of short ups and downs.

.7   A break in vegetation allows a limited view to the east. False hellebore and lily of the valley line the trail. In fact, these two plants continue to grow close to the pathway for the rest of its length. Descend steadily.

.8   This area almost has a rain forest feel as you enter a stand of towering hardwoods and go by moss- and lily-covered rocks.

1.2   Cross a small water run.

1.5   Cross a second stream on a footbridge. The bluets are especially vibrant as you round a spur ridge.

1.8   Continue through a fairly open forest with slight ups and downs.

2.2   Among rhododendron, birch, and galax, cross over a ridge line and descend.

2.4   Cross the stream and ascend.

2.6   Intersection. The Daniel Boone Scout Trail comes in from the left to join with the Tanawha Trail for a short distance. Payment of a fee and a permit are required to hike this trail! (See the section Trails of Grandfather Mountain in Chapter 6.) Keep to the right to continue on the Tanawha Trail.

2.8   Intersection. The Nuwati Trail comes in from the left. Once again, payment of a fee and a permit are required to hike on this trail. Keep right and descend to continue on the Tanawha Trail.

3.1   Intersection. Keep left where an access trail bears right to go under the BRP and descend to a parking area on US RT 221 in .4 mile. (This route is maintained by Grandfather Mountain trail crews but crosses BRP property so no permits are required.) Just after the intersection, cross over the very pretty falls of Boone Fork on a formidable footbridge and arrive at another intersection. Bear right to descend to the Boone Fork parking area. (The Tanawha Trail continues to the left.) When arriving at one last intersection in a few more feet, keep to the left. (The Upper Boone Fork Trail [BRP 82] goes right and parallels Boone Fork for .55 mile to arrive at the Calloway Peak Overlook.)

3.2   Boone Fork parking area.

Mile 300. Tanawha Trail (from Boone Fork Parking Area to Cold Prong Pond Parking Area at BRP Mile 299)

Length: 2 miles, one way

Difficulty: moderate

Recommended

Having traversed the length of Grandfather Mountain, the Tanawha Trail is no longer confined to staying within a few hundred yards of the Parkway. This section veers quite a distance away from the BRP, resulting in a welcome respite from automobile noise and an opportunity to enjoy the serenity of a lush, green, mature hardwood forest. Rhododendron and mountain laurel tunnels increase the sensation of seclusion.

This walk is recommended if you are in search of a little peace and quiet. It is one of the few isolated spots you can reach with such little effort.

.0 Ascend from the southern end of the Boone Fork parking area. Arrive at an intersection in just a short distance. Bear to the right. (The Upper Boone Fork Trail [BRP 82] descends to the left and parallels Boone Fork for .55 mile to arrive at the Calloway Peak Overlook, BRP mile 299.7.)

.1 Intersection. Turn to the right and ascend. (The Tanawha Trail also goes to the left and arrives at the Raven Rocks Overlook in 3.1 miles.)

.2 Come onto an old railroad grade lined with Solomon's seal. Descend gradually.

.3 Cross a small water run. Dwarf iris are abundant in early spring.

.5 The old railroad grade ends. Ascend.

.7 Cross over a ridge line and continue to ascend through rhododendron tunnels.

.8 Arrive at the high point and begin to descend in a more open forest. Wildflowers are everywhere! Look for Solomon's seal, lily of the valley, galax, dwarf iris, violets, mayapple, jack-in-the-pulpit, false hellebore, chickweed, and painted trillium.

1.1 Reenter rhododendron and switch back to the right.

1.5 Cross a small water run on a footbridge.

1.7 Cross a second water run.

1.8 Intersection. Bear right to descend to the Cold Prong Pond parking area. (The Tanawha Trail continues to the left.)

2   Arrive at the Cold Prong Pond parking area. The
     Cold Prong Pond Trail [BRP 81] leaves the parking
     area to encircle the pond.

Mile 299. Tanawha Trail (from Cold Prong Pond Parking Area to the Julian Price Memorial Park Campground at BRP Mile 297.2)

Length: 3.8 miles, one way

Difficulty: moderate

Human changes to the landscape now make their
mark on the Tanawha Trail. On this portion the mature
forest yields to open meadows of gently rolling pastureland. Weaving in and out of small wooded areas, the route
enters three different stock-grazing fields. Each contains
its own set of wildflowers and perspective on the surrounding scenery.

To help you visualize the full length of the Tanawha
Trail, there are views of Grandfather Mountain from a
couple of the meadows.

A segment of the Mountains to Sea Trail (see Appendix G) currently begins in this section, following the
Boone Fork Trail [BRP 79] where it splits northward from
the Tanawha Trail.

.0   Take the trail near the end of the Cold Prong Pond
     parking area. (Do not follow the Cold Prong Pond
     Trail [BRP 81], which goes around the pond.) Ascend
     slightly and descend through rhododendron. Soon
     cross a small water run and begin a series of slight
     ups and downs.

.2   Intersection. Turn right. (The Tanawha Trail also
     goes to the left and arrives at Boone Fork parking
     area, BRP mile 300, in 1.8 miles.) Descend into rho-
     dodendron tunnels.

.3   Cross a small water run and ascend gradually.

.6   A break in the vegetation permits a limited view to
     the east and of a portion of Grandfather Mountain.
     With painted trillium lining the trail, descend into
     more rhododendron.

.8   A more open area in the woods allows bluets, wild
     mustard, violets, and cinquefoil to spread out across
     the forest floor.

1   Switch back to the right.

1.1 Pass through a fence stile and follow trail posts

through the field, enjoying the open views. Soon come onto an old roadway.

1.25 Enter a small wooded area.

1.4 Be alert! As you are about to enter a field, the trail makes a hard turn to the left, staying on the edge of the woods. It leaves the forest in 250 feet to ascend into the meadow. In early spring you can admire the cinquefoil, violets, and buttercups; enjoy some wild strawberries later in the summer.

1.6 Enter a wooded area.

1.7 Ascend in a patch of mayapple, staying just below the summit of a knob.

1.8 Enter another meadow and soon pass through a fence stile. Catch a good view of Grandfather Mountain before descending.

2.2 Pass through a fence stile and cross Halloway Mountain Road. (The BRP, mile 298.6, is about 1 mile to the right.) Pass through another fence stile and follow trail posts as they ascend the pasture.

2.3 Pass through a fence stile, turn right, and come onto a dirt road that enters the woods.

2.5 Pass under utility lines.

2.6 Be alert! The trail leaves the roadway to the left on a path lined with rhododendron and painted trillium.

2.7 Pass through yet another fence stile and follow the descending dirt road, not the one that ascends into the meadow. Go through a rhododendron tunnel and begin to follow trail posts, bearing to the left in an open meadow. This spot is peacefully secluded, good for soaking up a bit of sun. Soon you must be alert! Just before coming to a dip between two pastures, the trail makes a sudden, almost unapparent, switchback to the right and descends through apple trees, where the trail becomes apparent once again.

3.1 Pass by an old fence stile and cross a small water run on a footbridge. Enter the woods and walk along a fence line, soon crossing another small stream. Ascend.

3.3 Intersection. The Boone Fork Trail [BRP 79] comes in from the left to run concurrently with the Tanawha Trail for a short distance. At this point a segment of the Mountains to Sea Trail (see Appendix G) begins, following the Boone Fork Trail to the left. Bear right to continue on the Tanawha Trail, pass through a fence stile, and enter a wide and dark rhododendron tunnel.

3.4 Intersection. The Boone Fork Trail [BRP 79] goes to the left. Bear right to continue on the Tanawha Trail.

3.5 Intersection. Pass by a connector trail to the Boone Fork Trail and bear right to continue on the Tanawha Trail.

3.7 The Julian Price Memorial Park campground is visible to your left. Come into a bottomland covered with Solomon's seal, mayapple, chickweed, and wild geranium. There are many small pathways going left to the campground. Stay on the main trail.

3.8 Arrive at campground site 46. The campground entrance is a few hundred feet to your left on the paved roadway. A short trail to the right would allow you to cross the BRP and come into the Price Lake section of the campground.

6

Julian Price Memorial Park to

U.S. Route 441

BLUE RIDGE PARKWAY MILES 297–469.1

Leaving the gentle highland plateau of the central Blue Ridge Mountains, the Parkway continues southward onto a landscape increasingly more elevated and rugged. No longer are there large rolling meadows such as those in Doughton Park. The topography is now inappropriate for farming or for establishing working estates like Moses H. Cone did. Instead, there is the spiny, rocky, mile-high ridge line of Grandfather Mountain and the narrow, vertical confines of Linville Gorge. Six-thousand-foot summits become commonplace in the Black Mountains. Near its southern terminus the Parkway takes its leave of the main crest of the Blue Ridges and traverses a hodgepodge jumble of steep slopes and high pinnacles created by a series of cross ranges.

Due to the increasing altitude, the further south you go on the BRP the further north you appear to be. Between 4,000 and 5,000 feet the forest takes on the countenance of a hardwood forest common in New England. Beech, white birch, and similar trees begin to grow along the BRP in increasing numbers. Near the 6,000-foot level Parkway travelers enter a spruce-fir forest – an environment more like Canada than the southern United States.

Pisgah National Forest surrounds a major portion of this section of the BRP. Its large network of pathways intersect many of the Parkway's trails to create an almost limitless array of overnight backpacking experiences. A couple of Forest Service trails (BRP miles 351.9 and 359.8) provide excellent spots for establishing base camps. From these you could spends days on further walks and explorations. (Backcountry camping is permitted almost anywhere in the national forest.)

This large expanse of public land furnishes many trails that are free of, or have minimum signs of, any human impact. Views (BRP mile 422.4) are unobstructed by housing developments, roadways, or even relay towers. Hidden coves (BRP miles 359.8 and 407.6) give the impression that you may be one of the first people to ever walk through them. Do remember, though, that the Forest Service and other non-Parkway trails in this section may not be as regularly maintained as the Parkway trails.

Other Parkway trails descend to permit intimate contact with rushing waterfalls (BRP miles 316.4, 339.5, and 418.8) or ascend for stunning views from prominent points (BRP miles 407.6, 422.4, and 451.2). Self-guiding trails (BRP miles 308.2 and 431) provide interesting details to add to your enjoyment and knowledge of the Parkway's natural surroundings. Balds, a unique Southern Appalachian phenomenon and natural mystery, may be observed and investigated firsthand (BRP miles 364.1 and 364.6).

Reminders of history will also be encountered while walking upon the trails of this section of the BRP. George W. Vanderbilt's 125,000-acre estate once encompassed much of what is now Pisgah National Forest. The over-16-mile Shut-In Trail (BRP miles 393.7 to 407.6) was originally constructed by Vanderbilt as a route from the Manor House in Asheville to his Buck Springs Hunting Lodge near Mount Pisgah. Devastating fires swept over many of these mountainsides in the first half of the twentieth century, and their effect on the land is still evident today (BRP mile 418.8). The Linville area (BRP mile 316.4) was named for a man and his son who were murdered by marauding Indians in the 1700s, while Mount Pisgah's (mile 407.6) name is linked with a history as old as the Bible.

Mile 299. Cold Prong Pond Loop Trail [BRP 81]

Length: .3 mile, round-trip

Difficulty: easy leg stretcher

Strawberries! That word describes this short, level loop around Cold Prong Pond. The area next to the trail and the small meadow around the pond are saturated by the strawberries' white blossoms in late spring. The succulent little berries become edible a few weeks later.

Strawberries are not, however, the only reason to leave your automobile and take this leg stretcher. Other wildflowers, such as cinquefoil and violets, line the pathway. Turtles may be spotted sunning themselves on small logs or other floating debris in the pond. Water snakes glide across the surface, creating ripples that glisten in the sun.

Activity around the pond slows as the cooler weather approaches, but you can enjoy the softly muted earthtones of the underbrush as it nears the end of its life cycle. Watch for a raccoon emerging from the woods in search of an early evening meal.

.o   Follow a pathway of rhododendron, wild mustard, and violets from the north end of the overlook. (Do not follow an access trail to the Tanawha Trail [see Chapter 5] that also leaves from the overlook.)

.05 Bear right at the loop-trail intersection.

.15 Swing around the pond and start looking for a few of the wild strawberries.

.2   Veer away from the pond and follow trail posts through a small field. Wild strawberries are everywhere!

.3   Return to the loop-trail intersection, bear right, and arrive back at the Cold Prong Pond parking area.

Mile 299.7. Upper Boone Fork Trail [BRP 82]

Length: .55 mile, one way

Difficulty: moderately easy

This may be the perfect path to let your restless children escape the car for a while and work off some excess energy. It is only .5 mile long and ends at the very next parking area (BRP mile 300). The kids will enjoy watching the stream descend in small cascades as they climb up and over boulders lying about on the forest floor. Just before ending, the trail passes through one of the most easily reached stands of birch along the Parkway.

.o   Descend from the Calloway Peak Overlook on a rhododendron-lined path and almost immediately turn left.

.1   Cross a small side stream.

.2   Walk right next to Boone Fork as it descends in small ripples and spills. Rhododendron opens up as you progress into a boulder-strewn landscape. Ascend along the stream.

.35   The trail swings to the right, away from the stream, and enters a wonderful stand of birch.

.4   Cross under the BRP.

.5   Intersection. Bear right to descend to the Upper Boone Fork parking area. The path to the left is an access trail to the Tanawha Trail (see Chapter 5).

.55   Arrive at Upper Boone Fork parking area.

Trails of Grandfather Mountain, Blue Ridge Parkway Mile 305.1

Rising almost 2,000 feet above the Parkway, the 5,964-foot summit of Grandfather Mountain is the highest point of the Blue Ridge Mountains. On clear days, when visibility is not obscured by haze, peaks almost 100 miles away may be seen from its rugged, quartzite ridge line.

Hikers of Grandfather Mountain's trails will experience almost every type of environment to be encountered along the BRP. Birch forests, along with stands of hemlock and spruce, cover the moist lower slopes. Rhododendron thickets and blueberry patches thrive on many places around the mountain. Rushing streams start in the evergreen Canadian Forest zone on the ridge and tumble past caves whose entrances may be adorned with verdant growths of mosses and ferns. Rock outcroppings provide outstanding vistas, while dense jungles of hardwood almost prevent sunshine from reaching abundant wildflowers growing on the forest floor.

One of North Carolina's most popular tourist attractions, Grandfather Mountain is also a nature preserve. Its environmental habitat houses deer, black bear, cougar, and bald eagle in their natural habitat. In addition, a paved road allows visitors to easily reach the mountain's lofty heights. Picnic tables and scenic turnouts provide a chance to enjoy the landscape as you ascend. A visitor center, museum, snack bar, souvenir shop, and rest rooms are located at the top of the road.

More information on Grandfather Mountain may be acquired by writing or calling:

Grandfather Mountain
P.O. Box 128
Linville, NC 28646
(704) 733-2013

Please note: Grandfather Mountain is privately owned. Permits and payment of a fee are required before hiking along any of the trails. Camping is permitted only at designated sites or a trailside shelter.

Permits (and the easiest automobile access from the Parkway) may be obtained at the entrance station on US RT 221, several miles west of the BRP at mile 305.1. Permits may also be obtained at the Grandfather Mountain Country Store at the US RT 221/Holloway Mountain Road junction, at Connect 4 Sports at the intersection of NC RT 105 and NC RT 184 between Boone and Linville, and in various other locations. Be aware that permit outlets vary from time to time. A list of current outlets, as well as up-to-date trail and campsite information, may be obtained by contacting the backcountry manager at the above address or phone number.

The following descriptions are provided just to acquaint you with the trails on Grandfather Mountain. Upon purchase of a permit you will be given a detailed map, descriptions of the trails, and a complete list of regulations. Rangers patrol the trails to enforce regulations and make sure hikers have valid permits.

Grandfather Trail

Length: 2.2 miles, one way

Difficulty: very strenuous

Markings: blue blazes

This National Recreation Trail is probably the most spectacular excursion to be taken on the private property of Grandfather Mountain. Leads from the trailhead at Swinging Bridge near the visitor center and crosses the alpine summit ridge. Terminates as it connects with Daniel Boone Scout Trail near Calloway Peak, highest point on the mountain. Do not underestimate the Grandfather Trail's difficulty; at times it makes use of ladders or cables to scale steep, rocky cliffs!

Underwood Trail

Length: .5 mile, one way

Difficulty: strenuous

Markings: yellow blazes

Leaves the Grandfather Trail about .5 mile from the Swinging Bridge trailhead and rejoins it just past MacRae

Peak. Provides easier passage than the more strenuous route of the Grandfather Trail and is an alternative to that trail's exposure during high winds, thunderstorms, or other inclement weather.

Black Rock Trail

Length: 1 mile, one way

Difficulty: moderate

Markings: yellow blazes

Drops gradually from a parking area on the road that goes to the visitor center and Swinging Bridge. Somewhat rocky. Ends in a small loop providing views to the east overlooking portions of the Tanawha Trail and the BRP.

Profile Trail

Length: 2.7 miles, one way

Difficulty: lower section is moderate; upper section becomes moderately strenuous

Markings: none

Ascends from NC RT 105 (.7 mile north of the intersection of NC RT 184 with NC RT 105) and passes almost directly below the Grandfather profile. Terminates at Shanty Spring where the Calloway Trail begins. The Profile Trail can be used as a route to Calloway Peak, but still requires you to use portions of the strenuous Calloway, Grandfather, and Daniel Boone trails to reach the summit.

Calloway Trail

Length: .4 mile, one way

Difficulty: strenuous

Markings: red blazes

A short, steep, and rocky connector trail between the end of the Profile Trail at Shanty Spring and the Grandfather Trail in Calloway Gap.

Daniel Boone Scout Trail

Length: 2.8 miles, one way

Difficulty: strenuous

Markings: white blazes

A National Recreation Trail, this pathway is most easily reached by taking the access trail from the Boone

Fork parking area (BRP mile 300) to – and then turning left onto – the Tanawha Trail (see Chapter 5), passing by the Nuwati Trail and arriving at the Daniel Boone Scout Trail in .6 mile from the parking area. (Another access route – .8 mile in length – is to turn left onto the Tanawha Trail after ascending on a trail from the parking area on US RT 221 at Serenity Farm, 8.8 miles north of the Grandfather Mountain entrance road.) From the Tanawha Trail, Daniel Boone Scout Trail climbs an evergreen-covered ridge to cross Calloway Peak, 5,964 feet above sea level. Continuing on, it connects with the Grandfather Trail near Watauga View.

Nuwati Trail

Length: 1.3 miles, one way

Difficulty: moderate

Markings: blue blazes

Begins at an intersection on the Tanawha Trail (see Chapter 5), about .4 mile from the Boone Fork parking area (BRP mile 300). Rocky, but fairly gentle. Ends at a view of Boone Fork Bowl, an isolated valley believed to have been glacially carved.

Cragway Trail

Length: 1 mile, one way

Difficulty: strenuous

Markings: orange blazes

A connector trail that covers the steep, rocky, and open landscape between the Nuwati Trail and the Daniel Boone Scout Trail. The easiest way to traverse this rugged route would be to ascend on the Daniel Boone Scout Trail and descend on the Cragway Trail, enjoying the views.

Mile 305.2. Beacon Heights Trail [BRP 83]

Length: .35 mile, one way

Difficulty: moderate

Ascend this extended leg stretcher to the 4,200-foot quartzite summit of Beacon Heights for the best views available of the landscape the BRP will pass through as you drive southward. Ridge after ridge rises toward the horizon, each a little higher than its predecessor as the mountains become progressively taller the further south you gaze. From a second viewpoint, the ridge line of Grandfather Mountain is visible.

The Mountains to Sea Trail (see Appendix G) makes use of the Beacon Heights Trail for a short distance.

.0   From the southern end of the Beacon Heights parking area, cross, diagonally to the left, a paved service road. Ascend on a path marked for the Tanawha Trail. Galax, rhododendron, and trillium line the trail.

.05   Intersection. The Tanawha Trail (see Chapter 5) and the Mountains to Sea Trail (see Appendix G) descend to the left. Bear right to continue on the Beacon Heights Trail.

.1   Pass by a bench.

.2   The Mountains to Sea Trail comes in from the right; bear left.

.3   Come to a bench at an intersection. Bear right for 100 feet to come onto a flat rock outcropping. Excellent views to the south and a wonderful spot to be for sunrise. Return to the intersection and bear right.

.35   Arrive at another flat rock overlook. This time enjoy a vista of Grandfather Mountain.

Mile 308.2. Flat Rock Self-Guiding Loop Trail [BRP 84]

Length: .7 mile, round-trip

Difficulty: moderately easy

Highly recommended

Signs along the trail identify and describe much of the plant life in the Blue Ridge Mountains. Take your time to walk this one; the detailed information will enrich your knowledge of the Parkway environment.

The signs, however, are not the only highlights of the Flat Rock Self-Guiding Loop Trail. Flat Rock, a quartzite outcropping on the western side of Grandfather Mountain, permits a stirring outlook of Linville Valley and of Roan Mountain and other 5,000- to 6,000-foot summits far to the west in Cherokee National Forest.

.0   Begin at the trail sign in the center of the Flat Rock parking area.

.05 Bear left at the loop-trail intersection. In a few feet is a sign supplying information about chestnut and oak.

.1 A sign about the American chestnut. The pathway is lined by Solomon's seal and wood anemones.

.2 Signs concerning mountain winterberry and galax. In a few feet pass by a bench and signs describing cucumber (magnolia) trees and witherod. Begin walking on a path of smooth rock.

.25 Come onto Flat Rock, a quartzite outcropping laced with white quartzite. Swing around the rock for grand views of Black, Yellow, Hawk, Big Yellow, and Roan mountains. Below is a large rock quarry in Linville Valley. Follow the trail arrows painted on the rock.

.3 Come to another view. This one is of Hump Mountain and the Blue Ridge Mountains to the south. Grandfather Mountain looms far above you. Begin a gradual descent.

.35 Pass by a sign identifying rhododendron, and in a few feet come to other signs about hobblebush, viburnum, red maple, and striped maple.

.55 Signs concerning Fraser magnolia and white oak.

.65 Bear left at the loop-trail intersection.

.7 Return to the Flat Rock parking area.

Mile 312.2. Unpaved NC RT 1514 descends east from the Parkway into the Wilson Creek Area of Pisgah National Forest. More than twenty-five trails in this section of the national forest provide ample opportunity for exploration and overnight camping. A map with descriptions of some of the trails may be purchased at the book shop inside the Linville Falls Recreation Area, BRP mile 316.4.

Maps and additional information on the Wilson Creek Area may be obtained by contacting:

District Ranger
Grandfather Ranger District, USFS
P.O. Box 519
Marion, NC 28752

North Carolina Hiking Trails, by Allen de Hart, describes the trails in detail.

Mile 315.5. Camp Creek Trail [BRP 85]

Length: .06 mile, one way

Difficulty: easy leg stretcher

The Camp Creek Trail, a short leg stretcher, descends steeply from the middle of the overlook in a corridor of mountain laurel and rhododendron. It soon arrives at a favorite local fishing spot on Camp Creek. The stream was named for the Camp brothers who logged the area in the early 1900s.

Cool air rising from the rippling waters and deep shade provided by the lush vegetation might, on a hot summer day, cause you to linger longer than you had intended.

Trails of the Linville Falls Recreation Area, Blue Ridge Parkway Miles 316.4–316.5

The Linville River and Falls receive their name from William Linville. In 1766, while on a hunting trip in the area, he and his son were attacked and killed by Indians. A sixteen-year-old companion lived to tell the world of the bloody incident.

Having wound its way through the Linville Valley, the river, like the James River far to the north in Virginia, has punched its way through the main ridge of the Blue Ridge Mountains to become an easterly flowing stream. The falls make an impressive ninety-foot drop to enter the twelve-mile-long Linville Gorge.

The gorge is a favorite spot for both amateur and professional geologists. Millions of years ago, as the earth's crustal plates were colliding, large slabs of land slid under other large slabs. This action can clearly be seen on the steep walls of the gorge, for different layers of rock are piled on top of one another. Interestingly, the falls expose a layer of cranberry gneiss (a metamorphic rock) sitting atop a shelf of rock believed to be 500 million years younger.

Three of the recreation area's trails lead to overlooks of the river and falls. The area also contains an extensive variety of plant life, including a virgin stand of hemlock. One of the overlooks has six types of heath growing nearby. Two of those, the Carolina and catawba rhododendron, grow profusely on the precipitous walls of the gorge. Their many flowers, usually blooming about early May, attract hundreds of visitors yearly.

Plants and water are also the focus of the recreation area's other two trails. A short loop weaves over a moist forest floor to pass by the Duggers Creek Falls, and a leg stretcher descends to the banks of the Linville River.

Except for the Linville River Bridge Trail, all of the trails in the recreation area emanate from the parking area at the end of the Linville Falls Spur Road (BRP mile 316.4).

Land for the Linville Falls Recreation Area was donated by John D. Rockefeller, Jr. The area contains a Park Service campground, picnic area, small book shop, and rest rooms.

Mile 316.4. Linville Falls Trail [BRP 86]

Length: 2.1 miles, round-trip

Difficulty: moderate

Recommended

Four side trails descend from this main pathway to views of the falls. The first overlooks the upper falls; the other three furnish varying perspectives on the lower falls. An additional side trail provides access to a Forest Service parking area on NC RT 1238.

The main trail begins by crossing the Linville River on a concrete and steel footbridge. It then passes through a small field dotted by dogwood trees before entering a dense forest. Even though this area was heavily logged before becoming BRP property, a small stand of virgin hemlocks still exists, and the trail is routed below their towering crowns.

This trail is recommended because it is a much easier walk for a view of the falls and gorge than either the Linville Gorge [BRP 87] or Plunge Basin Overlook [BRP 88] trails.

.0 From the book shop and rest rooms, cross over the Linville River on an extravagant footbridge and walk away from the river.

.2 Pass through a field of dogwood. The rapids on the river soon become audible.

.3 A pleasant spot to look at a bend in the river.

.4 Intersection. The trail to the right ascends to a Forest Service parking area on NC RT 1238. NC RT 1238 borders the Linville Gorge Wilderness Area (see BRP mile 317.5). Bear left to continue on the Linville Falls Trail. In 100 feet come to another intersection and turn left, descending along the trail bordered by a rail fence.

.5   Arrive at the view of the upper falls. The wide river is now channeled between a narrow cleft in the rock facing. The walls of the gorge are covered with mountain laurel and rhododendron. Retrace your steps and turn left at the intersection.

.6   Intersection. Bear left and ascend steadily into a majestic hemlock and hardwood forest.

.7   Pass by a bench.

.8   Arrive at a high point and descend. Come to a rest shelter in 300 feet and bear to the left to the Chimney View Overlook.

.9   Come to an overlook and in 100 feet arrive at a second overlook. The scene spread out below you is well worth the walking you've done to reach it: The upper falls plunges twelve feet down the rock facing while the lower falls drops more than sixty feet in a narrow channel. Rhododendron and mountain laurel appear to grow on every inch of the gorge. Retrace your steps back to the main trail.

1   Bear left at the intersection and ascend; the trail becomes a little steeper and rockier. Pass by a bench.

1.1   Arrive at a pleasant view out across the valley of the gorge. Take the side trail to another view of the falls – the most spectacular on the Linville Falls Trail. You are now high above the falls, with the peaks and ridges of the surrounding mountains soaring above you. Retrace your steps.

2.1   Arrive back at the book shop, rest rooms, and parking area.

Mile 316.4. Linville Gorge Trail [BRP 87]

Length: .7 mile, one way

Difficulty: moderately strenuous

A little rougher and not quite as heavily traveled as the Linville Falls Trail [BRP 86], the Linville Gorge Trail descends from the rest rooms and parking area through attractive growths of rhododendron. It arrives at the Linville River's edge in the basin of the lower falls. Flat rocks near the bank invite you to lie back, enjoy the sunshine, and wile away the day. The river itself will compel

Looking into Linville Gorge. (Photograph by Jim Page, courtesy of the North Carolina Division of Travel and Tourism)

you to contemplate its power to carve such a deep channel through solid, hard rock.

.0   Ascend the steps to the left of the rest rooms. Arrive at an intersection in 100 feet. The Duggers Creek Trail [BRP 89] goes off to the left. Bear right and ascend to continue on the Linville Gorge Trail.

.2   Cross a (usually) dry water run and descend very gradually.

.35   Intersection. The Plunge Basin Overlook Trail [BRP 88] is to the right. Bear left uphill through mountain laurel tunnels to continue on the Linville Gorge Trail. Soon, however, descend along a rock facing.

.5   Descend steeply on a staircase of twenty-seven steps and switch back to the right. The rock facing you just came down is directly above you. The trail here is very steep, rough, and rocky.

.7   Arrive at the river's edge below the lower falls. Magnolia, rhododendron, and mountain laurel cling to the sides of the gorge.

Mile 316.4. Plunge Basin Overlook Trail [BRP 88]

Length: .2 mile, one way, plus .35 mile to access the trail

Difficulty: moderate

The Plunge Basin Overlook Trail is the shortest route you can take to view the lower falls. From this point you may readily observe how the river is gradually eroding the rock facing behind the falls.

To reach this trail, follow the Linville Gorge Trail [BRP 87] for .35 mile from the rest rooms and parking area. Remember to include that distance when figuring how far you must really walk in order to reach the lower falls overlook.

.0   Bear right onto the beginning of the Plunge Basin Overlook Trail.

.1   Pass by a bench, where the trail becomes a little steeper and follows a series of steps.

.2   Arrive at the overlook of the lower falls.

Mile 316.4. Duggers Creek Loop Trail [BRP 89]

Length: .25 mile, round-trip

Difficulty: easy

Recommended

The Duggers Creek Loop Trail is an interpretive trail of a different kind. The signs along the pathway do not identify plants and animals or provide historical information; instead, quotes by John Muir, Edwin Wayne Teal, and others help set a mood and instill an appreciation of the natural world.

The trail also enters a "mini Linville Gorge" lined with ferns and mosses as Duggers Creek drops from Jonas Ridge to the Linville River.

This easy trail is a most pleasant walk.

.0 Ascend the steps to the left of the rest rooms and parking area, and in 100 feet arrive at an intersection. The Linville Gorge Trail [BRP 87] is to the right. Bear left to walk on the Duggers Creek Loop Trail.

.1 Be alert! Bear right slightly uphill and then bear left toward the pavement, but go uphill on the dirt pathway. Ascend through rhododendron tunnels. Soon you will cross Duggers Creek as it falls into a narrow ravine. Beyond the creek ascend steps lined by galax; then almost immediately descend via switchbacks.

.23 Be alert! The trail makes a hard left to cross the creek.

.25 Arrive at the far end of the parking area. The rest rooms are just a few feet ahead.

Mile 316.5. Linville River Bridge Trail [BRP 90]

Length: .1 mile, one way

Difficulty: easy leg stretcher

Dropping easily through rhododendron and giant hemlocks, this trail passes by a trail that connects with the Linville Falls Recreation Area picnic grounds before coming to the banks of the Linville River. At the end of the trail, you will be standing almost directly below one of the Parkway's largest stone arch bridges, which crosses the river on three spans of eighty feet each. Though the waters of the river are wide and slow moving here, they will be rushing and plunging into the confines of the Linville Gorge just a few miles downstream.

Mile 317.5. A left turn onto US RT 221 and another left onto NC RT 183 will bring you to NC RT 1238 (Kistler Memorial Highway). This unpaved road is on the edge of the Linville Gorge Wilderness. Trails on both sides of the gorge and along the river open the area up for hiking and overnight camping. Permits are required to enter the wilderness at certain times of the year. Permits, maps, and information may be obtained at the Forest Service's Linville Falls Visitor Center on NC RT 1238 (about a mile from the junction with NC RT 183).

Maps and permits may also be procured by contacting:

> District Ranger
> Grandfather Ranger District, USFS
> P.O. Box 519
> Marion, NC 28752

The Linville Gorge Wilderness trails are described in detail in *North Carolina Hiking Trails*, by Allen de Hart.

Mile 320.8. Chestoa View Loop Trail [BRP 91]

Length: .8 mile, round-trip

Difficulty: easy

On a ledge of Humpback Mountain, the Chestoa View Loop Trail (Chestoa is a Cherokee word meaning rabbit) is an almost perfectly level path. It passes by vistas across the North Fork Catawba River Valley to the upper reaches of the Linville Gorge Wilderness and to higher peaks in the north. Hawks are often seen soaring and riding the warm updrafts rising from the valley.

No better place is there to begin a day than at one of the viewpoints, where you can watch the morning sunlight quietly spread out across the valley and slowly brighten the distant ridge lines.

.0   Begin on the trail under oaks and hickory at the far end of the parking area.

.05   Reach the first view of the valley. Table Rock is prominent to the north. Descend very slightly on a gravel trail lined with chickweed and Solomon's seal.

.3   Bear to the left at the loop-trail intersection.

.35   Arrive at an even better view – US RT 221 snakes its way into the valley, and high and lofty Grandfather

Crabtree Falls, in the Crabtree Meadows Recreation Area. (Photograph by Clay Nolen, courtesy of the North Carolina Division of Travel and Tourism)

Mountain forms a backdrop for the rest of the scenery. Continue to loop around the very edge of the rock ledge for additional views.

.6 Arrive back at the loop-trail intersection and bear left.

.8 Return to the Chestoa View parking area.

Mile 339.5. Crabtree Falls Loop Trail [BRP 92]

Length: 2.5 miles, round-trip

Difficulty: strenuous

The Crabtree Falls Loop Trail is located within the Crabtree Meadows Recreation Area. In early spring the abundance and variety of wildflowers are almost overwhelming as the trail drops from the campground to the falls. Be forewarned, however; the climb back up from the falls is strenuous.

Also contained within the Crabtree Meadows Recreation Area are the Park Service campground, a picnic area, camp store, snack bar, gift shop, and gasoline station.

.0 Descend from a parking area in the campground on a wide and graveled path. Watch for yellow lady slippers, dwarf iris, mayapple, buttercup, and false hellebore.

.15 Loop-trail intersection; bear right.

.4 Pass by a bench and descend some steps. The falls soon become audible.

.5 Cross a water run on a wooden plank and descend forty-five stone steps.

.7 Pass by another bench, continuing to descend on a switchback.

.9 Arrive at Crabtree Falls, which plunges down a rhododendron-, hemlock- and birch-lined rock facing. Walk the short side trail to stand just below the falls to experience the power and force of the falling water. Return to the main trail and cross the stream on a wooden bridge. Ascend on steps and then on switchbacks bordered by bloodroot, Solomon's seal, and ferns.

1 Pass by an old bench and, in a few steps as you ascend on a switchback, be looking for a couple of jack-in-the-pulpits. Ascend steeply below a rock facing.

1.1　Pass by another bench as the ascent becomes a little more gradual.

1.2　At a small waterfall in the creek, the pathway begins, once again, to ascend steeply.

1.3　Cross the stream on a wooden bridge and, in a few hundred feet, cross it again as the rhododendron-lined creek drops in pretty little cascades.

1.6　Reach the top of a ridge line and descend for a few steps. Ascend and pass by a wonderful field of white trillium.

1.8　Cross the stream.

2　Bench.

2.1　Intersection. Loop B of the campground is to the right. Bear left, ascend, and then walk on a level trail through rhododendron tunnels.

2.3　Loop-trail intersection. Switch back to the right and ascend.

2.4　Cross the campground's Loop A roadway and walk by a water fountain and rest rooms.

2.5　Arrive back at the parking area in the campground.

Mile 344.1. Woods Mountain Trail Access Trail [BRP 93]

Length: 2.1 miles, one way

Difficulty: moderate

Staying within BRP boundaries but bordering Pisgah National Forest lands, an unpaved service road provides access to the Forest Service's primitive Woods Mountain Trail.

Even though it is just a dirt road, the Woods Mountain Trail access trail is, nonetheless, a worthwhile walk. Its ascents and descents are gradual and bordered by rhododendron, dogwood, and galax. The road passes through a plush hardwood forest, the changing leaves making this a very colorful jaunt in the fall.

The road begins and ends at points on the BRP (miles 344.1 and 342). You could be dropped off at one end and picked up at the other, refreshed by the natural world and ready to drive a few more miles along the Parkway. You might also want to consider walking this route in the opposite direction than described below. It would be a gentler trip, as the road tends to descend from the north to the south.

The Mountains to Sea Trail (see Appendix G) follows portions of this road and the Woods Mountain Trail, from Buck Creek Gap to US RT 221 at the Woodlawn Rest Area.

.0 Exit the Parkway at mile 344.1 and immediately park at the Buck Creek Overlook. Follow the old dirt road uphill and parallel the BRP through a hardwood forest. The dogwood is especially pretty along this road.

.3 Swing around a spur ridge as the road becomes lined with rhododendron. The pungent smell of galax assaults your sense of smell.

.5 The road levels out and then begins to gradually descend.

.7 Stay on the road and ascend as the Woods Mountain Trail comes in from the right.

• The Woods Mountain Trail [FS 218] follows the ridge line of Woods Mountain for several miles. Along the way it junctions with two other Forest Service trails – Armstrong Creek [FS 223] and Bad Fork [FS 227]. All of these trails are primitive and receive little maintenance. Camping is allowed anywhere along them.

.9 Swing around another spur ridge and continue to ascend. The BRP is almost directly below you.

1.3 Avoid the grassy woods road that comes in from the right.

1.4 Pass by a small radio relay antenna and in 200 feet avoid the dirt road to the right.

1.5 At the sight of the Good Cemetery, avoid another spur of the dirt road that comes in from the right. Descend gradually.

1.8 Reach a gap and ascend.

1.9 Level out and then ascend slightly to the Parkway.

2.1 Arrive at BRP mile 342.

Mile 347.6. FSR 482 descends from the Parkway to the east to reach a Forest Service campground and several trails (camping allowed along any of them) in the Curtis Creek Area of Pisgah National Forest. Information on the trails and campground may be obtained by contacting:

District Ranger
Grandfather Ranger District, USFS
P.O. Box 519
Marion, NC 28752

Curtis Creek Area trails are described in detail in *North
Carolina Hiking Trails*, by Allen de Hart.

Mile 350.4. Lost Cove Ridge Trail [FS 182] (also known as Green Knob Trail)

Length: 3.1 miles, one way

Difficulty: moderate; moderately strenuous if hiked
in the opposite direction than the one described

The Lost Cove Trail, a Forest Service trail that begins on BRP property, rises for the first .5 mile from the
Parkway to the Green Knob Lookout for views of prominent Mount Mitchell and other peaks and ridges of the
Black Mountain range. The trail then enters Pisgah National Forest to begin a long, gradual descent along an undulating ridge line. (Once you leave BRP property at the
lookout tower, camping is permitted anywhere along the
trail. Good sites, however, are very limited.) The route
passes through varying stands of evergreens and hardwoods, with Mount Mitchell visible much of the way. It
ends at the Forest Service's Black Mountain campground
on FSR 472.

The campground and far trailhead may be reached
by automobile by driving south on the Parkway from the
Green Knob Overlook. Exit at BRP mile 351.9 in Deep
Gap to follow unpaved FSR 472 as it drops along scenic
South Toe River. The campground is 5 miles from the
Parkway. (Camping is also permitted along the Forest Ser-
vice road.)

If you are staying in the Forest Service campground,
the Lost Cove Ridge Trail would make a fine walk for the
latter part of the day. Begin the hike a few hours before
sunset, saunter down the ridge watching shadows grow
longer, and arrive at the campground in time to enjoy din-
ner and an evening around the campfire.

.0   Begin at the Green Knob Overlook and follow a trail
through rhododendron and over a small rise next to
the Parkway.

.1   Diagonally cross the BRP and ascend via switchbacks
on a white-blazed trail.

.4   Avoid the faint trail to the right and continue straight; the trail becomes steeper.

.5   Arrive on Green Knob. The lookout tower is just to the left. Bear right on the trail and descend on a pathway being overtaken by rhododendron and mountain laurel. Views of Mount Mitchell continue as you descend.

.6   Be careful as you pass through a loose-boulder field.

.75 Level out and pass by a few small spots that could be used for tent sites (no water available, of course).

.85 Descend steeply.

1.1 The descent mellows out as you enter an evergreen forest and proceed via switchbacks. Trail is lined with false hellebore.

1.2 Descend steeply for a short while only to level out a little later.

1.5 The trail makes a hard turn to the right and resumes the steep descent for .1 mile before leveling out in a lovely evergreen forest.

1.7 Ascend for the first time since leaving the lookout tower.

1.8 Reach the top of the rise and descend through rhododendron, enjoying the sweet and pungent odor of the galax covering the ground.

2   Descend steeply to reach a small gap and walk level for a short distance.

2.1 Rise steeply.

2.3 Reach the top of a rise where Mount Mitchell is clearly visible. Descend.

2.7 Level out and then descend gradually through rhododendron tunnels beneath towering evergreens.

2.8 The sound of the river is clearly audible.

3   Turn right and descend on long switchbacks.

3.1 Arrive at the Forest Service's Black Mountain campground.

Mile 350.4. Snooks Nose Trail [FS 211]

Length: approximately 4 miles, one way

Difficulty: strenuous

As this trail does not receive regular maintenance, it may be hard to locate. Those who need a clearly defined pathway may want to forgo hiking it. Look to the east of the Parkway and you'll eventually find an indication of the route. It descends a rugged ridge line (with a few views) to

FSR 482 at the south edge of Curtis Creek Campground. Camping is prohibited on BRP property, but permitted on national forest land. Suitable sites are limited and may not be encountered until near the end of the trail.

The Curtis Creek Campground is reached by automobile by driving north on the Parkway. In Big Laurel Gap, BRP mile 347.6, turn right onto FSR 482 and descend several miles to the campground.

Mile 351.9. Deep Gap Trail [FS 210]

Length: 2 miles, one way

Difficulty: moderate; moderately strenuous if hiked in the opposite direction than the one described

Recommended

Another Forest Service pathway, the Deep Gap Trail makes long, fairly gentle switchbacks to enter a bowl nestled between Chute Branch and Newberry Creek. Woodpeckers and other birds seem to be a little more numerous here than in many other parts of the national forest. Abundant at the beginning of the trail, ferns, mosses, and other plants of the understory become lusher as the route loses elevation. This trail is recommended because of the ease of walking, beauty of the forest, and perception of isolation.

Once you are beyond BRP property, camping is permitted anywhere along the way. Several nice sites may be found near the end of the trail.

Automobile access to the far trailhead is obtained by driving north on the Parkway to Big Laurel Gap, BRP mile 347.6. Descend east on FSR 482, go past the Forest Service's Curtis Creek campground, and turn right onto FSR 482A. This road ascends through the first tract of national forest land purchased under the Weeks Act on March 1, 1911. Arrive at a gate, which may be locked. If so, you will need to walk the final distance of approximately 1.5 miles to the trailhead.

.0   Directly across the BRP from FSR 472, begin to descend through a hardwood forest on a narrow pathway.

.2   Switch back to the left and listen for woodpeckers and songbirds, which appear to enjoy this portion of the forest. The trail is barely defined in some places.

.4   Switch back to the right among a number of dogwood trees, and just before coming to a water run make a switchback to the left.

.5   Switch back right. The vegetation continues to grow lusher as you progress.

.6   Make three more switchbacks.

.8   Switch back right under a forest of poplar and maple.

1.1   Cross a good-sized water run and then pass over a spur ridge.

1.2   Begin walking through rhododendron and mountain laurel as galax becomes the dominant ground cover.

1.4   Switch back right and then left.

1.7   Cross another water run. The trailside vegetation has grown even lusher.

1.8   Walk next to a creek and by an old structure.

2   Cross the creek and arrive at the parking area on FSR 482A.

Mile 355. Bald Knob Ridge Trail [FS 186]

Length: 2.8 miles, one way

Difficulty: moderate

Another Forest Service trail, this is an excellent walk into large and magnificent stands of virgin spruce and fir. The vegetation is so lush in this forest primeval that at times you could almost believe you were traipsing through a deep and dark rain forest. Hardwoods replace the evergreens once the trail begins to descend on long, gentle switchbacks to FSR 472.

Camping is allowed anywhere along this trail once you get past BRP property (about .2 mile into the walk). Several pleasant, grassy, and level spots would serve as favorable campsites.

Automobiles may reach the trail's end by following the BRP north from Black Mountain Gap to Deep Mountain Gap at BRP mile 351.9. Descend on FSR 472. The trailhead is just beyond a wide curve where the road crosses the South Toe River for the first time.

.0   Descend to the left from the parking area in Black Mountain Gap into an evergreen forest.

.1   The vegetation is already quite verdant and lush as the trail becomes level for a short distance. Pass by an old cabin.

.2   Descend.

.4   There are some good wintertime views to the right

of the trail as the descent becomes more gradual. Also, several level grassy spots could make good tent sites.

.8   Enter a virgin forest.

1.1   Emerge from the virgin timber and enter a rhododendron tunnel.

1.3   Descend a little more rapidly.

1.5   Pass through more rhododendron tunnels; swing around the ridge line. Descend via long switchbacks in a forest that becomes progressively more hardwoods than evergreens.

2   Follow the old road for a very short distance then leave it.

2.4   Again follow an old road for just a very short distance. The tumbling waters of South Toe River become audible.

2.6   Turn right onto a wide old road.

2.8   Arrive at FSR 472.

Mile 355.4. NC RT 128 ascends from the Parkway to enter Mount Mitchell State Park. The park, designated as North Carolina's first state park in 1915, offers a restaurant and lounge, museum, concession stand, small tent-camping area, and several hiking trails.

The highest point in the eastern United States, Mount Mitchell is the focal point of the Black Mountain range. The mountains are so named because the dark green spruce and fir covering the slopes appear almost black when viewed from a distance. The area is reminiscent of the alpine environment of Canada.

The trails of the state park emanate from Mount Mitchell's 6,684-foot summit. One follows the main crest of the Black Mountain range, rarely dropping below 6,000 feet. It offers spectacular views of three intersecting mountain ranges – the Blue Ridge, Black, and Great Craggy mountains. Another trail drops from Mount Mitchell's summit, enters Pisgah National Forest, and ends at the Forest Service's Black Mountain campground on FSR 472. Other trails connect the park office with the restaurant and tent camping area and join with longer trails in the Pisgah National Forest.

Backcountry camping is prohibited in the state park. However, as stated, park trails do connect with national forest trails where camping is permitted. A

couple of Forest Service trailside shelters are located
on pathways within a couple of miles of the park's
boundary. Automobiles may be left overnight in the
state park but must be registered.

A map and more information on the state park and its
trails may be obtained by contacting:

Mount Mitchell State Park
Route 5, Box 700
Burnsville, NC 28714

Information on the national forest trails that connect with
state park trails may be obtained by contacting:

District Ranger
Toecane Ranger District, USFS
P.O. Box 128
Burnsville, NC 28714

Mile 359.8. Big Butt Trail [FS 161]

Length: 6 miles, one way

Difficulty: moderately strenuous

The trailhead is located in Balsam Gap, the joining
point of the Black Mountains and the Great Craggy
Mountains. This pathway is one of the few Forest Service
trails connecting to the Parkway that actually has a number of spots that would be suitable campsites. One even
has water available! It would make a great place for a base
camp. There are no other trails connecting with the Big
Butt Trail, but do not let this deter you from exploring the
area on your own. Please note: land to the right of the trail
(as viewed when walking in the direction described) is private property.

The trail descends through a variety of vegetations
and terrains. The pathway stays on the ridge line, but the
ridge is at some points narrow, rocky, and steep and at
others wide, lushly vegetated, and gently rolling. Large
stands of evergreens, complete with a luxuriant understory
of ferns and moist mosses, invoke memories of rain forests in the Pacific Northwest. A diversity of hardwoods
assures a colorful walk when leaves begin to change in the
fall. Don't be surprised, in the spring, to meet a few locals
carrying trowels and large sacks. They are gathering a delicious Southern Appalachian delicacy. Ramps grow pro-

fusely in large gardens along much of the length of this trail. You might even be tempted to try a few with your evening meal.

The trail ends on NC RT 197 in Cane River Gap. Reaching this far trailhead from the BRP involves quite a bit of driving. Head south on the Parkway to Bee Tree Gap, BRP mile 367.6. Exit the BRP and descend on an unpaved road through a lovely rhododendron and hemlock forest. The dirt road eventually becomes paved NC RT 2178. At the junction with NC RT 2173 turn left onto NC RT 2173 and arrive in the small hamlet of Barnardsville. Bear right onto paved NC RT 197 (which will eventually turn to dirt) for almost 10 miles to come to Cane River Gap. Be alert! There really is nothing here, except a wide pullout at the top of the rise, to identify the trailhead.

.0   Begin to the left in the parking area on a pathway behind the trail sign. (Do not mistakenly follow the old road that goes from the middle of the parking area.) Descend through red trillium, mayapple, and Solomon's seal.

.1   Enter an evergreen forest and come onto the ridge line that you will be following the rest of the way.

.2   Pass by an old hunter's camp in rain forest–type lushness.

.3   Begin ascent to a knob.

.5   Reach the high point of the knob, which is covered by red trillium. Just beyond the knob several spots would make nice campsites.

.7   Descend on a pathway being overtaken by briers.

.8   Low point in a gap. There are limited views to the right of the trail.

1.4   Having passed through a mossy, evergreen forest, rise and enter hardwoods.

1.5   At the top of the knob be sure to swing to the left on the blazed trail and not to the right on a faint pathway. Descend steeply via switchbacks. The red trillium is outrageously abundant.

1.8   The descent levels out somewhat.

2.1   Reach a gap where you might find a few level campsites. Ascend steeply on switchbacks along a rock facing of the knob. Be careful – the rock is slippery and dangerous in wet weather.

2.4   The open area on top of the knob permits a wonderful view of Mount Mitchell, the Black Mountain range, and Cane River Valley. Follow the up-and-down undulations of the narrowing ridge line. There are occasional good views.

2.7 Ascend steeply on an overgrown, but still visible, path.

2.8 Swing to the left side of the ridge. Ramps are plentiful here. Views from the narrow ridge continue to get better as you ascend. Graggy Dome and the Pinnacle may be seen to the south. Heath is crowding in on the pathway.

3.0 Swing to the right of the ridge to miss the summit of Big Butt. Walk along a brier-infested trail and begin to descend.

3.2 Enter wide and rolling Flat Spring Gap with a spring to the right of the trail. A perfect spot to establish a base camp. Red trillium, mayapple, and ramps carpet the forest floor.

3.6 Reach another gap and other good campsites. Ascend and slab to the left of a knob on a pathway being used and abused by all-terrain vehicles.

3.8 Descend.

4 The ridge line widens out, making a few more nice campsites. The trail is most definitely headed into its final descent.

4.2 The ridge line narrows.

4.6 Be alert! The all-terrain vehicles have established a trail that cuts straight down the hill to the right. Look for your pathway to the left and descend on a long series of switchbacks.

5 Do not become confused by the maze of trails and faint roads. Continue down the ridge line and rejoin the switchbacks.

5.6 A logging road is visible below. Violets and white violets appear.

5.8 The trail begins to follow a jeep road.

6 Arrive at Cane River Gap on NC RT 197.

Mile 361.2. Glassmine Falls Trail [BRP 94]

Length: .05 mile, one way

Difficulty: easy leg stretcher

A very short stretch to a view of Glassmine Falls. The 200-foot falls drops quickly and steeply down the side of Horse Range Ridge. Exploiting an abundant local natural resource, a mica mine operated at the base of the falls in the early part of this century.

Trails of the Craggy Gardens Recreation Area, Blue Ridge Parkway Miles 364.1–367.6

The Craggy Gardens are actually small grassy balds intermingled with large heath balds. They are the most easily accessed balds along the BRP. The scientific community still disagrees as to how and why balds exist. They are not above tree line. Many occur well below peaks adorned by spruce and fir. Research data has provided a number of theories attempting to explain this phenomenon, but unfortunately, information also exists to refute each one of these theories. David T. Catlin, in *A Naturalist's Blue Ridge Parkway*, discusses the varying theories.

Whatever the reason for the balds, Catawba rhododendron is the dominant plant in the Craggy Gardens. About a month after the rhododendron has bloomed in the lower elevations of the Parkway, the gardens become ablaze with acre upon acre of the plant's pink and purple blossoms. If you are in the area in mid-June to early July, do not pass up the chance to enjoy this dazzling natural display that has delighted visitors from around the world.

One of the recreation area's trails ascends to the 5,840-foot Craggy Pinnacle for a view across the heath balds and out to the surrounding mountains. A self-guiding pathway winds in and among the voluminous rhododendron, and a Forest Service trail provides access to two tumbling waterfalls.

In addition to the trails, the Craggy Gardens Recreation Area contains a Park Service visitor center, book shop, and picnic area.

Mile 364.1. Craggy Pinnacle Trail [BRP 95]

Length: 1.2 miles, round-trip

Difficulty: moderate

The Craggy Pinnacle Trail ascends in a true heath bald. Lining the trail are mountain laurel, rhododendron, blueberry, and mountain cranberry – all members of the heath family.

High winds and elevation can sometimes combine to make extraordinary conditions on the exposed summit. The valleys and lower ridge lines may be bathed in warm temperatures and sunshine, while the rhododendron and mountain laurel on the pinnacle are covered in a thick layer of rime ice.

This is also the trail to walk if you want to appreciate the full effect of the gardens in bloom in June and early July.

.0   Begin on the steps in the Craggy Dome Overlook and ascend through rhododendron.

.1   Pass by a bench.

.2   Arrive at an old box spring.

.3   Come to a bench with a grand view to the west. Intersection. Bear right and descend.

.4   Arrive at a view overlooking the visitor center and Craggy Flats. Retrace your steps.

.5   Bear right at the intersection and ascend.

.7   Arrive at the summit for an extensive 360-degree view of the Asheville Reservoir, Craggy Flats, Craggy Dome, Mount Mitchell, Big Butt, and Ogle Meadow. On a clear day you may even be able to see the mountains of Tennessee to the northeast. Retrace you steps, staying to the right at the intersection.

1.2   Arrive back at the Craggy Dome Overlook.

Mile 364.6. Douglas Falls Trail [FS 162] (also known as the Halfway Trail)

Length: 4 miles, one way

Difficulty: strenuous

This Forest Service trail descends, steeply in places, to pass by Cascade Falls and Douglas Falls. The trail ends at a parking area on FSR 74. Be advised that most people who utilize this trail hike in from FSR 74 to Douglas Falls and then make use of another Forest Service trail to return to FSR 74 for a circuit hike of about 2 miles. The upper portion of the Douglas Falls Trail is less traveled, rough, and not as well maintained as the lower section. Also, the Park Service has plans to relocate the trailhead away from the visitor center parking area. Check at the visitor center for the most up-to-date information.

Reaching the far trailhead on FSR 74 by automobile is rather involved. Drive south on the Parkway and exit in Bee Tree Gap, BRP mile 367.6. Descend on dirt FSR 63 which, at a lower elevation, becomes paved NC RT 2178. Turn right on NC RT 2173, which becomes dirt FSR 74, and ascend to the trailhead. Allow at least fifty to sixty minutes of driving from the Parkway to reach this point.

Mile 364.6. Craggy Gardens Self-Guiding Trail [BRP 96]

Length: 1 mile, one way

Difficulty: moderate

A pleasant walk from the visitor center to the picnic area, this self-guiding trail winds through rhododendron tunnels and ascends to an observation platform on Craggy Flats. It then descends to the picnic area. Signs identify plant life and discuss the different species of heath.

If you don't mind carrying your supplies, the two shelters (no tables) along the trail might actually be more desirable spots to enjoy your meal instead of the picnic area. The views are certainly better.

A segment of the Mountains to Sea Trail (see Appendix G) begins at the Craggy Gardens Picnic Area.

.0 Begin at the trail sign on the southern end of the visitor center parking area.

.05 Pass by a bench with a limited view. Ascend.

.1 Come to another bench and enter a thick rhododendron tunnel.

.15 Pass by a spring and another bench.

.3 Arrive in open Craggy Flats with excellent views of Craggy Pinnacle and Craggy Dome. Bear left through stunted rhododendron.

.4 Arrive at the observation platform for a vista to the southeast. Retrace your steps.

.5 Bear left at the intersection and go through the shelter and descend. The view to the east is quite wonderful. Descend.

.6 Enter woods.

.7 Pass by another shelter to the right. The descent becomes a little more gradual.

.8 Swing around the mountain for a different perspective on Craggy Pinnacle. Descend rapidly.

1 Pass by a bench and soon arrive in the picnic area, BRP mile 367.6 (rest rooms and water).

Mile 367.7. Mountains to Sea Trail. See Chapter 7.

Mile 374.4. Mountains to Sea Access Trail [BRP 97] (also known as the Rattlesnake Lodge Trail)

Length: .4 mile, one way

Difficulty: strenuous

Markings: orange blazes

The access trail ascends from a small parking area at the southern end of the Tanbark Ridge Tunnel. Rising steeply along a rhododendron-lined stream, it junctions with an old carriage road that serves as the route of the Mountains to Sea Trail (see Appendix G) in this area. The pathway ends at the ruins of buildings that were the summer home of a prominent Asheville citizen near the turn of the century.

.0   Begin at the small pull-off area and ascend steeply along the stream through rhododendron and mountain laurel.

.1   Level out a little and enjoy the small waterfalls of the creek.

.2   Cross a water run.

.25   Cross a larger stream.

.3   Wild geranium are prolific as the path becomes steeper.

.4   Arrive at the Mountains to Sea Trail and the ruins of a number of buildings. A little exploring here may turn up the spring that was the water source for the homestead. A few iris grow in the area.

Mile 382. Folk Art Center

A massive native stone and wood structure, the Folk Art Center (operated by the Southern Highland Handicraft Guild) provides a showplace for master artisans.

Even during a short visit to the center you can watch a dull lump of clay being turned into a hand-formed drinking goblet unique in shape and style, see intricate patterns emerge as a weaver works her loom, or be delighted when nimble fingers transform bits of discarded cloth into a colorful and useful patchwork quilt. Dulcimer makers fill the center with sweet sounds of old-time music.

The center features sales of the crafts, a museum, a library of Appalachian literature, and live folk dancing, music concerts, and interpretive programs are presented on an irregular basis. A Park Service visitor center provides Parkway information, rest rooms, and water.

The Mountains to Sea Trail crosses the center's entrance road. Northward the pathway begins a long climb toward Craggy Gardens. To the south it parallels the BRP, descending to the French Broad River to connect with the Shut-In Trail.

See Appendix G for more information on the Mountains to Sea Trail.

The Shut-In Trail,
Blue Ridge Parkway Miles 393.6–407.6

Originally the Shut-In Trail, now a national recreation trail, stretched from George W. Vanderbilt's Biltmore Estate in Asheville to his Buck Springs Hunting Lodge near Mount Pisgah. Built in the last decade of the 1800s, the route fell into disrepair, and portions were destroyed by the establishment of the BRP. Volunteers helped reclaim old sections and build new paths to create the Shut-In Trail of today – running from the French Broad River to the Mount Pisgah Recreation Area.

One can easily envision a Vanderbilt hunting party ascending the mountains in noisy anticipation. The men, riding and leading horses laden with provisions, talk excitedly about the events of the next few days while the dogs run ahead scaring up squirrels, chipmunks, and deer.

It is believed the trail's name comes from the copious rhododendron thickets that "shut-in" the trail, limiting vistas to just a few. As you hike the different portions of the trail, you will no doubt be able to contemplate the effort and toil the builders of this route expended as they had to cut, uproot, and hack their way through the tough, twisting rhododendron wood. Also take note of the rock wall foundations shoring up the steep sections of the trail. It took foresight to see the need for the walls and craftsmanship to ensure their durability.

A couple of side trails permit access to the Forest Service's system of trails in the Bent Creek Experimental Forest. (See BRP mile 400.3.) Also, the Shut-In Trail is a part of the Mountains to Sea Trail. (See Appendix G.)

The elevation of the Shut-In Trail rises from 2,025 feet at the French Broad River to almost 5,000 feet at its southern terminus near Mount Pisgah. To make it a little easier on yourself, you might want to consider walking some sections of the trail in the opposite direction than described.

Mile 393.6. Shut-In Trail [BRP 98] (from Bent Creek Experimental Forest to Walnut Cove Overlook, BRP Mile 396.4)

Length: 3.1 miles, one way

Difficulty: moderately strenuous

For the initial ascent from near the French Broad River, the Shut-In Trail is able to rise fairly gently on a system of old roadways. There are limited wintertime views of the river as you ascend. Also, the forest is a little more open on this section than on others; rhododendron thickets don't become numerous until you gain a bit more elevation.

The Shut-In Trail does not actually begin on the Parkway. The trailhead may be reached by exiting the Parkway at BRP mile 393.6. In just a few feet turn left onto FSR 479. After .3 mile make a left onto FSR 80 and arrive, in 500 feet, at a parking area and the beginning of the trail.

.0   Begin to rise from the parking area. In 100 feet the Mountains to Sea Trail (see Appendix G) comes in from the left. It will follow the Shut-In Trail all of the way to the Mount Pisgah Recreation Area. Enter a rhododendron tunnel for a short distance.

.2   Cross a small stream. Enter a mountain laurel tunnel.

.3   Emerge from the mountain laurel and ascend quickly.

.4   Come onto an old road with wintertime views of the French Broad River. Even though you are on a road, the ascent is still rather steep.

.7   Descend gradually.

1   Resume a gradual ascent in an open forest of poplar, maple, oak, and dogwood.

1.1   Turn left to join a different woods road and ascend gradually.

1.6   Bear left onto another old roadway and descend.

1.8   Turn left onto a dirt road and walk next to the BRP.

1.9   The trail leaves the road and ascends quickly.

2   Turn left onto yet another old woods road.

2.1   The road makes a switchback to the right and then one to the left. Ascend, and be cautious around the poison ivy growing in profusion along the road. Here are more wintertime views of the French Broad River.

2.5 Begin a gentle descent. The road here feels like an old country lane – vegetation on the forest floor is lush and green, and poplars line the wide roadway.

2.7 Reach a low point and gradually ascend.

2.8 Resume a gradual descent, watching out once again for the abundant poison ivy.

3.1 Arrive at the Parkway and turn right to come to the Walnut Cove Overlook.

Mile 396.4. Shut-In Trail [BRP 99] (from Walnut Cove Overlook to Sleepy Gap Overlook, BRP Mile 397.3)

Length: 1.8 miles, one way

Difficulty: moderate

No longer on old roads, this section of the Shut-In Trail makes a rather stiff ascent over a knob. The route continues to pass through hardwoods. Wildflowers become a little more plentiful. This section also junctions with the Forest Service's Grassy Knob Trail [FS 338], providing access to the Bent Tree Experimental Forest trail system. (See BRP mile 400.3.)

.0 Walk north from the Walnut Cove Overlook and cross the BRP in 200 feet. Enter the woods behind the trail sign and ascend to the left. (The Shut-In Trail also goes right for 3.1 miles to FSR 80, BRP mile 393.6.)

.1 The mayapple are particularly large and abundant here. Ascend via switchbacks in a vine-choked forest.

.3 The ascent becomes almost level. Beware of voluminous poison ivy lining the trail.

.5 Reach the top of the knob and descend on a couple of switchbacks, after which the descent is rather steep. Once again watch out for the poison ivy.

.8 Walk next to the BRP for a short distance.

1.25 Intersection. Keep to the left.

• The Grassy Knob Trail [FS 338] descends into the Bent Creek Experimental Forest of the Pisgah National Forest.

  Cross a small water run (may be dry in summer) in 200 feet.

1.4 Cross an even smaller water run. Slab to the right of

a knob through tunnels of mountain laurel.

1.8   Arrive at the Sleepy Gap Overlook.

Mile 397.3. Grassy Knob and Sleepy Gap Trail [FS 338 and FS 339]

Length: 1 mile, one way

Difficulty: strenuous

This Forest Service trail descends steeply for 1 mile from the Sleepy Gap Overlook before intersecting other trails in the Bent Creek Experimental Forest of Pisgah National Forest (see BRP mile 400.3).

Mile 397.3. Shut-In Trail [BRP 100] (from Sleepy Gap Overlook to Chestnut Cove Overlook, BRP Mile 398.3)

Length: .9 mile, one way

Difficulty: moderately strenuous

The hardwood trees seem to become even larger on this portion of the Shut-In Trail. Pay particular attention to the venerable old oaks growing on the summit of Grassy Knob. Be prepared for a couple of stiff ascents as the route traverses two high knobs.

.0   Ascend from the southern end of the overlook on switchbacks through tunnels of mountain laurel. (The Shut-In Trail also goes northward from the overlook for 1.8 miles to the Walnut Cove Overlook, BRP mile 396.4.)

.3   Attain the top of a knob and descend gradually through more mountain laurel.

.45   Reach a gap; ascend steeply.

.6   Reach the summit of 3,300-foot Grassy Knob. The forest is quite old here, and the trees have attained some very admirable dimensions. Descend somewhat steeply.

.8   Bear left.

.9   Arrive at the Chestnut Cove Overlook.

Mile 398.3. Shut-In Trail [BRP 101] (from Chestnut Cove Overlook to Bent Creek Gap, BRP Mile 400.3)

Length: 2.8 miles, one way

Difficulty: strenuous

The Shut-In Trail now truly lives up to its name. Mountain laurel and rhododendron close in, forming tunnels and dark corridors for much of the way. The route moves the Shut-In Trail far away from the Parkway, making one long descent into Chestnut Cove. This remoteness from automobile traffic, and the shadowy caverns provided by the twisting rhododendron and mountain laurel branches, instills a quiet and sense of isolation not possible on other stretches of the Shut-In Trail. However, there is a price to be paid for this retreat – be ready for a lengthy ascent out of the cove to return to the Parkway.

.0   Cross the BRP from the Chestnut Cove Overlook, enter the woods, and turn left to descend away from the Parkway. (The Shut-In Trail also goes right for .9 mile to arrive at the Sleepy Gap Overlook, BRP mile 397.3.)

.5   Cross a stream and follow an old roadbed for 250 feet before leaving it for a pathway to the left. Mountain laurel and rhododendron arc over the trail.

.7   Emerge from the heath tunnel and enter a hardwood forest of oak, maple, dogwood, and sassafras.

.9   Cross over a spur ridge and continue to descend.

1.1 Come onto a woods road and bear left.

1.4 Come into Chestnut Cove, cross the creek, and ascend for the first time since leaving the Parkway. Rhododendron tunnels reappear.

1.6 As the old road begins to fade, look for a few jack-in-the-pulpits along the trail. Emerge from the rhododendron into a mixed hardwood forest.

1.8 Swing around a spur ridge and continue to ascend on a wide pathway.

2   Cross a small water run.

2.4 Cross another small creek and continue with the long ascent through hardwoods and mountain laurel tunnels.

2.8 Arrive at FSR 479 in Bent Tree Gap. The BRP is just to your left.

Mile 400.3. FSR 479 provides access to trails in two different areas of Pisgah National Forest. To the west it enters Bent Creek Experimental Forest. To the east of the Parkway the road descends to the North Mills River Area. Both places have a number of excellent hiking trails for extended excursions, and each has a Forest Service campground.

Information on the trails and campgrounds may be obtained by contacting:

District Ranger
Pisgah Ranger District, USFS
101 Pisgah Highway
Pisgah Forest, NC 28768

Mile 400.3. Shut-In Trail [BRP 102] (from Bent Creek Gap to Beaver Dam Gap Overlook, BRP Mile 401.7)

Length: 1.9 miles, one way

Difficulty: moderately strenuous

You'll finally get a view or two from this section of the Shut-In Trail. The path makes one long climb to the 4,064-foot summit of Ferrin Knob only to immediately make a steep descent back to the Parkway.

.0   The trail ascends south from FSR 479 at the sign identifying the Southeastern Forest Experiment Station. (The Shut-In Trail also goes north from the road for 2.8 miles to the Chestnut Cove Overlook, BRP 398.3.) Turn right onto an old road in 250 feet.

.5   Pass by a delicious-tasting spring, which unfortunately may not be running at the end of a long, dry summer season. Continue to ascend gradually.

.9   Make a switchback to the left.

1.3   Attain the summit of Ferrin Knob, where there used to be a fire tower. Enjoy the view to the northeast. Begin a steep descent through a beautiful display of mayapple.

1.5   Level out for a short distance in a wildflower-crowded gap. Then continue to descend gradually through abundant dogwood trees and swing around to the right of a knob.

1.9   Arrive at Beaver Dam Gap Overlook.

Mile 401.7. Shut-In Trail [BRP 103] (from Beaver Dam Gap Overlook to Stoney Bald Overlook, BRP Mile 402.6)

Length: .9 mile, one way

Difficulty: strenuous

Even though the trail stays close to the BRP for the entire length of the section, it definitely does not rise at the same easy grade as the Parkway. Three times, in only .9 mile, the route will bring you quickly over a knob or ridge and then plummet downhill.

Take note of the excellent work the trail builders have done with rock cribbing to stabilize the steep hillsides.

.0 From the Beaver Dam Gap Overlook turn left onto the trail and begin an immediate ascent. (The Shut-In Trail also bears to the right for 1.9 miles to go to Bent Tree Gap Overlook, BRP mile 400.3.)

1.5 Reach the top of a knob and promptly descend.

.2 In a gap covered in poison ivy begin to rise once again.

.3 Attain the high point, but abruptly descend via switchbacks secured by rock walls. Looking down on the Parkway slab to the right of a knob.

.5 Arrive at the low point in a gap and ascend very steeply. Cancer root and violets line the pathway.

.7 Reach the ridge line and descend on steep switchbacks. Buttercups and orchids are abundant on this hillside.

.9 Cross the BRP and arrive at Stoney Bald Overlook.

Mile 402.6. Shut-In Trail [BRP 104] (from Stoney Bald Overlook to Big Ridge Overlook, BRP Mile 403.6)

Length: 1.2 miles, one way

Difficulty: moderately strenuous

Once again, there is nothing particularly spectacular about this section of the Shut-In Trail. It climbs several knobs through a hardwood forest before coming to an end at another overlook. The route does pass by a few wildflowers that have not been seen in any great numbers until now.

.0 Take a couple of steps down from the south end of the Stoney Bald Overlook, then immediately begin to ascend. (The Shut-In Trail also goes to the north by crossing the BRP, entering the woods, and traveling .9 mile to Beaver Dam Gap Overlook, BRP mile 401.7.)

.4   Reach the top of a knoll. Descend and slab around the left side of a small knoll.

.6   Begin a very rapid descent.

.7   Cross the BRP (no parking or pull-off area) and slab to the right of a knob. Pass a few jack-in-the-pulpits.

.9   Cross over a low ridge and descend. Rattlesnake plantain, bellwort, robin plantain, and trailing arbutus are all abundant.

1.2   Cross the BRP and arrive at Big Ridge Overlook.

Mile 403.6. Shut-In Trail [BRP 105] (from Big Ridge Overlook to Mills River Valley Overlook, BRP Mile 404.5)

Length: 1.1 miles, one way

Difficulty: moderate

The Shut-In Trail now swings away to the east to traverse a cross ridge of the main crest of the mountains. This provides a pleasant break from being right next to the Parkway like much of the rest of the trail. The ascents are a little gentler than on the previous section.

.0   Descend the steps at the southern end of the overlook and enter the woods. (The Shut-In Trail also heads north by crossing the BRP, entering the woods, and going 1.2 miles to Stoney Bald Overlook, BRP mile 402.6.) Ascend gradually; a number of cancer roots and bloodroot line the trail.

.1   Solomon's seal and false Solomon's seal are abundant, as is lousewort.

.3   Cross over a flat ridge and continue with minor ups and downs. Blueberries, in season, may slow your progress. In fact, let them slow your progress. Take the time to enjoy a few.

.5   Begin to rise at a steadily increasing rate.

.7   Attain the ridge line and follow it, slabbing to the right of a high knob.

.8   Walk along a narrowing ridge line and gradually descend through a hardwood forest.

1.1   Arrive in Mills River Valley Overlook.

Mile 404.5. Shut-In Trail [BRP 106] (from Mills River Valley Overlook to Elk Pasture Gap, BRP Mile 405.5)

Length: 1.2 miles, one way

Difficulty: moderate

There is only one short, steep ascent on this section of the Shut-In Trail. Once you complete this climb, the pathway follows a wavy ridge line with very minor changes in elevation. A spring will supply liquid refreshment.

.0   Follow the trail from the southern end of the overlook and immediately begin a stiff climb. (The Shut-In Trail also leaves from the northern end of the overlook. It will reach Big Ridge Overlook, BRP mile 403.6, in 1.1 miles.) False hellebore, star chickweed, and Solomon's seal grow well here. Pass by a splendid array of lily of the valley.

.15   Slab to the left of a knob, going by a cluster of white trillium.

.3   Come to a spring.

.5   Cross onto the ridge line and now continue with only slight ups and downs.

.9   The trail-building techniques are striking here, as the rock walls supporting the trail are solid and well built.

1   Cross over a small rise and parallel the BRP.

1.2   Cross the Parkway in Elk Pasture Gap and arrive at NC RT 151.

Mile 405.5. Shut-In Trail [BRP 107] (from Elk Pasture Gap to Mount Pisgah Trailhead, BRP Mile 407.6)

Length: 1.9 miles, one way

Difficulty: strenuous

Elk Pasture Gap is at an elevation of 4,200 feet. The Mount Pisgah Trailhead lies at almost 5,000 feet. You will gain all of that elevation in the final section of the Shut-In Trail. However, you will also be able to enjoy several outstanding views of Mount Pisgah and numerous other peaks and valleys. In addition, in late summer a large berry patch awaits those who expend the energy to reach it.

.0   Enter the woods to the south from NC RT 151 and pass by violets and wood anemone. (The Shut-In

Trail also goes to the north. Cross the BRP and follow the trail 1.2 miles to Mill River Overlook, BRP mile 404.5.) Steeply ascend by bloodroot and white trillium.

.2   Come into a large patch of mayapple.

.35   Finally reach the top of the knob and the end of a stiff climb. However, begin immediately to descend.

.45   Arrive in a wide, flat gap.

.5   The BRP is almost directly below; large-flowered trillium and wood anemone abound.

.7   Rise steeply once again.

.8   A break in the vegetation permits a view to the east overlooking Mills River Valley. Continue with the steady ascent.

.9   Level out somewhat as you enter a large patch of delicious berries.

1.1   The climb begins in earnest once again and will become even steeper as you progress. Note that with a change in elevation also comes a change in vegetation.

1.5   Finally reach the ridge line, where there is a nice view to the east. Also, Mount Pisgah soars high above on your right.

1.6   Attain a small knob with limited views to the north and east. Descend into a thicket of mountain laurel.

1.9   Arrive at the Mount Pisgah Trailhead parking area and the southern terminus of the Shut-In Trail on the Mount Pisgah Inn extension road. The Mount Pisgah Trail [BRP 108] begins to your right.

Trails of the Mount Pisgah Area, Blue Ridge Parkway Miles 407.6–408.8

According to the Bible, Moses first sighted the "promised land of milk and honey" from a land mass called Mount Pisgah. Local folklore maintains that in 1776, Reverend James Hall ascended a North Carolina peak and delighted in the beauty of the surrounding countryside. Remembering the biblical account of Moses, he named the summit Mount Pisgah and proclaimed that he, too, had been privileged to look out upon a land of milk and honey.

Near the turn of the twentieth century Mount Pisgah was a part of George W. Vanderbilt's 125,000-acre estate. He and his associates often wandered over the mountainsides to spend time at his Buck Springs Hunting Lodge. Hired to manage the vast timber resources of the estate, Gifford Pinchot developed many forestry practices that are still in use today. In 1895, Vanderbilt employed Dr. Carl A. Schenck, who established the first forestry school in America in the valley below Mount Pisgah. (See BRP mile 411.9 for more information.) Many of his students became some of the initial Forest Service employees.

Upon Vanderbilt's death, his heirs sold a huge tract of land, including Mount Pisgah, in 1914 to the federal government. This property became the basis of the Pisgah National Forest.

The Mount Pisgah area presents many wonderful opportunities for walking and hiking experiences. The Shut-In Trail, of course, may be followed for more than 16 miles from the eastern side of Mount Pisgah to the banks of the French Broad River. Those with stout legs and healthy lungs may climb to the observation platform on Mount Pisgah for their own view of a promised land. Easy and short, but also pleasurable, pathways provide links to the picnic area, campground, and lodge. Several Forest Service trails snake eastward along sloping ridge lines into Pisgah National Forest to permit lengthy overnight trips and interesting campsites.

The Mount Pisgah area contains a Park Service picnic area, campground, camp store, gas station, gift shop, restaurant, and the Pisgah Inn.

Mile 407.6. Mount Pisgah Trail [BRP 108]

Length: 1.25 miles, one way

Difficulty: strenuous

The view of a "land of milk and honey" from the summit of Mount Pisgah certainly lives up to its descriptive name. Be forewarned, however; this is not an excursion for those who are out of shape. The final .75 mile is, more or less, one long set of steep stairs. The trail builders deserve praise and appreciation for the planning and hard work that obviously went into creating this pathway over such rugged terrain.

Notwithstanding the warning, do take at least the first half of the Mount Pisgah Trail. The pathway is wide, level, and, in springtime, lined with more than its fair share of wildflowers.

.0 Begin at the trail sign at the end of the Mount Pisgah extension road. (The Mount Pisgah Trailhead to the Picnic Area Connector Trail [BRP 113] immediately drops off to the left.) Walk very gently, ascending on a wide pathway and admiring the deluge of wildflowers – bed straw, lousewort, star chickweed, white violet, jewelweed, and ragwort.

.15 Pass by a large rock facing; rhododendron and mountain laurel close in on the trail.

.4 Come to a gushing double springs.

.55 The ascent becomes less gradual as you walk onto a narrowing ridge line.

.8 Pass by an old bench. The tangy smell of galax will become apparent as you begin huffing and puffing up the rougher and steeper trail.

1 Arrive at a bench with a limited view. Good spot to take a break, as the trail will become even steeper and more rugged.

1.1 Note that the vegetation becomes stunted as you gain elevation. The trail is now very rough and eroded.

1.25 Arrive at the observation platform on the 5,721-foot summit of Mount Pisgah. Rest, relax, and savor the fruits of your labors – a 360-degree view of the land of milk and honey.

Mile 407.6. Mount Pisgah Trailhead to Picnic Area Connector Trail [BRP 109]

Length: .5 mile, one way

Difficulty: easy leg stretcher

This is an extended easy walk connecting the Mount Pisgah Trail with the picnic area. In just .5 mile it passes through several distinct vegetation areas – oak and beech forest, rhododendron tunnels, and damp, marshy areas. Spring wildflowers are abundant.

This would make a relaxing stroll after a hearty cookout in the picnic area.

.0 Begin on the Mount Pisgah Trail [BRP 112], but almost immediately bear to the left on the descending pathway through oak, beech, and rhododendron.

.1 The rhododendron gives way to a very open forest. Bluets, lousewort, and violets add color to the ground. Soon pass by the Buck Spring Gap Tunnel

Hikers on Mount Pisgah. (Photograph by Jim Page, courtesy of the North Carolina Division of Travel and Tourism)

entrance on the BRP and then walk below the Parkway on a narrow trail.

.3   Galax is the dominant ground cover. Painted trillium also grows well here.

.4   The trailside is almost inundated by the great number of false hellebore. Begin ascending through a field, looking for a few of the succulent wild strawberries sure to be growing in late summer.

.5   Arrive in the picnic parking area.

Mile 407.7. Buck Spring Gap Overlook to the Shut-In Trailhead [BRP 110]

Length: .3 mile, one way; .5 mile, round-trip

Difficulty: moderately easy

The Mountains to Sea Trail (see Appendix G) and this trail start together, separate for a short distance, and then rejoin. They would make a quick but energetic circuit walk of .5 mile. There are a couple of limited views along the way.

This is one of the shortest sections of the Mountains to Sea Trail. Therefore, you may want to walk it just to be able to brag to friends that you have walked a portion of this soon-to-be famous trail. Also, as the Mountains to Sea Trail is a fairly new pathway, you will be one of the first people to walk upon it!

.0   Ascend the steps at the northern end of the Buck Spring Gap Overlook. Rise steeply, passing numerous strawberry plants.

.1   The Mountains to Sea Trail bears to the left; keep right.

.15 Reach the top of the knob for a somewhat limited view. Bear left and descend.

.2   Rejoin the Mountains to Sea Trail.

.3   Come to the Mount Pisgah extension road. The Shut-In Trail [BRP 107] (which the Mountains to Sea Trail follows) is a few feet ahead. The Mount Pisgah Trail [BRP 108] is to your left at the end of the road.

Mile 407.8. Picnic Area Loop Trail [BRP 111]

Length: .3 mile, round-trip

Difficulty: easy

Following the Picnic Area Loop Trail is the only way to reach the accommodations (tables, rest rooms, and water fountain) in Mount Pisgah's picnic area. Of course you would not have to walk the whole trail just to enjoy your outdoor meal, but the pathway would make a pleasant after-lunch jaunt. You might even let nature supply your dessert. Blueberries may be found along a section of the trail in mid to late summer.

.0 Begin near the southern end of the picnic parking area next to the gated road. Ascend very gradually on a paved trail through rhododendron.

.05 Come into the open field of the picnic area and pass by the rest rooms. Continue on a dirt road.

.1 Bear right at the intersection and walk by picnic tables hidden among the rhododendron and mountain laurel. Be watching for your chance to savor a few wild blueberries.

.2 Do not follow the dirt road into the open meadow; rather, take the trail into the rhododendron tunnel.

.3 Return to the parking area.

Mile 407.8. Picnic Area to Mount Pisgah Campground Connector Trail [BRP 112]

Length: 1 mile, one way

Difficulty: moderately easy

This connector pathway turns out to be a real surprise. On trail maps of the Mount Pisgah area it looks like a dull, noisy, right-next-to-the-highway type of trail. However, the route quickly drops below the BRP into a dense forest of hemlock and rhododendron. If you didn't know you were so close to the Pisgah Inn, you might believe you were walking through a hidden and isolated cove. The rhododendron forms long, dark tunnels, and the extensive evergreens muffle any road noise. Moss, growing right on the treadway, bears witness to the fact that this trail receives very little use.

.0 Begin at the trail post on the southern end of the picnic area parking lot and descend into a deep forest of hemlock and rhododendron where galax spreads across the earth.

.25 The galax leaves grow to a rare large size here. Pass by a few painted trillium and cross a couple of small water runs.

.35 Emerge from the rhododendron into a more open forest and ascend gradually.

.6 Cross over the campground loop trail and continue straight. (The campground loop trail is just what it says – it encircles the campground to provide access to the various campsites.)

.7 Pass steps leading up to the BRP and several camp-sites. Continue straight, crossing a stone-paved drainage ditch.

.9 Arrive at and follow the campground road.

1 Reach the campground entrance station, BRP mile 408.8.

Mile 408.6. Buck Spring Trail (FS Portion) [FS 104]

Length: 6.2 miles, one way

Difficulty: moderate

Highly recommended

This just may be the world's most perfect walking path! The route descends from the Pisgah Inn to US RT 271. The rate of descent is so gradual that you can barely perceive that you are dropping. However, your body appreciates it. There are no jolts to your ankles as there would be if you were dropping at a rapid pace, no pressure on your knees from trying to keep yourself from going downhill too fast, and no fatigue to your calf muscles from having to ascend for long periods of time. The one or two ascents are short and extremely gradual. They, in fact, provide a sort of welcome change from the ever-descending trail.

There are no appreciable views along the way, but the many little waterfalls, cascades, and wildflowers make up for that. Shade, courtesy of rhododendron groves and a thick hardwood forest, will keep the hot summer sun off your brow.

You enter Pisgah National Forest in a couple of tenths of a mile after leaving the Pisgah Inn. Camping is allowed anywhere in the national forest. Although water is plentiful along this route, you would be very hard pressed to find any suitable, level campsites.

The Mountains to Sea Trail (see Appendix G) follows the Buck Spring Trail from the Pisgah Inn to mile point 5.1.

The far trailhead may be reached by automobile by driving south on the Parkway to BRP mile 411.9. Descend east on US RT 276 for almost 2.5 miles to arrive at the wide trailhead parking area on the left side of the road.

.0   Ascend the steps at the northern end of the Pisgah Inn parking lot and turn right in 150 feet.

.1   Bear right again and walk below the Pisgah Inn on a wide, grassy roadway. Arrive at an intersection. The old Thompson Creek Trail drops to the left and eventually ends on FSR 1206. (This trail is rough, overgrown, and no longer maintained; it should probably not be hiked.) Bear right to continue on the Buck Spring Trail. There are excellent views to the east and out across the ridge you will be descending.

.4   Leave the roadbed and descend on a series of switchbacks. Cancer root is prevalent.

.6   Cross a small cascading water run and continue via switchbacks.

.7   Recross the same water run and continue on a gently sloping pathway.

.8   Cross another small stream.

1   Blackberries and raspberries abound!

1.1   Cross over a small water run that has an especially pretty little waterfall.

1.2   Cross a water run lined by rhododendron.

1.3   False hellebore grows well around another water run you need to cross.

1.6   Swing around a spur ridge, enjoying the bountiful blueberries.

1.9   As you cross this water run, be sure to look uphill to see the water tumbling down a forty- to fifty-foot rock facing.

2.1   Bell flowers appear in great numbers around the trail.

2.3   Cross another water run with small cascades uphill.

2.4   Pass by a large patch of lousewort and enter a blueberry and mountain laurel tunnel.

2.5   Cross a rhododendron-lined stream.

2.7   Cross the largest water run so far; bloodroot and Solomon's seal make an occasional appearance.

3.1   In the early spring the azalea stands out, and the dogwood trees add a splash of white in an otherwise green forest.

3.2   Cross a rhododendron-crowned spur ridge that
      might provide a few, small tent sites.

3.5   Cross a stream.

3.7   Cross another stream. The trail becomes a little
      rough and overgrown.

4.4   Cross a large stream.

4.7   Swing around a spur ridge that is covered in dog-
      wood and azalea. Soon cross another stream.

5.1   The Mountains to Sea Trail veers off to the left.
      Bear right to continue on the Buck Spring Trail.

5.3   Cross stream.

5.7   Cross a large stream that possesses a rushing
      waterfall.

5.9   Cross the final stream.

6   Pass by a field of giant mayapple and wake robin tril-
      lium. Striped maple is the dominant low bush. Begin
      a gradual rise.

6.2   Arrive at US RT 271.

Mile 408.6. Buck Spring Trail (BRP Portion) [BRP 113]

Length: 1.1 miles, one way

Difficulty: moderately easy

An excellent choice for an early morning or early
evening stroll from the Pisgah Inn. The trail takes an easy
route along the side and top of East Fork Ridge. It passes
through a mixed forest of oak, hemlock, and rhododendron on its way to the former site of the Buck Spring
Lodge. Just as George W. Vanderbilt once did, you, too,
can enjoy the panorama of a morning sun rising over the
ridge lines in the east.

The trail is intersected by two Forest Service trails
that, in turn, provide access to a large area of the Pisgah
National Forest. Camping is permitted on either of the
routes, giving rise to several overnight-hike possibilities.
(See BRP 411.9 for more information on Pisgah National
Forest trails.)

The Mountains to Sea Trail (see Appendix G) makes
use of the route of the Buck Spring Trail.

.0   Begin at the northern end of the Pisgah Inn parking
      lot. Ascend the steps next to the trail sign, bear left,
      and pass by several lodge buildings. Rise into a for-
      est of wind-stunted trees and shrubs.

.15   Cross over a rock outcropping that provides limited

wintertime views. Slab the steep hillside on a wide, level trail.

.3 Begin walking on the top of the ridge line and continue with minor ups and downs. In season, blackberries and blueberries make this a delicious section of trail to walk.

.45 Descend gradually.

.6 Intersection.

- The Pilot Rock Trail [FS 321] goes to the right .2 mile to the summit of Little Bald Mountain and 2.3 miles more to end on Yellow Gap Road (FSR 1206). The far trailhead can be reached by car by following the Parkway south and exiting at BRP mile 411.9. Descend on US RT 276 for several miles and turn left onto FSR 1206. Continue for almost 4 miles to reach the trailhead.

Bear to the left and descend into rhododendron tunnels to continue on the Buck Spring Trail.

.7 Intersection.

- The Laurel Mountain Trail [FS 121] bears to the right for 7.1 miles to Yellow Gap Road. The far trailhead may be reached by using the above directions to the far trailhead of Pilot Rock Trail. Continue 4.5 miles beyond the Pilot Rock Trailhead on FSR 1206 to reach the Laurel Mountain Trailhead.

Bear left and walk on a galax-lined trail to continue on the Buck Spring Trail.

.9 Enter a thick rhododendron tunnel.

1 Arrive at the site of Vanderbilt's Buck Spring Lodge, which was used as a hunting and entertaining retreat around the turn of the century. You'll find pleasing views to the east. Continue straight; the Mountains to Sea Trail drops to the left.

1.1 Arrive at the Buck Spring Gap Overlook on the Mount Pisgah extension road.

Mile 408.8. Frying Pan Mountain Trail [BRP 114]

Length: 1.9 miles, one way

Difficulty: moderately strenuous

Along this route you can observe the effects of the harsher weather of an upland environment. The vegetation is strong and healthy near the campground but becomes gnarled and stunted as you cross over an exposed knob.

The Frying Pan Mountain Trail would be a suitable walk to the fire tower to enjoy either sunrise or sunset. In the morning you could watch the sunlight slowly spread across the Mills River and Davidson River valleys. In the evening dark shadows begin to creep up from the Pigeon River to cover Frying Pan Mountain and Mount Pisgah.

.0   Begin at the trail sign on the campground entrance road. Pass by a couple of service buildings and ascend into an oak forest.

.2   Follow the ridge line to the left.

.4   Coming close to the edge of the ridge, obtain a limited view to the southeast. The trees become smaller and wind gnarled as you ascend.

.6   Passing by a few evergreens, begin to descend.

.8   Your objective, the fire tower, can be seen through the vegetation.

1.1   Drop into Frying Pan Gap, so named because local herders used to camp and cook here. The Parkway (BRP mile 409.6) is just to your left. Follow the dirt road uphill.

1.3   Avoid the old road that bears right.

1.5   Cross under a utility line and by a gated dirt road to the right.

1.6   The road levels out for a short distance; the fire tower is directly ahead.

1.9   Arrive at the fire tower for a 360-degree view that includes the BRP almost directly below and Mount Pisgah to the north.

Mile 411.9. Three miles to the west on US RT 276 will bring you to the trailheads of Old Butt Knob [FS 363], Shining Creek [FS 357], Big East Fork [FS 332] trails. All of these trails intersect other pathways in the Shining Rock Wilderness.

East on US RT 276 permits access to the Cradle of Forestry, a Forest Service visitor center with exhibits portraying Dr. Carl A. Schenck's establishment of the first forestry school in America. Included are two short, easy interpretive trails. A small entrance fee is charged for this worthwhile side trip from the BRP.

A little further east on US RT 276 is the Davidson River Area of the Pisgah National Forest, which has a Forest Service campground and a network of hiking trails.

Information on all of the attractions along US RT 276 may be obtained by contacting:

District Ranger
Pisgah Ranger District, USFS
101 Pisgah Highway
Pisgah Forest, NC 28768

Mile 415.9. Case Camp Ridge Trail [FS 119]

Length: 1.5 miles, one way

Difficulty: moderate

This little-used trail drops along a ridge line for slightly over 1.5 miles to FSR 475B. (The closest place to park on the Parkway is .2 mile to the north at Cherry Cove Overlook, BRP mile 415.7.) Since it is on national forest land, camping is allowed anywhere along the route. Suitable sites and water, however, may be hard to locate.

The far trailhead may be reached by driving north on the Parkway to BRP mile 411.9. Descend east on US RT 276 and soon after the Cradle of Forestry Visitor Center, turn right onto FSR 475B. The trailhead is .9 mile out this road.

Mile 417. East Fork Trail Access [BRP 115]

Length: about .2 mile, one way

Difficulty: easy

A hard-to-find and unmaintained trail enters the forest just a few feet north of the Looking Glass Rock Overlook. If you are able to find and follow the trail, it will eventually bring you into the Shining Rock Wilderness and connect with the East Fork Trail. (See BRP mile 420.2 for information on the trails in the Shining Rock Wilderness.) There are good campsites along the stream.

Mile 418.8. Graveyard Fields Loop Trail [BRP 116]

Length: 2.2 miles, round-trip

Difficulty: moderately easy

All of the Shining Rock Wilderness is somewhat reminiscent of the Rocky Mountains along the Continental Divide, and Graveyard Fields is no exception. Even the name of the stream and falls, Yellowstone, evokes the Rockies.

The fields obtained their name from the hundreds of dead tree trunks lying on the ground, resembling gravestones, after a fire swept across more than 25,000 acres in 1925.

The trail parallels the wide and shallow river, winding through mountain laurel, rhododendron, serviceberry, and open grasslands. A short side trail drops to the base of impressive Yellowstone Falls. Also, the Graveyard Ridge Trail [FS 336] intersects the loop trail to provide easy access to the wilderness.

.0   Descend through mountain laurel and rhododendron on the steps at the northern end of the overlook. Follow a paved trail.

.1   The pavement ends.

.15   Cross the cascading waters of a small creek.

.3   Pass by a rock outcropping with a small cave; the trail then switches back rather precipitously on a badly eroded pathway. Cross the river on a footbridge and turn right on a short side trail to see Second Falls. Retrace your steps.

.5   Do not recross the bridge; follow the trail upstream and ascend where serviceberry blossoms dot the trail.

•   Almost immediately the Graveyard Ridge Trail [FS 336] bears to the right.

Keep left to continue on the Graveyard Loop Trail.

.6   Walk along the bank where the river is wide and shallow.

.85   Pass by a rock dam that has created a shallow wading pool. Cross a side stream and wind through rhododendron and mountain laurel.

1   Cross a small side stream twice. Galax covers the ground like ivy.

Second Falls, on the Graveyard Fields Loop Trail.
(Photograph by Clay Nolen, courtesy of the North
Carolina Division of Travel and Tourism)

1.2   The valley is very wide and open here, affording a view of the surrounding bald mountains.

1.4   Intersection.

•   An unmaintained trail goes straight for about .5 mile to the Upper Falls.

      Bear left, boulder hop part of the river, and cross the rest of the stream on a wooden footbridge. Cross a second bridge to continue on the Graveyard Loop Trail.

1.6   Pass through a damp and muddy area and gradually ascend into rhododendron thickets. Continue with minor ups and downs.

2   Cross a marshy spot on a 100-foot-long log bridge. The trail then becomes rough and rocky.

2.2   Ascend the steps and return to the overlook.

Mile 419.4. John Rock Trail [BRP 117]. Several short leg stretcher trails emanate from the overlook to the edge of the ridge line for a view into the Davidson River Valley. For safety's sake, and to prevent erosion, do not take any of the unauthorized trails that descend steeply over the mountainside.

Mile 420.2. FSR 816 permits access to the Shining Rock Wilderness, an area intensely rugged and well suited for overnight hiking. Some trails lace the open bald mountains, created by logging at the turn of the century and catastrophic fires in 1925 and again in 1942. Other pathways cross over narrow ridge lines, some of which have peaks attaining heights over 5,000 and 6,000 feet. All of the trails connect in some way or another and even permit access to additional routes in the Middle Prong Wilderness and other portions of Pisgah National Forest. The unique conditions in this area make it a highly recommended place to spend some time.

Maps and further information on Shining Rock Wilderness may be obtained by contacting:

District Ranger
Pisgah Ranger District, USFS
101 Pisgah Highway
Pisgah Forest, NC 28768

Mile 421.2. Art Loeb Trail [FS 146]. The 30-mile-long Art Loeb Trail, a national recreation trail, crosses the BRP here. The closest parking area on the Parkway is .5 mile to the south at the Fetterbush Overlook, BRP mile 421.7. Connecting with a myriad of trails in the Shining Rock Wilderness and Pisgah National Forest, the Art Loeb Trail provides almost unlimited options for extended overnight excursions.

East of the Parkway the trail crosses the heavily wooded slopes and hollows of Pisgah National Forest for 17.5 miles before arriving at US RT 276 just east of the Pisgah Ranger Station. (US RT 276 connects with the Parkway at BRP mile 411.9.)

On the western side of the Parkway the trail passes through wonderfully open heath and grass balds to traverse the main ridge line in the Shining Rock Wilderness. The trail ends at a Boy Scout camp on NC RT 1129. Automobile access to this far trailhead may be obtained by exiting the Parkway at BRP mile 423.2. Follow NC RT 215 for 13 miles to the west, and turn right onto NC RT 1129 for 4 miles to the Boy Scout camp.

The Art Loeb Trail is described in detail in *North Carolina Hiking Trails*, by Allen de Hart.

The Mountains to Sea Trail (see Appendix G) makes use of a large portion of the Art Loeb Trail.

Mile 422.4. Devil's Courthouse Trail [BRP 118]

Length: .43 mile, one way

Difficulty: moderately strenuous

Highly recommended

The Cherokee Indians believed that the evil spirit, Judaculla, once held court inside this massive rock outcropping. You won't have to face this giant devil to enjoy the magnificent view, but the mountain will make you huff and puff to attain it. Fortunately the trail is fairly short and the effort worthwhile.

The trail passes through a highland forest of spruce and fir. The Fraser fir trees have been as devastated by the woolly aphid as those near Richland Balsam.

The viewpoint is a favorite spot with the locals for watching hawks (and an occasional eagle or falcon) riding the hot air currents that rise from the valleys below.

A short side trail provides access to the Mountains to Sea Trail. (See Appendix G.)

.0 Walk next to the Parkway on the paved sidewalk.

.1 Turn away from the BRP, enter the woods, and ascend rather steeply into a forest of stately evergreens. This is a good spot to enjoy several different songbirds early in the morning. Pass by a bench.

.25 A second bench.

.3 Arrive at another bench – a nice spot to watch the hawks soaring high above. Intersection.

• A short trail to the left connects with the Mountains to Sea Trail.

   Bear right and ascend to continue on the Devil's Courthouse Trail.

.4 Ascend on stone steps. Rhododendron and other shrubs close in on the trail.

.43 Attain the high point of the trail for a grand 360-degree view from which you can see three different states. To the south is South Carolina, to the southwest Georgia, and to the west Snow Bird Mountain in Tennessee. The BRP snakes southward onto the Balsam Range. Nearby are Sam Knob in the Shining Rock Wilderness, Richland Balsam, Rich Mountain, and Pilot Mountain. There are almost no signs of civilization!

Mile 425.4. Mountains to Sea Trail Access [BRP 119]

Length: .15 mile, one way

Difficulty: moderately easy

A short leg stretcher through a cool, shaded forest, this pathway intersects the Mountains to Sea Trail (see Appendix G). The Mountains to Sea Trail in this area provides access to many of the trails in the Middle Prong Wilderness, where camping is allowed along any of the routes.

.0 Begin across the BRP from the southern end of the Rough Butt Overlook. Enter a cool, shaded forest whose understory includes rhododendron and trillium.

.05 Cross a murmuring brook and ascend.

.1 The forest floor becomes very open.

.15 Intersect the Mountains to Sea Trail.

Mile 426.5. Haywood Gap Trail [FS 142]. The closest Parkway parking area to this trailhead is Bear Pen parking area, BRP mile 427.6. The Haywood Gap Trail enters the Middle Prong Wilderness and descends west from the Parkway for 3 miles to intersect FSR 97. Along the way it passes by the Mountains to Sea Trail (see Appendix G) and Buckeye Gap Trail [FS 126]. FSR 97 is gated and must be walked 2.5 miles to arrive at the Forest Service's Sunburst Recreation Area and campground on NC RT 215. The recreation area may be reached by exiting the Parkway at BRP mile 423.2 and driving west on NC RT 215 for 8.5 miles.

Mile 427.6. Bear Pen Gap Trail [BRP 120]

Length: 2.8 miles, one way

Difficulty: moderate

Only the first .2 mile of this trail is actually the BRP's Bear Pen Gap Trail. The rest is a part of the Mountains to Sea Trail (see Appendix G). It is a most pleasant walk, as the first half is on an old, almost level roadway lined, in early spring, by abundant wildflowers. The remainder of the route slabs the side of a knob rich with hemlock and rhododendron. There are also two excellent campsites along the route.

.0 Begin on the unmarked trail at the northern end of the overlook. Descend on a well-established trail.

.1 The trail develops into an old woods road.

.2 Spring beauties, trailing arbutus, and trout lilies abound.

.4 Cross a moss-lined water run that descends in small cascades.

.6 A dirt road comes in from the right. Bear left to continue on the trail.

.7 Pass through a Forest Service gate and be alert! Make a left turn uphill at the road intersection.

.8 Descend very gradually.

1 Begin a gentle rise.

1.2 Be alert! As you enter an open field, the trail leaves the road, makes a hard left, and descends. (The field would be an excellent campsite. The lack of water is compensated by flat land to pitch a tent and wonderfully open views to the east and south. Also, the meadow provides wild strawberries for a snack or

dessert.) The route now continues as a narrow pathway bordered by bluets. Slab around the steep hillside. Cross a rock slide in which the builders of this
trail have done an excellent job of smoothing the way
for you.

1.6 The trail makes a couple of quick, short switchbacks.

1.7 Cross a second rock field and ascend via
switchbacks.

1.8 The route levels out and then gradually descends
into an evergreen forest.

2 Come into a small meadow that also provides a couple of vistas and a few nice, dry campsites. Enter a
hemlock forest and ascend.

2.3 Leave the evergreens behind and gradually descend
through a hardwood forest.

2.7 Rhododendron closes in on the pathway.

2.8 Arrive at the Parkway in Haywood Gap, BRP mile
426.5. The Mountains to Sea Trail crosses the Parkway and continues via the Haywood Gap Trail [FS
142].

Mile 431. Richland Balsam Self-Guiding Trail
[BRP 121]

Length: 1.4 miles, round-trip

Difficulty: moderate

Here is a chance to observe a forest in transition.
Fraser fir was once the dominant tree on this lofty peak.
Sadly, perhaps weakened by acid rain and the balsam
woolly aphid, these stately giants are crashing to the forest
floor. Some scientists estimate 80 percent of the Fraser fir
along this portion of the Parkway have succumbed. Plants
(such as certain mosses) that depended on the moist conditions the firs provided are dying and being replaced by
shrubs and briers.

A brochure, keyed to numbered stations on the trail,
is available at the beginning of the route (or from a
ranger). It describes plants and trees and discusses the effects of the change in the forest.

A walk along the Richland Balsam Self-Guiding
Trail may raise many questions in your mind. Is this a
natural process taking place? Could it have been pre-
vented? Will the Fraser firs eventually reestablish themselves? If not, what type of environment will nature now
provide?

.0   Begin on a paved trail at the southern end of the Haywood-Jackson Overlook and ascend through an amazingly thick undergrowth.

.1   Just after the pavement ends, arrive at a bench.

.15 At the loop-trail intersection, bear right and ascend a little more steeply.

.2   Another bench; bluets line the trail.

.3   Another bench; moss is thick and fiddleheads appear in May.

.4   Arrive at a bench with a limited view to the west. Begin to walk on a narrow ridge line as the trail ascends a little more gradually.

.5   Yet another bench; the trail begins its final climb.

.6   Arrive at a bench on the 6,292-foot summit of Richland Balsam. Breath deeply and enjoy the wonderful fragrance provided by the fir trees. You will soon pass another bench and begin to descend. The rocks, mosses, and evergreens along the route may remind you of trails in the mountains of Maine.

.75 Bench. Rhododendron grows well next to the trail.

.1   A break in the vegetation permits a slight view to the east.

1.1 A bench overlooking the BRP. The trail passes through an evergreen tunnel and makes a short rise.

1.2 Come to a bench with a wonderful view to the east. Descend once more.

1.3 Return to the loop-trail intersection. Bear right.

1.4 Arrive back at the overlook.

Mile 451.2. Waterrock Knob Trail [BRP 122]

Length: .55 mile, one way

Difficulty: moderately strenuous

Very highly recommended

While the view from the parking area is breathtaking, it will pale in comparison to the exhilaration of ascending the Waterrock Knob Trail. Every step upward reveals a new vista or perspective overlooking the expanse of Pisgah National Forest. Ridge lines rise and fall far into the distance, unspoiled by any signs of human activity. Hiking up the strenuous pathway, you will smell – almost taste – the rich aroma of red spruce and Fraser fir with each breath.

An additional attraction of the Waterrock Knob Trail is that it attains the highest elevation of all of the BRP trails. The summit is higher than the surrounding ground, giving you a free and soaring feeling. The knob is the joining point of the Plott Balsam and Great Balsam ranges.

Don't miss this one!

.0 Follow the paved trail steeply uphill.

.1 Pass by a bench.

.15 Come to a second bench and a set of steps overlooking the BRP. The pavement ends soon at a vista to the south and east.

.3 Pass by a spring gushing from under a rock.

.35 Come to a bench with a view to the west. The trail now becomes eroded and steeper.

.45 Pass by a rock facing and switch back to the right on a set of steps.

.55 Arrive at the 6,400-foot summit of Waterrock Knob. Views to the southeast are of the Cowee and Nantahala mountains and to the northeast of the Newfound Mountains.

Mile 458.2. The 9-mile-long Heintooga Spur Road provides access from the Parkway to a southeastern corner of the Great Smoky Mountains National Park. An access trail leading to a network of the park's trails, most notably the Cataloochee Divide, Rough Fork, and Polls Gap trails, is 6.5 miles out the spur road. About 2 miles further is the national park's Balsam Mountain campground (8.6 miles from the BRP). A picnic area is .4 mile beyond the campground.

Two trails emanate from the picnic area. The Flat Rock Creek Falls Trail winds for 2.5 miles through a spruce and birch forest. It passes by Flat Rock Creek Falls and ends at a point on the spur road 3.1 miles from the picnic area. The self-guiding Balsam Mountain Nature Trail (.6 mile) connects the picnic area with the campground.

Mile 469.1. Arrive at US RT 441 and the southern terminus of the Blue Ridge Parkway. The Great Smoky Mountains National Park Oconaluftee Visitor Center is located on US RT 411. The Great Smokies, of course, offer a large network of hiking and walking trails.

More information on the Great Smoky Mountains National Park may be obtained by contacting:

Superintendent
Great Smoky Mountains National Park
Gatlinburg, TN 37738

There is a wide variety of guides to the trails of the Great
Smoky Mountains National Park. Probably the most
comprehensive is the *Hiker's Guide to the Smokies*, by
Dick Murlless and Constance Stallings.

Appendixes

Appendix A. Mileage Log and
Features of the Blue Ridge Parkway

.0   Rockfish Gap. US RT 250 and I-64. Tourist infor-
        mation center, motels, and restaurants located just
        off BRP. Access to Waynesboro (4 miles) and Char-
        lottesville (16 miles). Appalachian Trail.

.2   Afton Overlook.

1.5   Rockfish Valley Overlook.

2.2   Access to VA RT 610.

2.9   Shenandoah Valley Overlook.

4.4   Access to VA RT 610.

5.9   Humpback Rocks Visitor Center. Water, rest
        rooms. Mountain Farm Trail [BRP 1].

6   Humpback Gap parking area. Humpback Rocks
        and Mountain Trail [BRP 2] and Appalachian Trail.

8.4   Humpback Rocks picnic area. Water, rest rooms.
        Blue-blazed side trail [BRP 3] to the Appalachian
        Trail and Cotoctin Trail [BRP 4].

8.8   Greenstone Overlook. Greenstone Trail [BRP 5].

9.2   Laurel Springs Gap.

9.6   Dripping Rock parking area. Appalachian Trail.

10.4   Rockpoint Overlook.

10.7   Raven's Roost Overlook. Picnic table.

11.7   Hickory Spring parking area.

13.1   Three Ridges Overlook. Picnic table. Appalachian
        Trail.

13.7	Reeds Gap. VA RT 664 with access to VA RT 814 and US RT 29. Appalachian Trail.
15.4	Love Gap.
16	VA RT 814 and access to Massie's Mill.
17.6	Priest Overlook. Picnic table. The Priest Overlook Trail [BRP 6].
18.5	White Rock Gap. White Rock Falls Trail [BRP 7] and White Rock Gap Trail [FS 480].
19	20 Minute Cliff Overlook. Picnic table.
20	The Slacks Overlook. Slacks Overlook Trail [FS 480A].
22	Bald Mountain parking area. FSR 162 to Bald Mountain. Torry Ridge Trail [FS 507], Slacks Overlook Trail [FS 480A], and Bald Mountain Trail [FS 500E].
23	Fork Mountain Overlook.
23.4	Elevation 3,333.7 feet, highest point on the BRP north of the James River.
25.6	Spy Run Gap and VA RT 686.
26.3	Big Spy Overlook. Big Spy Mountain Overlook Trail [BRP 8].
27.2	Tye River Gap and VA RT 56. Access to Montebello and Vesuvius.
29	Whetstone Ridge. Ranger office, restaurant, gift shop, and gas station. Whetstone Ridge Trail [FS 523]. VA RT 603.
31.4	Still-House Hollow parking area. Picnic table and water fountain.
31.9	VA RT 686.
33	Yankee Fence Exhibit.
34.4	Yankee Horse parking area. Picnic table. Yankee Horse Overlook Trail [BRP 9].
34.8	Yankee Horse Ridge.
37.4	Irish Gap.
37.5	VA RT 605. Access to Irish Creek, Buena Vista, Amherst, and US RT 60.
38.8	Boston Knob parking area. Picnic table. Boston Knob Trail [BRP 10].
39.9	Clark Cemetery Road.
40	Clarks Gap.
42.2	Irish Creek Valley parking area.
44.4	Whites Gap Overlook. Picnic table.
44.9	Chimney Rock parking area.
45.6	Humphries Gap and US RT 60. Access to Buena Vista (5 miles) and Amherst.

45.7	Buena Vista Overlook.
47.5	Indian Gap parking area. Indian Gap Trail [BRP 11].
48.9	Licklog Spring Gap.
49.3	House Mountain Overlook.
50.5	Robinson Gap.
51.5	Appalachian Trail crossing and parking area.
52.8	Bluff Mountain Overlook.
53.1	Bluff Mountain Tunnel.
53.6	Rice Mountain Overlook.
54.1	Brown's Creek.
55.1	White Oak Flats Overlook. Picnic table. White Oak Flats Trail [BRP 12].
55.2	Otter Creek.
55.9	Dancing Creek Overlook. Picnic table.
56.6	Otter Creek Bridge #1.
57.6	Upper Otter Creek Overlook.
58.2	Otter Creek Flats Overlook. Picnic table.
58.5	Otter Creek Bridge #2.
59.1	Otter Creek Bridge #3.
59.6	Otter Creek Bridge #4.
59.7	Otter Creek Overlook.
59.8	Otter Creek Bridge #5.
60.4	The Riffles Overlook.
60.8	Otter Creek campground, restaurant, gift shop, rest rooms, and water. Otter Creek Trail [BRP 13].
61	Otter Creek Bridge #6.
61.4	Terrapin Hill Overlook and VA RT 130. Access to US RT 501 and Glasgow (8 miles), Natural Bridge (15 miles), and Lynchburg (22 miles).
61.5	Otter Creek Bridge #7.
61.6	Otter Creek Bridge #8.
62.1	Otter Creek Bridge #9.
62.5	Lower Otter Creek Overlook. Picnic table.
63.1	Otter Lake Overlook. Otter Lake Trail [BRP 14].
63.2	Elevation 646.4 feet, lowest on the Parkway.
63.6	James River Overlook and Visitor Center. Trail of Trees Self-Guiding Trail [BRP 15] and James River Self-Guiding Trail [BRP 16].
63.7	James River Bridge. US RT 501. Access to Glasgow (9 miles), Natural Bridge (15 miles), and Lynchburg (22 miles).
66.3	Ranger office.
66.6	Falling Rock Creek.
67.1	Falling Rock Creek.
67.9	Billy's Branch.

68.7   Bellamy Creek.

69.1   James River Overlook. Picnic table. FSR 951.

71   Petites Gap. Cave Mountain Lake Recreation Area 8 miles via FSR 35. Glenwood Horse Trail.

71.1   Appalachian Trail.

72.6   Terrapin Mountain parking area.

74.7   Thunder Ridge Overlook. Picnic table. Thunder Ridge Trail [BRP 17] and Appalachian Trail.

74.9   Hunting Creek Trail [FS 3].

75.2   Arnold Valley parking area.

76.3   Appalachian Trail.

76.5   Apple Orchard parking area.

76.7   Highest point on BRP in Virginia. Elevation 3,950 feet.

78.4   FSR 812. Access to Forest Service's North Creek campground. Appalachian Trail.

78.7   Sunset Field Overlook. Apple Orchard Falls Trail [BRP 18 and FS 17].

79.7   Onion Mountain Overlook. Picnic table. Onion Mountain Loop Trail [BRP 19].

79.9   Black Rock Hill parking area.

80.5   FSR 190. Glenwood Horse Trail.

81.9   Headforemost parking area.

83.1   Fallingwater Cascades parking area. Fallingwater Cascades Trail [BRP 20].

83.5   Flat Top Trail [BRP 21] and parking area.

85.7   Peaks of Otter Lodge. Abbot Lake Loop Trail [BRP 22] and Peaks of Otter Picnic Area Trail [BRP 23].

85.9   Peaks of Otter Visitor Center and Ranger Office. Rest rooms and water. Elk Run Self-Guiding Trail [BRP 24], Johnson Farm Loop Trail [BRP 25], and Harkening Hill Trail [BRP 26].

86   VA RT 43 with access to Bedford, Peaks of Otter campground, camp store, rest rooms, water, bus station for bus to summit of Sharp Top, and picnic area. Sharp Top Trail [BRP 27].

89.1   Powell's Gap. VA RT 618 and access to Forest Service's North Creek campground.

89.4   Upper Goose Creek parking area.

90   Porter's Mountain Overlook.

90.9   Bear Wallow Gap and Porter's Mountain Overlook. VA RT 695 to Montvale and VA RT 43 to Buchanan. Appalachian Trail.

91.8   Mills Gap parking area. Picnic table.

92.1	Purgatory Mountain parking area.
92.5	Sharp Top parking area. Appalachian Trail.
93.1	Bobblet's Gap Overlook. Appalachian Trail. Glenwood Horse Trail.
95.2	Pine Tree Overlook.
95.3	Harveys Knob Overlook. Appalachian Trail.
95.9	Montvale Overlook. Appalachian Trail.
96	Spec Mine Trail [FS 28].
96.2	Iron Mine Hollow parking area.
97	Taylor Mountain Overlook. Appalachian Trail.
97.7	Black Horse Gap. Appalachian Trail.
99.6	The Great Valley Overlook. Picnic table.
100.9	The Quarry Parking Overlook.
101.5	Curry Gap. FSR 191, with access to US RT 460.
105.8	US RT 460. Access to Roanoke (9 miles) and Bedford (21 miles).
106.9	N & W Railroad Overlook.
107	Coyner Mountain Overlook.
107.6	Glade Creek.
109.8	Read Mountain Overlook.
110.6	Stewarts Knob Overlook. Stewarts Knob Trail [BRP 28] and Roanoke Valley Horse Trail [BRP 29].
112	Ranger office. Roanoke Valley Horse Trail [BRP 30].
112.2	VA RT 24. Food, gas, lodging, and phone located just off BRP. Access to Roanoke (5 miles), Vinton (2 miles), and Stewartsville (4 miles).
112.9	Roanoke Basin Overlook.
114.7	Roanoke River Bridge.
114.9	Roanoke River Overlook. Roanoke River Self-Guiding Trail [BRP 31].
115.1	Pine Mountain parking area.
116.4	Roanoke Valley Horse Trail [BRP 32].
118	Roanoke Valley Horse Trail [BRP 33].
120.4	Roanoke Mountain Loop Road. Roanoke Mountain Summit Trail [BRP 34].
120.5	Mill Mountain Spur Road.
.1	Gum Spring Overlook.
1.1	Chestnut Ridge Overlook. Chestnut Ridge Trail [BRP 35].
1.3	Roanoke Mountain campground.
2.5	End BRP jurisdiction. Left to Mill Mountain Park, Playhouse, and Zoo. Right on J. B. Fishburn Parkway to city of Roanoke (2 miles).

121.4	US RT 220. Food, gas, lodging, and phone located just off BRP. Access to Roanoke (5 miles) and Rocky Mount (21 miles).
123.2	Buck Spring Overlook. Buck Mountain Trail [BRP 36].
126.6	Masons Knob Overlook.
128.7	Metz Run Overlook.
129.3	Poages Mill Overlook.
129.6	Roanoke Valley Overlook. Water fountain.
129.9	Lost Mountain Overlook.
132.9	Slings Gap Overlook.
133.6	Bull Run Knob Overlook.
134.9	Poor Mountain Overlook.
135.9	US RT 221. Food, gas, and phone located just off BRP. Access to Roanoke (19 miles). Also access to VA RT 602.
139	Cahas Knob Overlook.
143.9	Devils Backbone Overlook.
144.8	Pine Spur Overlook.
145.7	VA RT 791.
146.4	VA RT 642.
148.1	VA RT 641.
148.4	VA RT 663.
149.1	VA RT 640.
150.5	VA RT 639 and VA RT 221, with access to Roanoke.
150.9	VA RT 681 and VA RT 640.
152	VA RT 888.
153.6	VA RT 993.
154.1	Smart View Overlook.
154.5	Smart View picnic area. Rest rooms and water fountains. Smart View Loop Trail [BRP 37].
155.3	VA RT 793. Access to Endicott (4 miles) and VA RT 680.
156.3	VA RT 635.
157.6	Shortt's Knob Overlook.
158.9	VA RT 637. Access to Floyd.
159.3	VA RT 860. Access to Floyd, Endicott, and Ferrum.
161.2	VA RT 708.
162.1	VA RT 711.
162.4	Rakes Mill Pond Overlook [BRP 38].
162.9	VA RT 710.
163.2	VA RT 797.
163.5	VA RT 709.
165.3	Tuggle Gap. VA RT 8. Food, gas, and lodging

	located just off BRP. Access to Floyd (6 miles) and Stuart (21 miles).
167.1	Rocky Knob Recreation Area. Ranger office, campground, rest rooms, and water. Rock Castle Gorge Trail [BRP 39] (includes the Hardwood Cove Self-Guiding Nature Trail).
168	Saddle Overlook.
168.8	Rock Castle Gorge Overlook.
169	Rocky Knob picnic area, ranger office, rest rooms, and water fountains. Rocky Knob Picnic Loop Trail [BRP 40], Woodland Trail [BRP 41], and Black Ridge Trail [BRP 42].
169.1	12 O'Clock Knob Overlook.
170.4	VA RT 720.
171.3	VA RT 720.
171.7	VA RT 729.
174	Rock Castle Gap. VA RT 799 and access to Willis and Hubbards Mill.
174.1	VA RT 758 and access to Rocky Knob Cabins and Meadows of Dan.
174.2	VA RT 758 and VA RT 778.
174.7	VA RT 778.
175.9	VA RT 603.
176.2	Mabry Mill. Coffee shop, gift shop, rest rooms, and phone. Mountain Industry Trail [BRP 43].
176.3	VA RT 603.
177.7	Meadows of Dan. US RT 58. Food, gas, lodging, and phone located just off BRP. Access to Stuart (16 miles) and Hillsville (21 miles).
178.8	VA RT 744.
179.2	Round Meadow Overlook. Round Meadow Creek Trail [BRP 44].
179.4	Round Meadow Creek.
180.1	VA RT 600.
180.5	VA RT 634. Gas, mountain crafts, and antiques located just off BRP.
183.4	Pinnacles of Dan, elevation 2,875 feet.
183.9	VA RT 614 and access to Mount Airy, North Carolina.
186.7	VA RT 631 and access to Laurel Fork.
187.7	VA RT 639.
188.8	Groundhog Mountain picnic area. Rest rooms and water. Groundhog Mountain Picnic Area Observation Tower [BRP 45].

189.1   Pilot Mountain Overlook.
189.2   VA RT 608. Food, gas, lodging, and phone located just off BRP.
189.9   Puckett Cabin parking area. Puckett Cabin Walk [BRP 46].
190.6   VA RT 910.
191.4   VA RT 910.
192.3   VA RT 648.
193.7   VA RT 691. Food, gas, and phone located just off BRP. Access to Hillsville, Virginia, and Mount Airy, North Carolina.
194.7   VA RT 608.
198.4   VA RT 685 with access to VA RT 608.
198.9   VA RT 608.
199.1   VA RT 608.
199.4   Fancy Gap. US RT 52. Ranger office, food, gas, lodging, and phone located just off BRP. Access to Hillsville, Virginia, and Mount Airy, North Carolina.
199.9   VA RT 778.
202.2   VA RT 608.
202.8   Granite Quarry Overlook.
203.9   Piedmont Overlook.
204.8   VA RT 700.
206.3   VA RT 608 with access to VA RT 620, VA RT 97, and VA RT 775.
207.7   VA RT 608.
209.3   Parsons Gap. VA RT 715 and access to Galax.
209.8   VA RT 716.
211.1   VA RT 612 and access to Galax.
213.3   VA RT 612.
215.3   VA RT 799.
215.8   VA RT 89. Access to Galax, Virginia (7 miles), and Mount Airy, North Carolina (22 miles).
216.9   Virginia–North Carolina state line.
217.3   NC RT 18. Access to Sparta (15 miles) and Mount Airy (22 miles).
217.5   Cumberland Knob Visitor Center and picnic area. Rest rooms and water fountains. Gully Creek Trail [BRP 47] and Cumberland Knob Trail [BRP 48].
218.6   Fox Hunter's Paradise Overlook. Fox Hunter's Paradise Trail [BRP 49].
220.4   NC RT 1460.
220.5   NC RT 1461.
221.8   NC RT 1461.

222.8	Pine Creek Bridge #1.
223.1	Pine Creek Bridge #2 and NC RT 1486.
223.8	Pine Creek Bridge #3.
224.1	Pine Creek Bridge #4.
224.2	Pine Creek Bridge #5.
224.8	Pine Creek Bridge #6.
225	Pine Creek Bridge #7.
225.3	Hare Mill Pond and NC RT 1463.
226.3	NC RT 1433.
227.4	Brush Creek Bridge.
227.6	NC RT 1433 and NC RT 1472.
228.1	Little Glade Bridge.
229.2	NC RT 1468 and Little Glade Bridge.
229.7	US RT 21 and access to Sparta (7 miles) and Elkin (21 miles).
229.9	Little Glade Bridge.
230.1	Little Glade Mill Pond Overlook. Picnic tables. Little Glade Mill Pond Trail [BRP 50].
230.5	Little Glade Bridge.
230.9	NC RT 1108 and NC RT 1111 and access to Sparta.
231.5	NC RT 1109.
231.8	NC RT 1110.
232.5	Stone Mountain Overlook.
233.7	Bullhead Mountain Overlook.
234	Bullhead Gap. NC RT 1115.
235	Mahogany Rock Overlook.
235.7	Devils Garden Overlook.
236.9	Air Bellows Gap Overlook.
238.5	Brinegar Cabin Overlook. Brinegar Cabin Walk [BRP 51], Cedar Ridge Trail [BRP 52], and Bluff Mountain Trail [BRP 53].
239.3	Doughton Park campground.
241	Doughton Park coffee shop, gas station, rest rooms, and picnic area. Fodder Stack Trail [BRP 54], Wildcat Rocks Trail [BRP 55], and Bluff Ridge Trail [BRP 56].
242	Ice Rock.
242.4	Alligator Back Overlook.
243.4	Bluff Mountain Overlook.
243.7	Grassy Gap Fire Road (gated). Basin Creek Trail [BRP 57] and Grassy Gap Fire Road [BRP 58].
244.7	Basin Cove Overlook. Flat Rock Ridge Trail [BRP 59].
245.5	Ranger office.
246.1	NC RT 1143, with access to NC RT 18.

246.9   NC RT 1144.

247.2   NC RT 1175 (Miller's Campground Road).

248   NC RT 18. Food, gas, and lodging located just off BRP. Access to Laurel Springs (2 miles) and North Wilkesboro (24 miles).

248.9   Laurel Fork Viaduct.

249.3   NC RT 1613.

250   NC RT 1615.

250.8   NC RT 1617 and NC RT 1620.

251.5   Alder Gap.

252.4   NC RT 1619.

252.8   Sheets Gap Overlook and NC RT 1568.

255.2   NC RT 1567 and NC RT 1622.

256   NC RT 1624.

256.5   NC RT 1628.

256.9   NC RT 1628 and access to coffee shop, gift shop, and gas station.

257.7   NC RT 1628 and NC RT 1630.

258.7   Old NC RT 16 and Northwest Trading Post (gift shop).

259.2   NC RT 1633.

259.8   NC RT 1634.

260.3   Jumpinoff Rocks parking area. Jumpinoff Rocks Trail [BRP 60].

261.2   Horse Gap. NC RT 16 and access to West Jefferson (12 miles) and North Wilkesboro (22 miles).

262.2   NC RT 1165 and NC RT 1360.

264.4   The Lump Overlook. The Lump Trail [BRP 61].

265.1   Calloway Gap and NC RT 1360.

266.8   Mount Jefferson Overlook.

267.6   NC RT 1167.

267.8   Betsey's Rock Falls Overlook.

268   NC RT 1166.

269.7   NC RT 1365.

269.8   NC RT 1168.

270.2   Lewis Fork Overlook.

271.9   Cascades Overlook and picnic area. Cascades Trail [BRP 62].

272.5   Tompkins Knob parking area. Tompkins Knob Trail [BRP 63].

274.3   Elk Mountain Overlook.

276.4   Deep Gap. US RT 421 and access to Boone (12 miles) and North Wilkesboro (26 miles).

277.3   Stoney Fork Valley Overlook.

277.9   Osborne Mountain View Overlook.

278.3	Carroll Gap Overlook.
280.9	US RT 421 and US RT 221. Access to Deep Gap (4 miles) and Boone (7 miles).
281.4	Grandview Overlook.
285.1	Boone's Trace Overlook.
285.5	Access road to Boone.
286.4	Goshen Creek Bridge.
288.1	Public road crossing.
289.5	Raven Rocks Overlook.
289.8	Yadkin Valley Overlook.
290.4	Thunder Hill Overlook.
290.7	Green Hill Road.
291.8	US RT 321 and US RT 221. Access to Boone (7 miles) and Blowing Rock (2 miles).
293.5	Moses H. Cone Overlook.
294	Moses H. Cone Manor House. Water and rest rooms. Rich Mountain Carriage Trail [BRP 64], Flat Top Mountain Carriage Trail [BRP 65], Watkins Carriage Road [BRP 66], Black Bottom Carriage Road [BRP 67], Bass Lake Carriage Road [BRP 68], Deer Park Carriage Road [BRP 69], The Maze [BRP 70], Apple Barn Connector Road [BRP 71], Duncan Carriage Road [BRP 72], Rock Creek Bridge Carriage Road [BRP 73], and Figure Eight Trail [BRP 74].
294.6	Sandy Flat Gap. US RT 221 and access to ranger office and Blowing Rock (2 miles). Also access to Shulls Mill Road and Flannery Fork Road. Trout Lake Trail [BRP 75] and Shulls Mill Road extension of the Rich Mountain Carriage Trail [BRP 76].
295.4	Sims Creek Viaduct. Sims Creek Trail [BRP 77].
295.9	Sims Pond Overlook. Green Knob Trail [BRP 78].
296.5	Price Memorial Park picnic area. Boone Fork Trail [BRP 79].
296.7	Price Lake Overlook.
296.9	Price Memorial Park campground. Price Lake Loop Trail [BRP 80].
298.6	Holloway Mountain Road and access to US RT 221.
299	Cold Prong Pond Overlook. Cold Prong Pond Loop Trail [BRP 81] and Tanawha Trail.
299.7	View of Calloway Peak. Upper Boone Fork Trail [BRP 82].
300	Boone Fork parking area. Tanawha Trail.
300.6	Green Mountain Overlook.

301.8	Pilot Ridge Overlook.
302.1	View of Wilson Creek Valley.
302.4	Raven Rocks Overlook. Tanawha Trail.
302.9	Rough Ridge parking area. Tanawha Trail.
303.7	Wilson Creek Overlook. Tanawha Trail.
303.9	Yonahlossee Overlook.
304.4	Linn Cove Information Center. Tanawha Trail (the first .15 mile has handicap access).
304.8	Stack Rock parking area. Tanawha Trail.
305.1	US RT 221 and access to Blowing Rock and Grandfather Mountain Entrance Station and trails.
305.2	Beacon Heights parking area. Tanawha Trail and Beacon Heights Trail [BRP 83].
306.6	Grandfather Mountain Overlook.
307.4	Grandmother parking area.
307.6	Parking area.
307.9	NC RT 1511 and access to Linville (2 miles).
308.2	Flat Rock parking area. Flat Rock Self-Guiding Loop Trail [BRP 84].
310	Lost Cove Cliffs Overlook.
310.3	NC RT 1519.
311.2	NC RT 1518.
312.2	NC RT 181 and access to Pineola (2 miles) and Morganton (32 miles).
312.9	Clark Road.
313.2	Rose Road.
314.2	Barrier Road.
314.6	Shuffler Road.
315.5	Camp Creek Overlook. Camp Creek Trail [BRP 85].
316.4	Linville Falls Recreation Area. Book shop and information center, campground, picnic area, rest rooms, and water. Linville Falls Trail [BRP 86], Linville Gorge Trail [BRP 87], Plunge Basin Overlook Trail [BRP 88], and Duggers Creek Loop Trail [BRP 89].
316.5	Linville River parking area. Linville River Bridge Trail [BRP 90].
316.6	Linville River Bridge.
317.5	US RT 221 and access to Spruce Pine (12 miles) and Linville Falls community (1 mile).
318.4	North Toe Valley Overlook.
319.8	Humpback Mountain Viaduct.

320.8	Chestoa View parking area. Chestoa View Loop Trail [BRP 91].
323	Bear Den Overlook.
324.7	Bear Den Road.
325.9	Heffner Gap Overlook.
327.3	North Cove Overlook.
327.5	Public road crossing. Access to Spruce Pine (5 miles).
328.3	Apple Orchard Road.
328.6	The Loops Overlook.
329.5	Swafford Gap. NC RT 1113.
329.8	Table Rock Overlook.
330.9	Gillespie Gap. NC RT 226. North Carolina Museum of Minerals and ranger office located just off BRP. Access to Spruce Pine (6 miles), Marion (14 miles), and NC RT 226A and Little Switzerland (3 miles).
333.4	Little Switzerland Tunnel.
333.9	Public road access.
336.3	Public road access.
336.8	Wildacres Tunnel.
337.2	Deer Lick Gap Overlook.
338.8	Three Knobs Overlook.
339.5	Crabtree Meadows. Campground, camp store, restaurant, gift shop, and gas station. Crabtree Falls Loop Trail [BRP 92].
340.2	Crabtree Meadows picnic area. Rest rooms and water fountains.
342.1	Victor Road.
342.2	Black Mountains Overlook.
344.1	Buck Creek Gap Overlook and NC RT 80. Access to Micaville (14 miles) and Marion (14 miles). Woods Mountain Trail Access Trail [BRP 93].
344.5	Twin Tunnel.
344.7	Twin Tunnel.
345.3	Singecat Ridge Overlook.
347.2	Big Laurel Mountain Viaduct.
347.6	Big Laurel Gap and FSR 482.
347.9	Hewat Overlook.
348.8	Curtis Valley Overlook.
349	Rough Ridge Tunnel.
349.2	Licklog Ridge Overlook.
349.9	Mount Mitchell Overlook.
350.4	Green Knob Overlook. Lost Cove Ridge Trail

	[FS 182] and Snooks Nose Trail [FS 211].
351.9	Deep Gap and FSR 472. Deep Gap Trail [FS 210].
352.4	Parking area.
354.8	Toe River Gap.
355	Bald Knob Ridge Trail [FS 186].
355.3	Black Mountain Gap. Ridge Junction Overlook and NC RT 128. Access to Mount Mitchell State Park.
358.5	Highest point on BRP north of Asheville. Elevation 5,676.5 feet.
359.8	Balsam Gap parking area. Big Butt Trail [FS 161].
361.2	Glassmine Falls Overlook. Glassmine Falls Trail [BRP 94].
363.4	Greybeard Mountain Overlook.
364.1	Craggy Dome Overlook. Craggy Pinnacle Trail [BRP 95].
364.4	Craggy Pinnacle Tunnel.
364.6	Craggy Gardens Visitor Center. Douglas Falls Trail [FS 162] and Craggy Gardens Self-Guiding Trail [BRP 96].
365.5	Craggy Flats Tunnel.
367.7	Bee Tree Gap and Craggy Gardens picnic area.
372.1	Lanes' Pinnacle Overlook.
373.8	Bull Creek Valley Overlook. Picnic table.
374.4	Tanbark Ridge Tunnel. Mountains to Sea Access Trail [BRP 97] (Rattlesnake Lodge Trail).
375.2	Bull Gap.
375.7	NC RT 694 and access to Weaverville (8 miles).
376.7	Tanbark Ridge Overlook.
377.4	Craven Gap and NC RT 694. Access to Asheville (7 miles). 380 Haw Creek Valley Overlook.
382	The Folk Art Center. Water and rest rooms.
382.3	Ranger office.
382.4	US RT 70. Access to Asheville (5 miles) and Black Mountain (9 miles).
383.5	Swannanoa River.
384.7	US RT 74. Access to Asheville (5 miles) and Bat Cave (17 miles).
388.8	US RT 25. Access to Asheville (5 miles) and Henderson (16 miles).
390.9	Dingle Creek.
393.5	French Broad River.
393.6	NC RT 191 and access to Asheville (9 miles). Shut-In Trail [BRP 98].

393.8 French Broad Overlook.

396.4 Walnut Cove Overlook. Shut-In Trail [BRP 99].

397.1 Grassy Knob Tunnel.

397.3 Sleepy Gap Overlook. Picnic table. Grassy Knob and Sleepy Gap Trail [FS 338 and FS 339] and Shut-In Trail [BRP 100].

398.3 Chestnut Cove Overlook. Shut-In Trail [BRP 101].

399.1 Pine Mountain Tunnel. Longest tunnel on the BRP (1,320 feet).

399.7 Bad Fork Valley Overlook.

400.3 Bent Creek Gap and FSR 479. Shut-In Trail [BRP 102].

400.9 Ferrin Knob Tunnel.

401.1 Wash Creek Valley Overlook.

401.3 Ferrin Knob Tunnel #1.

401.5 Ferrin Knob Tunnel #2.

401.7 Beaver Dam Gap Overlook. Shut-In Trail [BRP 103].

402.6 Stoney Bald Overlook. Shut-In Trail [BRP 104].

403 Young Pisgah Ridge Tunnel.

403.6 Big Ridge Overlook. Shut-In Trail [BRP 105].

404 Fork Mountain Tunnel.

404.2 Hominy Valley Overlook.

404.5 Mills Valley Overlook. Shut-In Trail [BRP 106].

405.5 Elk Pasture Gap. Shut-In Trail [BRP 107].

406.9 Little Pisgah Tunnel.

407.3 Buck Spring Tunnel.

407.6 Mount Pisgah parking area. Mount Pisgah Trail [BRP 108] and Mount Pisgah Trailhead to Picnic Area Connector Trail [BRP 109].

407.7 Buck Spring Gap Overlook. Buck Spring Gap Overlook to the Shut-In Trailhead [BRP 110].

407.8 Mount Pisgah picnic area. Picnic Area Loop Trail [BRP 111] and Picnic Area to Mount Pisgah Campground Connector Trail [BRP 112].

408.3 Parking area.

408.6 Mount Pisgah Inn, restaurant, gift shop, camp store, and gas station. Buck Spring Trail (BRP Portion) [BRP 113] and Buck Spring Trail (Forest Service Portion) [FS 104].

408.8 Mount Pisgah campground. Frying Pan Mountain Trail [BRP 114].

409.3 Funnel Top Overlook.

409.6 Frying Pan Gap.

410.1   Frying Pan Tunnel.

410.3   The Pink Beds Overlook.

411   The Cradle of Forestry Overlook.

411.8   Cold Mountain Overlook.

411.9   US RT 276 and access to Waynesville (22 miles) and Brevard (18 miles).

412.2   Wagon Road Gap Overlook.

413.2   Pounding Mill Overlook.

415.7   Cherry Cove Overlook.

415.9   Case Camp Ridge Trail [FS 119].

416.3   Log Hollow Overlook.

417   Looking Glass Rock Overlook. East Fork Access Trail [BRP 115].

417.9   Yellowstone Falls.

418.3   East Fork Overlook.

418.8   Graveyard Fields Overlook. Graveyard Fields Loop Trail [BRP 116].

419.4   John Rock Overlook. John Rock Trail [BRP 117].

420.2   Balsam Spring Gap. FSR 816.

421.1   Old Silver Mine.

421.2   Art Loeb Trail [FS 146].

421.7   Fetterbush Overlook.

422.1   Devil's Courthouse Tunnel.

422.4   Devil's Courthouse Overlook. Devil's Courthouse Trail [BRP 118].

422.8   Mount Hardy Overlook.

423.2   Beech Gap and NC RT 215. Access to Waynesville (23 miles) and Rosman (18 miles).

423.5   Courthouse Valley Overlook.

424.4   Herrin parking area.

424.8   Wolf Mountain Overlook.

425.4   Rough Butt Bald Overlook. Mountains to Sea Trail [BRP 119] Access.

426.5   Haywood Gap Trail [FS 142].

427.6   Bear Pen Gap parking area. Bear Pen Gap Trail [BRP 120].

427.8   Spot Knob Overlook.

428   Caney Fork Overlook.

428.5   Beartrap Gap Overlook.

430.4   Beartrail Ridge parking area.

430.7   Cowee Mountain Overlook.

431   Haywood-Jackson Overlook. Richland Balsam Self-Guiding Trail [BRP 121].

431.4   Richland Balsam Overlook. Highest point on the BRP. Elevation 6,053 feet.

432.7	Lone Bald Overlook.
433.3	Roy Taylor Forest Overlook.
435.3	Double Top Mountain Overlook.
435.7	Licklog Gap Overlook.
436.8	Grassy Ridge Mine Overlook.
438.9	Steestachee Bald Overlook.
439.4	Cove Field Ridge Overlook.
439.7	Pinnacle Ridge Tunnel.
440	Saunook Overlook.
440.9	Waynesville Overlook.
441.4	Standing Rock Overlook.
441.9	Rabb Knob Overlook.
442.2	Balsam Gap Overlook.
442.8	Ranger office.
443.1	Balsam Gap. US RT 74 and US RT 23. Access to Waynesville (8 miles) and Sylva (12 miles).
444.6	The Orchards Overlook.
445.2	Mount Lynn Lowry Overlook.
446	Woodfin Valley Overlook.
446.7	Woodfin Cascades Overlook.
448.1	Wesner Bald Overlook.
448.5	Scott Creek Overlook.
449	Fork Ridge Overlook.
450.2	Yellow Face Overlook.
451.2	Waterrock Knob Overlook. Rest rooms and water. Waterrock Knob Trail [BRP 122].
452.1	Cranberry Ridge Overlook.
452.3	Woolyback Overlook.
453.4	Hornbuckle Valley Overlook.
454.4	Thunderstruck Ridge Overlook.
455.1	Fed Cove Overlook.
455.5	Soco Gap Overlook.
455.7	Soco Gap and US RT 19. Access to Dellwood (8 miles) and Cherokee (12 miles).
456.2	Jonathan Creek Overlook.
457.7	Enter Cherokee Indian Reservation.
457.9	Plott Balsam Overlook.
458.2	Heintooga Spur Road.
	1.3 Mile High Overlook.
	1.4 Maggie Valley Overlook.
	2.3 Lake Junaluska Overlook.
	3.3 Horsetrough parking area.
	3.6 Black Camp Gap parking area and boundary of the Great Smoky Mountains National Park.

3.9	Parking overlook.
4.8	Parking overlook.
6.2	Parking overlook.
8.4	Balsam Mountain campground.
8.9	Heintooga Ridge picnic area.
9	Parking area and end of paved road. One-way motor nature road (gravel).
458.8	Lickstone Ridge Tunnel.
458.9	Lickstone Overlook.
459.3	Bunches Bald Tunnel.
459.5	Bunches Bald Overlook.
460.8	Jenkins Ridge Overlook.
461.2	Big Witch Tunnel.
461.6	Indian Road and Bunches Creek Road.
461.9	Big Witch Overlook.
462.3	Barnett Fire Tower Road.
463.9	Thomas Divide Overlook.
465.6	Rattlesnake Mountain Tunnel.
466.2	Sherill Cove Tunnel.
467.4	Ballhoot Scar Overlook.
467.9	Raven Fork Overlook.
468.4	Oconaluftee Overlook.
469.1	End of the Blue Ridge Parkway. US RT 441 and access to Cherokee, North Carolina (2 miles), and Gatlinburg, Tennessee (29 miles).

Appendix B. Blue Ridge Parkway Offices

Blue Ridge Parkway Central Office

The Blue Ridge Parkway
200 BB & T Building
One Pack Square
Asheville, NC 28801
704-298-0398

Blue Ridge Parkway Ranger Offices

The ranger offices are usually better equipped to supply you with detailed information about trails and conditions in their own districts than the central BRP office in Asheville. However, these offices are not staffed twenty-four hours a day. If you find an office closed in an emergency, you should call PARKWATCH at 800-727-5928.

JAMES RIVER DISTRICT (Miles 0–76.5)

Mile 29	Montebello Office RFD 1, Box 17 Vesuvius, VA 24483 703-377-2377
Mile 66.3	Big Island Office P.O. Box 345 Big Island, VA 24525 804-299-5941

PEAKS/VALLEY DISTRICT (Miles 76.5–144.3)

Mile 85.9	Peaks of Otter Office Route 2, Box 163 Bedford, VA 24523 703-586-4357
Mile 112	Vinton Office 2551 Mountain View Road Vinton, VA 24179 703-982-2490

ROCKY KNOB DISTRICT (Miles 144.3–216.9)

Mile 167.1   Rocky Knob Office
Route 1, Box 465
Floyd, VA 24179
703-745-9660

Mile 199.4   Fancy Gap Office
Route 2, Box 3
Fancy Gap, VA 24328
703-728-4511

BLUFFS DISTRICT (Miles 216.9–298.6)

Mile 245.5   Bluffs Office
Route 1, Box 263
Laurel Springs, NC 28644-9714
919-372-8568

Mile 294.4   Sandy Flats Office
Route 1, Box 565
Blowing Rock, NC 28605
704-295-7591

GILLESPIE GAP DISTRICT (Miles 298.6–359.8)

Mile 330.9   Gillespie Gap Office
Route 1, Box 798
Spruce Pine, NC 28777
704-765-6082

ASHEVILLE DISTRICT (Miles 359.8–470)

Mile 382.3   Oteen Office
P.O. Box 9098
Asheville, NC 28815
704-298-0262

Mile 442.8   Balsam Office
P.O. Box 99
Balsam, NC 28707
704-456-9530

Appendix C.
Inns, Lodges, and Cabins on the Blue Ridge Parkway

These facilities are operated by private concessionaires under contract with the Park Service. Contact the particular facility in order to make reservations or obtain detailed information.

Mile 86   Peaks of Otter Lodge (open year round)
           P.O. Box 489
           Bedford, VA 24523
           703-586-1081

Mile 169   Rocky Knob Cabins
           Meadows of Dan, VA 24120
           703-593-3503

Mile 241.1 Bluffs Lodge
           Laurel Springs, NC 28644
           919-372-4499

Mile 408.6 Pisgah Inn
           P.O. Drawer 749
           Waynesville, NC 28786
           704-235-8228

The Blue Ridge Parkway Association publishes a very complete directory of commercial accommodations, services, and attractions within easy driving range of the BRP. The directory is available free of charge at most Parkway facilities or by contacting:

Blue Ridge Parkway Association
P.O. Box 453
Asheville, NC 28802

Appendix D.
Campgrounds on the Blue Ridge Parkway

BRP campgrounds are usually open from May through October. Some sites do stay open year round, but these can change from year to year. Call 704-259-0701 for the most up-to-date information. Camping is permitted only in the designated campgrounds. Drinking water and rest rooms are provided; shower and laundry facilities are not. There are no hookups, but each campground does have a sanitary dumping station. Please remember that camping is prohibited along all of the "official" BRP trails.

Mile 60.9	Otter Creek
Mile 86	Peaks of Otter
Mile 120.4	Roanoke Mountain
Mile 169	Rocky Knob (backcountry camping also available)
Mile 241.1	Doughton Park (backcountry camping also available)
Mile 297.1	Julian Price Memorial Park
Mile 316.4	Linville Falls
Mile 339.5	Crabtree Meadows
Mile 408.6	Mount Pisgah

Appendix E.
Blue Ridge Parkway Roadside Bloom Calendar

This is a general guideline of the common and/or showy plants on the Parkway. There are other flowers on the Parkway not listed here, and blooming times will vary from year to year according to the weather. Usually flowers will appear in Virginia before they do in North Carolina, which is due to Virginia's lower average elevation. Use this guide whenever you can; seeking out and identifying certain plants will no doubt add to your enjoyment of the Parkway.

The plants are organized by blooming time, starting in February. The abbreviation *PA* indicates a picnic area.

This information is supplied courtesy of the National Park Service, Blue Ridge Parkway.

Flower	Peak Bloom	Mile Point or General Location
Skunk Cabbage *Symplocarpus foetidus*	February– March	176.1, 185.8, 217.0
Dandelion *Taraxacum officinale*	February– June	Common along road
Dwarf Iris *Iris verna*	March–April	260.5
Mayapple *Podophyllum peltatum*	March–April	76.2–76.4, 296– 297, 315–317, 320.8, 339.5
Spring Beauty *Claytonia caroliniana*	March–April	Craggy Gardens PA
Birdfoot Violet *Viola pedata*	March–May	147.4, 202, 260.5, 379
Serviceberry-Sarvis *Amelanchier arborea*	March–May	241–242, 294– 297, 308.3, 347.6, 368–370
Silver-Bell Tree *Halesia carolina*	March–May	344.1–355.3
Buttercups *Ranunculus hispidus*	March–June	Common along road
Wild Strawberry *Fragaria virginiana*	March–June	Common along road

Flower	Peak Bloom	Mile Point or General Location
Bloodroot *Sanguinaria canadensis*	April–May	85.6, 191–193, 198.7, 294
Crested Dwarf Iris *Iris cristata*	April–May	195, 198, 210, 250.8, 273.4, 379
Fringed Phacelia *Phacelia fimbriata*	April–May	365–370
Golden Groundsel *Senecio aureus*	April–May	29.1, 85.8 (PA), 330–340
Great Chickweed *Stellaria pubera*	April–May	Common in rich, moist woods
Indian Paintbrush *Castilleja coccinea*	April–May	369–371
Pinxter Flower *Rhododendron nudiflorum*	April–May	4, 92–97, 138.6, 145.5, 154.5 (PA), 162.9, 211.6
Princess Tree *Paulownia tomentosa*	April–May	100–123, 381–382, 396, 400
Solomon's Seal *Polyganatum biflorum*	April–May	Common in moist, wooded slopes and coves
Squirrel Corn *Dicentra canadensis*	April–May	Craggy Gardens PA, 458.2 (Heintooga Spur Road)
Trillium *Trillium spp.*	April–May	175, 200–216, 339–340, 364.6
Tulip Poplar *Liriodendron tulipifera*	April–May	Common in low woods and coves
Heal All *Prunella vulgaris*	April–frost	Common along road
Fetterbush *Leucothoe racemosa*	Late April–May	241.1, 379
Redbud *Cercia canadensis*	Late April–May	54–68
Black Locust *Robina pseudo-acacia*	April–June	100–123, 367–368, 383

Flower	Peak Bloom	Mile Point or General Location
Dutchman's Breeches *Dicentra cucullaria*	April–June	367.8 (PA), 458.2 (Heintooga Spur Road)
False Solomon's Seal *Smilacina racemosa*	April–June	Common along road
Foam Flower *Tiarella cordifolia*	April–June	269.9, 339.5, 369.7 (PA)
Witch Hobble- Hobblebush *Viburnum alnofolium*	April–June, August (fruit)	295.5, 362–367, higher elevations in rich, moist woods
Carolina Rhododendron *Rhododendron minus*	Late April– June	308–310, 404–411
Dogwood *Cornus florida*	May	6, 85.8 (PA), 154.5 (PA), 230–232, 217–219, 378–382
Fraser Magnolia *Magnolia fraseri*	May	173–174, 252–253
Large-Flowered Trilium *Trillium grandiflorum*	May	3–7, 64–85, 154.5 (PA), 168–169, 175, 330–340, 370–375
Allegheny Blackberry *Rubus allegheniensis*	May–June	6, 167.2, 239.9, 305–315, 339.5, 367.6 (PA)
Bead Lily *Clintonia umbellulata*	May–June	Common in rich, moist deciduous woods
Bittersweet *Calastrus orbiculatus*	May–June	242.4, 383, 394, 396
Bluets *Houstonia spp.*	May–June	200.2, 355–368 (PA)
Bowman's Root *Gillenia trifoliata*	May–June	24–45, 149.5, 260, 332, 368–369

Flower	Peak Bloom	Mile Point or General Location
Bristly Locust *Robinia hispida*	May–June	167–174, 308.3, 347.9
Field Hackweed *Hieracilum pratense*	May–June	6, 78.4, 165.5, 229.5, 325–330
Fire Pink *Silene virginica*	May–June	1–2, 85.8 (PA), 154.5 (PA), 241 (PA), 339.3 (PA), 367–375, 404–408
Flame Azalea *Rhododendron calendulaceum*	May–June	138.6, 144–145, 149.5, 164–166, 217–221, 308–310, 368–380, 412–423
Galax *Galax aphylla*	May–June	Common in deciduous forests and open rocky areas
Hawthorne *Crataegus spp.*	May–June	155–176, 365.6, 368
New Jersey Tea *Caenothus americanus*	May–June	42–43, 91–100, 138.4, 197, 211, 241, 328.6
Pinkshell *Rhododendron vaseyi*	May–June	305.2, 342–343, 349–351, 419–424
Red-Berried Elder *Sambucus pubens*	May–June	355–360, 369, 412–425, higher elevations in rich, moist woods
Small's Groundsel *Senecio smallii*	May–June	29.1, 85.8 (PA), 330–340
Staghorn Sumac *Rhus typhina*	May–June	Common along road in dry, rocky areas
Wild Geranium *Geranium maculatum*	May–June	84–86, 170–172, 211.6, 375
Columbine *Aquilegia canadensis*	May–July	74–75, 339.3 (PA), 370–378

Flower	Peak Bloom	Mile Point or General Location
Fly Poison *Amianthium muscaetoxicum*	May–July	210–216, 406–408
Phlox *Phlox carolina*	May–July	4, 79–82, 163–164, 200–202, 219–221, 339.3 (PA), 370–380
Bladder Campion *Silene cucubalus*	May–August	376–381
Queen Anne's Lace *Daucus carota*	May–September	Common along open fields and road
Virginia Spiderwort *Tradescantia subaspera*	Late May–July	85.8 (Sharp Top Trail), 380–381
Mountain Laurel *Kalmia latifolia*	Late May–June	130.5, 162.9, 347.9, 380, 400
Spiraea *Spiraea japonica*	June–July	368–378
Catawba Rhododendron *Rhododendron catawbiense*	June	44.9, 77–83, 130.5, 138.6, 239, 247, 266.8, 348–350, 364.1
Goat's Beard *Aruncus dioicus*	June	10–11, 24, 240, 337.6, 370–375
Sundrop *Oenothera fruticoas*	June	8–10, 89–91, 229, 270.6, 351–352, 355–360, 370–375
Tree of Heaven *Ailanthus altissima*	June	Common along road in Virginia, 382
Viper's Bugloss *Echium vulgare*	June	5–40
American Elder *Sambucus canadensis*	June–July	29, 85.8 (PA), 136–138, 272–275, 311.2
Beard Tongue *Penstemon spp.*	June–July	44.4, 89–91, 154.5 (PA), 254.5, 339–340, 370–372

Flower	Peak Bloom	Mile Point or General Location
Fragrant Thimbleberry *Rubus odoratus*	June–July	18, 74.7, 339.3 (PA), 369–372, 406–408
Mountain Ash *Sorbus americana*	June–July	Higher-elevation spruce-fir forests, Mount Mitchell, Mount Pisgah
Sourwood *Oxydendrum arboreum*	June–July	102–106, 231–232, 321–327, 375–380
White Rhododendron *Rhododendron maximum*	June–July	162.9, 169 (PA), 232–233, 339.3 (PA), 352–353, 455–456
Butter and Eggs *Linaria superbum*	June–August	Common along road and waste places
Butterfly Weed *Asclepias tuberosa*	June–August	63–65, 238–246
Coreopsis *Coreopsis pubescens*	June–August	29.6, 77, 157, 190, 306
Deptford Pink *Dianthus armeria*	June–August	Common along grassy roadsides
False Hellebore *Veratrum viride*	June–August	364.6, Craggy Gardens Nature Trail
Turkscap Lily *Lilium superbum*	June–August	187.6, 364–368, 406–411
Mullein *Verbascum thapsus*	June– September	Common along road on dry banks
Bull Thistle *Carduus lanceolatus*	Late June– frost	Common along road and pastures at lower elevations
Black Cohosh *Cimicifuga racemosa*	July	6, 85.8 (PA), 169 (PA), 374

Flower	Peak Bloom	Mile Point or General Location
Black-Eyed Susan *Rudbeckia hirta*	July	Common in fields and along road
Fleabane *Erigeron strigosus*	July	Common in fields and along road
Ox-Eye Daisy *Chrysanthemum leucanthemum*	July	Common in fields and along road
Tall Meadow-Rue *Thalictrum polyganum*	July	85.8 (PA), 155.2, 248
Yarrow *Achillea millefolium*	July	Common in fields and along road
Bergamot Beebalm *Monarda fistulosa*	July–August	38.8, 368–374
Common Milkweed *Asclepias syriaca*	July–August	85–86, 167–176
Oswego Tea *Monarda didyma*	July–August	Common in wet areas at higher elevations
Tall Coneflower *Rudbeckia laciniata*	July–August	36, 161.2, 228.1, 314, 359–368
Bellflower *Campanula americana*	July–September	370–375
Starry Campion *Silene stellata*	July–September	378–380
White Snakeroot *Eupatorium rugosum*	July–October	Common along road
Boneset *Eupatorium perfoliatum*	August	29.1, 85.8 (PA), 151, 247, 314
Cardinal Flower *Lobelia cardinalis*	August	Infrequently in wet areas
Ironweed *Veronia noveboracensis*	August	245, 248
Jewel Weed *Impatiens capensis*	August	Common along road in wet areas
Joe-Pye-Weed *Eupatorium pupureum*	August	6, 85.8 (PA), 146, 248, 339.3 (PA), 357–359
Pokeberry *Phytolacca americana*	August	6, 74.7, 151, 239.9, 323, 376.9

Flower	Peak Bloom	Mile Point or General Location
Virgins Bower *Clematis virginiana*	August	13.1, 85.8 (PA), 176.1, 285–289, 313–314
Angelica *Angelica triquinata*	August–September	295.7, 339.5, 355, Craggy Gardens Nature Trail
Blazing Star *Liatris spicata*	August–September	305.1, 369–370
Dodder or Love Vine *Cuscuta rostrata*	August–September	Common along road
Sneezeweed *Helenium autumnale*	August–September	29.1, 85.8 (PA), 176.1, 229, 313–314
Nodding Lady Tresses *Spiranthes cernua*	August–frost	365–368
Gentian *Gentiana quinquefolia*	Late August–frost	85.8, 363–368
Aster *Aster spp.*	September	Common in fields and along road
Goldenrod *Solidago spp.*	September	Common in fields and along road
Yellow Ironweed *Actinomeris alternifolia*	September–October	6, 88, 154.5, 271.9, 330.8
Witch Hazel *Hamaelis virginiana*	Late September–October	130.5, 293.3, 295, 305.1, 308.3, 339.5, 347.6, 367.7

Appendix F. Forest Service Maps

The vast majority of BRP trails are so short and well marked that you should not need a map to walk them. It would be helpful, though, to have a national forest map or two with you when driving along the Parkway, as they provide a number of details, such as optional roadways, additional trails, and possible campsites and campgrounds.

If you are going to be hiking any of the trails in the national forests, you are strongly advised to obtain a map. Many of the trails in the national forests are not well maintained or marked. They are also less used than BRP trails. A map will give you an overview of the area you will be hiking and present the options available to you.

The *George Washington National Forest Map* covers the Parkway from BRP mile 0 to 63.7. It may be obtained from:

Forest Supervisor
George Washington National Forest
P.O. Box 233
Harrisonburg, VA 22801

or

Pedlar Ranger District
2424 Magnolia Avenue
Buena Vista, VA 24416

The *Jefferson National Forest, Glenwood Ranger District Map* covers the Parkway from BRP mile 63.9 to 104.3. It may be obtained from:

U.S. Forest Service
Jefferson National Forest
5162 Valleypointe Parkway
Roanoke, VA 24019

or

Glenwood Ranger District
P.O. Box 10
Natural Bridge Station, VA 24579

The *Pisgah National Forest, Grandfather, Toecane, and French Broad Ranger Districts Map* covers the Parkway from BRP mile 295.4 to 367.6. It may be obtained from:

Forest Supervisor
National Forests in North Carolina
P.O. Box 2750
Asheville, NC 28802

or

Grandfather Ranger District
P.O. Box 519
Marion, NC 28752

or

Toecane Ranger District
P.O. Box 128
Burnsville, NC 28714

The *Pisgah National Forest, Pisgah Ranger District Map* covers the Parkway from BRP mile 393.6 to 431.4. It may be obtained from the forest supervisor (see above) or from:

Pisgah Ranger District
101 Pisgah Highway
Pisgah Forest, NC 28768

The Pisgah National Forest offers a number of very detailed trail maps of the following sections of the national forest:

Trails of the Wilson Creek Area, accessible from BRP mile 307.9, NC RT 1511 (Grandfather Ranger District)
Linville Gorge trails, accessible from BRP mile 317.5, US RT 221 (Grandfather Ranger District)
Trails in the South Toe River Area, accessible from BRP mile 351.9, FSR 472 (Toecane Ranger District)

The maps may be obtained from the forest supervisor in Asheville, North Carolina, or from the individual ranger districts (see above for location of the ranger districts).

The *Shining Rock Wilderness and Middle Prong Wilderness Map* covers Parkway miles 393.6–431.4 (Pisgah Ranger District).

Appendix G.
The Mountains to Sea Trail

The Mountains to Sea Trail is one of the most exciting trail projects currently underway in North America. The idea was originally proposed in 1977 by Howard N. Lee, secretary of the North Carolina Department of Natural Resources and Community Development. His concept was further developed with the aid of the Department of Natural Resources and Community Development, the North Carolina Trails Committee, and the North Carolina Trails Association. The result of all of this collaboration is a proposed route that will someday stretch approximately 700 miles from spruce- and fir-covered Clingman's Dome high atop the Great Smoky Mountains National Park to the rolling surf and white sand beach of Nags Head on the Outer Banks jutting out into the Atlantic Ocean.

Aided by the provisions of the 1973 North Carolina Trails System Act and a publicly funded State Trails Coordinator, volunteer citizen task forces are gradually building new pathways to connect with existing trails. As a result of a 1979 agreement between the State of North Carolina and the U.S. government, much of the route will be passing through federal lands such as the Great Smoky Mountains National Park, the Nantahala National Forest, the Pisgah National Forest, the Croatan National Forest, and the Cape Hatteras National Seashore.

Many local governments and agencies are helping the trail by arranging routes through numerous state parks and, possibly, county and city parks. By the end of 1993, more than 300 miles of trail had been officially designated as parts of the Mountains to Sea Trail. Many of those miles lie within close proximity to the BRP. In fact, portions of a number of the Parkway's paths, such as the Shut-In Trail and the Watkins Carriage Road, are now considered components of the Mountains to Sea Trail.

There is not, however, one long continuous route that parallels the Parkway. Rather, there exists a hodgepodge of trails that will someday be connected to make up the full length of the Mountains to Sea Trail. Gaps of twenty miles or more sometimes occur between designated or completed sections of the trail along the Parkway. Since the trail is still in the development stage, new sections will continually be added and other sections may be changed or rerouted.

If you wish to obtain more information on the Mountains to Sea Trail or to aid its development, contact:

State Trails Coordinator
Department of Environment, Health, and Natural Resources
Division of Parks and Recreation
P.O. Box 27687
Raleigh, NC 27611-7687

Suggested Readings and Field Guides

Bradley, Jeff. *A Traveler's Guide for the Smoky Mountain Region*. Boston: Harvard Common Press, 1985.

Brooks, Maurice. *The Appalachians*. Boston: Houghton Mifflin, 1965.

Bull, John, and John Farrand, Jr. *The Audubon Society Field Guide to North American Birds, Eastern Region*. New York: Alfred A. Knopf, 1977.

Byrd, Nathan, ed. *A Forester's Guide to Observing Animal Use in the South*. Atlanta, Ga.: Forest Service, U.S. Department of Agriculture, 1981.

Catlin, David T. *A Naturalist's Blue Ridge Parkway*. Knoxville: University of Tennessee Press, 1984.

De Hart, Allen. *Hiking the Old Dominion*. San Francisco, Calif.: Sierra Club Books, 1984.

————. *North Carolina Hiking Trails*. Boston: AMC Books, 1988.

Fletcher, Colin. *The Complete Walker III*. New York: Alfred A. Knopf, 1987.

Gupton, Oscar W., and Fred W. Swope. *Fall Wildflowers of the Blue Ridge and Great Smoky Mountains*. Charlottesville: University Press of Virginia, 1987.

————. *Wildflowers of the Shenandoah Valley and Blue Ridge Mountains*. Charlottesville: University Press of Virginia, 1979.

Johnson, Randy. *Southern Snow*. Boston: AMC Books, 1986.

Jolley, Harley E. *The Blue Ridge Parkway*. Knoxville: University of Tennessee Press, 1969.

Justice, William S., and C. Ritchie Bell. *Wildflowers of North Carolina*. Chapel Hill: University of North Carolina Press, 1968.

Kephart, Horace. *Our Southern Highlanders*. 1929. Reprint. Knoxville: University of Tennessee Press, 1976 and 1984.

Little, Elbert L. *The Audubon Society Field Guide to North American Trees*. New York: Alfred A. Knopf, 1980.

Lord, William. *Blue Ridge Parkway Guide*. Asheville, N.C.: Hexagon, 1976.

Martof, Bernard S., William M. Palmer, Joseph R. Bailey, and Julian R. Harrison. *Amphibians and Reptiles of the Carolinas and Virginia*. Chapel Hill: University of North Carolina Press, 1980.

Mulford, Carolyn, and Betty L. Ford. *Adventure Vacations in Five Middle Atlantic States*. McLean, Va.: EPM Publications, 1987.

Murlless, Dick, and Constance Stallings. *Hiker's Guide to the Smokies*. San Francisco, Calif.: Sierra Club Books, 1973.

Peterson, Roger T. *Field Guide to Eastern Birds: A Field Guide to Birds East of the Rockies*. Boston: Houghton Mifflin, 1984.

Petrides, George A. *A Field Guide to Trees and Shrubs*. Boston: Houghton Mifflin, 1988.

Potter, Eloise F., James F. Parnell, and Robert P. Teulings. *Birds of the Carolinas*. Chapel Hill: University of North Carolina Press, 1986.

Radford, Albert E., Harry E. Ahles, and C. Ritchie Bell. *Manual of the Vascular Flora of the Carolinas*. Chapel Hill: University of North Carolina Press, 1968.

Rives, Margaret R. *Blue Ridge Parkway: The Story Behind the Scenery*. Las Vegas, Nev.: KC Publications, 1982.

Stokes, Donald W. *The Natural History of Wild Shrubs and Vines*. New York: Harper and Row, 1989.

Webster, William David, James F. Parnell, and Walter C. Biggs. *Mammals of the Carolinas, Virginia, and Maryland*. Chapel Hill: University of North Carolina Press, 1985.

Wenberg, Donald. *Blue Ridge Mountain Pleasures*. Chester, Conn.: Globe Pequot, 1988.

———. *Appalachian Trail Guide to Central Virginia*. Harpers Ferry, W.Va.: Appalachian Trail Conference, 1994.

————. *100 Favorite Trails of Great Smokies and Carolina Blue Ridge*. Skyland, N.C.: Hickory Printing, n.d.

————. *Trails in Southwest Virginia: James River to New River*. Blacksburg, Va.: Virginia Tech Outing Club, 1987.

Index

Italic page numbers indicate the detailed description of a trail.